T0381483

The Eve of Annihilation

Good and Evil
VOLUME III

We all drank beer!
And watched the Super-bowl

And watched the Super-bowl 2010
And watched the Super-bowl 2005
And watched the Super-bowl 2000
And watched the Super-bowl1995
And watched the Super-bowl 1990

Robert R. Fiedler

iUniverse, Inc.
Bloomington

Good and Evil Volume III
The Eve of Annihilation

iUniverse books may be ordered through booksellers or by contacting:

iUniverse
1663 Liberty Drive
Bloomington, IN 47403
www.iuniverse.com
1-800-Authors (1-800-288-4677)

ISBN: 978-1-4620-3112-2 (sc)
ISBN: 978-1-4620-3116-0 (e)

Printed in the United States of America

iUniverse rev. date: 9/15/2011

GOOD AND EVIL
The Eve of Annihilation

First, let us consider the good: Gifts, which we enjoy

SPACE, MATTER, MOVEMENT, TIME AND LIGHT

All of these gifts are phenomenal and they are freely given

No matter when one is born, these are very special gifts

Every single living being has the same opportunity

ALSO, THOSE HAVE THE SAME RESPONSIBILITY

Additionally those have a responsibility to each other

The Virtues can and should be learned and practiced

We must apply Virtue to our existence and avoid all

SIN

One small infraction can ruin a lifetime of goodness

We should not corrupt others with our personal Sins

Some of the Virtues: Patience, Temperance, Honesty and Truthfulness.

Humility is a cardinal virtue upon which many others are resting
A Liar is the greatest enemy of Civilization and of all people
Believe this, it is the truth

Always Consider Reality

As a complex
Multi-Faceted
SINGULARITY

The Nature of Being is
ALWAYS A SINGULARITY
A Civilization is always in Flux

Is this for Real?
Or is it a Nightmare?

The Eve of Annihilation
Is upon us
It is just ahead

On the Eve of Annihilation

We all drank beer!
And watched the Super-bowl
And watched the Super-bowl 2010
And watched the Super-bowl 2005
And watched the Super-bowl 2000
And watched the Super-bowl 1995
And watched the Super-bowl 1990

Contents

Head of Christ

The Image on the cover is of a Drawing I did which emphasizes the idea of photons moving in space. I consider this a very timely work which relates too much that is being done in Physics. The image is absolutely original and had come to being in a definite and singular act: it is totally intuitive.

A reproduction of this image, an eleven color printing, approximately 16" x 20" from a limited edition printing of 250 is available for $35.00 plus $10.50 for shipping and handling. Checks are acceptable however they must clear before shipment. Therefore allow four weeks for delivery. All sales are final: no refunds and no returns. When you purchase this print you will own a very unique and very limited work of Fine Art. The piece is unique and is timely relating to some of the most advanced work in optics and physics.

There does exist a prior printing of 1000 done for Don Bosco, New Rochelle, New York: it was done as a promotional piece.

Christ: Catholic

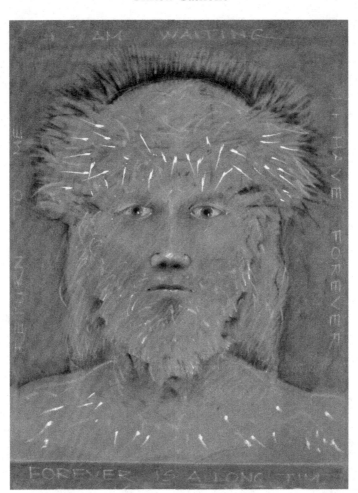

Introduction and some credits

First, I thank my immediate family for providing the love and patience necessary to raise a precocious son, especially my dad who had much of the malfeasance of government figured out in 1938. He was a farm boy very intelligent: the **best man I ever knew. Also my sister and my mom: later my wife the best of womanhood and her mother** who raised four children alone. She was my hero! Also the many good people whom I have met who have befriended me along the way.

Especially I thank Oswald Spengler, Philosopher, Historian and Prophet: his monumental _Decline of the West_, in two volumes, no doubt obviates one of the best minds of the past several hundred years. He was a superlative Scholar and Writer. I also thank Eustice Mullins, for his book on _The Order_ for his fine more current Historical research, in obviating what is wrong with the system and who made it as it is: and why. Also I recently, five years ago, discovered the writings of Mathias Chang, a Chinese Catholic, _Future Fast Forward, The Zionist Anglo-American Empire Meltdown,_ who has understandings that are current and have efficacy functioning at this point in time. I thank Francis Parker Yockey for his compelling book _Imperium._

Additionally I thank Nesta Webster for her writing on _the French Revolution_ and _World Revolution._ Both are classics on the subject with no holds barred. They should be required reading in our high Schools for insightful understanding of just what is a Revolution and why do we have "One" World Revolution. Who promotes this nonsense and how have the promoters gained control, of our economic and governmental institutions that function within our Civilization? For many reasons people are not necessarily the same and at times they attempt to express their dissimilarities in strange and malicious ways. I also thank E. C. Knuth, an engineer, for his _The Empire of the City,_ a startling expose of the role of England in attempting to destroy America. They are still fighting the Revolutionary War and at times seem to be winning.

Also I thank Olivia Marie O'Grady for her book _The Beasts of the Apocalypse._ This is an insightful and well-documented work, which should reach a wider audience for the history and continuity of the assault on Christianity and Western Civilization. I thank Father Vincent P. Micelli, S. J. for his book _The Antichrist._ Much that is happening has to do with the Antichrist and the Scriptures and Prophesies given by God. This is not something that is easily understood indeed it may be as much imagination as understanding. Not all believe in prophecy however some, in the future we imagine, will witness the power of the Creator who made the World and the Heavens above. Special thanks, is extended to E. Michael Jones, Ph.D. for his _Degenerate Moderns_ and others of his writing. He shows very clearly the outcome of the kind of thinking that has taken over our Civilization. We must change our ways or we are certainly doomed! I wish to thank Richard Gerber for his _Vibration Medicine,_ which obviates a profound and current understanding of the direction and methods of medical procedures.

I wish to thank Bruce Cathie for his book _The Bridge to Infinity_, a most compelling work on the nature and function of Space.

Finally, I extend my gratitude to the many authors found on my bibliography at the end of the book. I am somewhat of a Renaissance man and the authors mentioned have helped me along the way.

Preface

The Individual

You have been told by some that there are no ABSOLUTES

In fact there are many Absolutes there most certainly are: billions of them!
**Every single person is an absolutely singular human being, distinct from all others.
This is recorded in the DNA.**

This is an important part of God's Plan, the name and the DNA are distinct thus He will be able to identify every individual as such. **At present** we have discovered that every single human being is distinct, which distinction is recorded in the DNA. It is said that all of the DNA from the entire human race, up till now, if combined, would weigh less than a single aspirin. This understanding gives phenomenal evidence of the ability of God the Father, nevertheless many do not recognize this is a fact and others simply discount it. In this instance we have "stumbled" upon one of God's miraculous inventions. He may very well refer to this when and if we face Him during the Last Judgment. Who knows what will be the last judgment? This presents an issue beyond human knowing and understanding.

Millions of individuals believe in God, <u>one way or another</u>. This, as an **Idea**, ties in with the **Time/Space** phenomenon that many associate only with Physics. Some Physicists are atheistic or are not certain if there is a God Being, others are determinedly certain that this is not in the equation.[1] Those are confused in their own knowledge of all that is. Those prefer to concentrate on what those "imagine" and have discovered, as a part of reality, it is their Reality and those have used mathematics to explain what they do and what they have found in so doing.[2] Mathematics depends on a building of knowledge and is dependent upon the techniques employed and can be extended indefinitely with the discovery of new elements, or principles. Mathematicians have had profound consequence in the world of reality and are just now approaching "other" worlds as a consequence of a better understanding of time-space phenomenon. This, in fact is related to **Faith** and **Reason** and allows, or provides for much of what we do and for what we understand: also for what we cannot do and do not understand. Man seeks answers to questions and is often disappointed in the answers. Men, *"imagine"* much of, which is simply not true: their thinking carries them inside and out of the sphere of **Reality**. Those believe that eventually those will figure out what has happened, truthfully, in this Universe and exactly how it did happen.

----

1   **1 See our proof that** there must be a God and why this must be so (Chapter X). There must have been an omnipotence that had an **Idea** of reality. Without the word and the thought there would be no reality as we sense and know it to be. No one knows how the Universe came to be: however there are many interesting ideas.

2   **Mathematics** is limited by its use of numbers, which are finite and by Symbols, which may be misinterpreted. When one deals with what is infinite and timeless numbers will not suffice and the symbols are only abstractly indicative. So we cannot easily resolve the most important questions regarding issues of which we are only aware of a segment, a part, rather than a [the] totality.

It must be understood that this work deals with the "Ultimate Question." How far does Space extend so to support the total of Reality? "Infinite space is the ideal that the Western soul has always striven to find …" (Spengler, pg. 175) This is a very complex and somewhat mysterious Issue, involving much of what is known and unknown at the present time. *(See the drawing, at the end of the book: This drawing is my attempt to give graphic form to this idea. However, I do know, to do so is an impossible task, thus the image must remain as incomplete).* We can assume that any singular being does not have all of the necessary information and that much of the information is false or only partially correct and truthful.

To return to the ***ABSOLUTE*** nature of every person we must consider as fundamental the time/place factor of every single human being. In fact the question goes to the point of inception.[3] Interestingly some are not certain of when human life begins. Those are amongst the most confused of all that ponder this Issue. Nevertheless *when the genitals of two consenting adults touch and function as those are intended,* then a new life begins including physical, and spiritual components. Moral implications are varied, profound and far-reaching. Given the nature of what is physical such observations can be assumed rather directly however in the spiritual realm it is not so easy to understand the details. This is an obvious consequence of the divide and conquers Technique, as practiced and encouraged by Satan the Devil (an Idea), which is ongoing coincident with the reality of History. It is the effect in practice. Many Religions have entertained the need for making the Religion better, more compelling, and in responding to this need new Religions become a reality. ***The one Theology founded by Christ was and is perfect and cannot be improved.*** Misunderstanding has done much to confuse millions and it appears that the situation will not get much better, in the near future: perhaps never. Those that attempt to make it better simply *develop a new form of false or incomplete religion,* which others may choose to follow. Those do this not understanding the meaning of existentialism: What is religion? Keep in mind, there is a reason and need for man, as man, to be able to be assertive and to discover what it is that God has placed before him. Not all believe this however that does not change the facts of existence, which must be the truth. *Keep in mind no mortal knows what, precisely, is the truth?*

Finally, there are so many pedants that imagine those know something that any precise and correct inference, including the many and varied complexities, will probably be overlooked in the political clamor. Politicians have great problem with this "genre" of thought, what is absolute and existentially truthful, since self-interest and a form of obedience to other *"thought Systems"* is almost always an over-riding element. Political thought determined by false necessity and money-grubbing interests is ruining the processes that hold a Civilization together, or a new Civilization is being constructed to replace the present one, and the behaviors promoted by that same thinking will be a Disaster! The new form is called the "one World Order" and is a nearly established fact: the many wars being fought are, generally speaking, to gain what belongs to another. The people fight, presumably, in defense of an imagined freedom from the workings of this monstrosity.

---

3   **At inception** two persons, joined in the flesh release human substance *destined to become as those are,* more or less. There is a complex combining of the "flesh" in a way distinct in time that is absolute. There has been much discussion about gene splitting and related issues that combine in the forming of a person. This is mostly technical and some wonder what it might be like to have all perfect people. The Idea is *compelling however probably not wise.* The variation in individual physical make-up is not the only characteristic that we should be concerned with. Anxious scientists would hope to make money from such procedures. In this instance we are dealing with the corruption of the species: ***this is not a good Idea!***

Consider for example war:

All Wars are Evil however, for now, they are imagined as necessary.

To define the Soul of a man or of a community is a most challenging task, in reality impossible for most. A Soul exists and becomes as an accumulation over an extended period of time during which the individual is living or the community functioning with some form of continuity. The word continuity is important, which means *Tradition,* since individuals may and do change, which will affect how God will interpret their being. Keep in mind, it is believed by billions, that an all knowing God will act, with perfect understanding of each and every individual. This too is an **Idea** about living and cannot be extinguished. We believe that this suggests a part of what a God-Being is and what *[He?]* is able to do. To act with perfect understanding is an **"Idea"** about action and as such it *(as an Idea)* cannot be extinguished. *It can only be modified, considered differently, from many distinct points of view.* To know and to believe one thing or another is what places man in a peculiar and unique position. Keep in mind for every thinking person there is much more that is unknown than is known truthfully. Consider unknown Reality to be infinitely extensive whereas what is known by any individual is comparatively miniscule: near meaningless in a very short time. *Ideas in most minds stand as unproven, misunderstood or simply without veracity or conviction.*

What we consider at this juncture is difficult to contemplate however it is what makes life interesting, as life. Each life is different and the understandings that emanate there from are unique and may be profound. Every mind is saturated with the remains of various experiences and the imagination of a Godly being. The consequence of such saturation and imagination is not possible to know in advance and may very well be that, which propels the individual to discreet action. Politicians and World "Planners" do not understand the variety within the thought patterns of various populations. If those do understand, they prefer to categorize and *imagine what is simply not true.* If those succeed in their efforts the World will be made over to suite their imaginations. This would be an incomprehensible tragedy and should not happen: such as that cannot be allowed to happen.

There is much more to life than economics.
Economics are fleeting and have only coincidental effect.
Bottom line profit for corporations should be considered as secondary.
Actually it should be considered much less than secondary: it is only temporary.
All this must be reasoned with the genuine and honest serving of the People in mind.
What is moral has become secondary and is often forgotten in the maelstrom.
It often happens that what is moral and decent is overlooked or confused.
This occurs when economics are the driving force of the Civilization,
This of course relates to the becoming of sinfully driven excess.
We have deemed success to be related to what is excessive.

The driving force then becomes the Sin of Greed.

Greed is A Mortal Sin!

One of the seven deadly Sins, it is deadly.

The Eve of Annihilation
Is upon us

Is this for Real?
Or is it a Nightmare?

What follows is an explanation of the contents of this work.

This book is my attempt to place some Ideas in order and create relationships which are not always considered. Many aspects of our existence are interrelated in strange and unusual ways. Moments come and go and we are left with the memories which may or may not be understood. What is understood is more easily dealt with however what is not understood may be more affective on us and on our behavior and understanding. The brain and the mind are difficult to assess and to understand however much is knowable: given the proper means and technical education. Nevertheless the person changes from moment to moment and it is not always possible to understand what such change means and/or infers.

This work is written from a somewhat Catholic point of view: meaning it is universal and affects everyone. However it is not, strictly speaking a religious book. I see all forms of Christianity as having stemmed from the original presence of Christ on this earth. We have only the history of his existence however it has been, and is very compelling for hundreds of millions of individually concerned individuals: it has a two thousand year history, is as the present and will extend into the future. We speak of infinity and of forever rather casually, nevertheless both are very significant thoughts in respect to what has been what is and what will be in an unknown future: they project a sense of holiness not always appreciated or understood.

Many related Christian religions have come and gone.[4] They were the work of men, interpretations of what was imagined as being holy, or just: others were vain and selfish. They all derived some or much of their understanding from the Catholic faith which is what made them seem correct. However they were all works of common men, sometimes called prophets. All had many flaws. Even the Catholic Church and the theology that it projects have been influenced at times by worldly or manly influence. Nevertheless, the Catholic Church was the work of a divinely inspired deity: Christ, person of the Trinity become man. It is thus the most holy Institution, inviolate and perfect. What men have done to this institution is not always correct. We understand that over the past two thousand years the scribes have copied the sacred Catholic (Meaning, universally applicable) books without error. They are right now as they were written in the first century. Ultimately it is hoped that all people will understand the meaning of these sacred texts. When they do we will have a better and more fairly disposed existence. When they do all will be more like Christ.

Robert Fiedler April 26, 2001

---

4   ***Most Holy Family Monastery***, *A Voice Crying in the Wilderness,* Issues 1-2-3-4. 4425 Schneider Road, Fillmore, N. Y. 14735

Prologue

For the benefit of who will read this book some background information is provided hereunder. I, Robert Fiedler am an Emeritus Professor at California State University. I taught Fine Art Painting, Drawing and Graphics for forty-one years at that Institution. It was a wonderful experience and I met thousands of students some gifted and many amongst them taught me something that was and is very important to me.

As a Professor I had time to study and to learn about various things: this I did. As a young man I was an avid reader and interested in many disciplines. I have Degrees in Fine Art and the normal Bachelor of Science in Art and Biology. I also have attained an MA an MS and an MFA Degree. When I was a young man there was not so much emphasis on a Doctor's degree except in the Sciences, math, astronomy and related fields: for the Artists there was the MFA degree, which was considered the terminal Degree. I also studied at the Layton School of Art, Milwaukee, Wisconsin, The University of Heidelberg in West Germany and Scripps Graduate School, in California. In 1965 I was admitted to the University of Southern California, USC, School of Medicine, to study for an MD Degree. After a short time I determined that my family was more important than whatever I might learn in addition to what I knew and I abandoned my studies so to be able to be a better father. I hope I did succeed. The remainder of my education was self-imposed, between the more normal events of life. I am a self-trained architect and have completed over ninety residential architectural projects: mostly in California, two in Wisconsin, one in New York. In the early seventies I worked as a gold and silver broker. Additionally I have completed study work and writing for a degree in Economics however, I did not attempt to achieve the Doctor's Degree for various personal reasons.

I have been and am a well recognized artist. Between 1950 and 1990 I participated in over one-hundred important Regional, National and International exhibitions. My work has been toured by the Western Associations of Art Museums, The Library of Congress and the American Federation of Art. I completed a number of sculptural works and was a competent Ceramicist. In 1982 and 1983 I was invited to represent the United States in West Germany. For that I received the Commanding Generals award for excellence. I have been honored by my communities with Special Awards for my work. In addition I received two Congressional Citations one for my retrospective exhibit in 1997 and one other.

My work has found its way to Europe and Asia and there are many pieces in the United States in private collections. Nevertheless I am known by only a small number of Individuals. I was never a salesman and have never been beholden to the role of a Dealer who could make a profit from the sale of my works, many of which I have given as gifts. I have completed over twelve thousand various works, mostly drawings and prints, most done exclusively by my own hand. To me this is what Art is and should be: collaborations generally miss the point of the meaning of Art and compromise the form. I realize this is a personal opinion however it has a good pedigree behind it. I have worked with some Dealers thirteen come to mind in the selling and presentation of my output as an artist. Most all of my former Dealers are deceased.

My creative work and research spans about sixty-five years: during this time I have been an observer of a drastically changing Society, the Culture and the Civilization in general. The world is captured by money grubbers (for example George Soros and the Rockefellers) and vain

Politicians (for example Hillary and Bill Clinton and Hessian Obama, together with Nancy Pelosi and Harry Reid), many of who have little honor and no sense of National identity. They are known as being Internationalists: whatever that means is unclear. In fact, the word Traitor is generally a better description of what they are about. They should be tried on this charge and if found guilty should be removed from office. They are able to avoid and pervert most of the laws in place that should protect the people from their kind of manipulation. They are greedy and self-serving and are strangling the good people of this world. Their speech is mostly contrived for what they can gain for themselves and their like-minded colleagues. I don't see things improving much without a serious Intellectual Revolution: this is not likely: the money and the arms are in the wrong places.

Although Art can be sold that is not the reason for creating it. The reasons are personal and involve the soul and being of the Artist. The nonsense that one sees in the papers about paintings selling in the millions is simply an indication that many fools have too much money to waste on attempting to be the most prominent patron. Anyone who would pay one hundred million, more or less, for a Picasso is the biggest fool around. Picasso was not as good as is claimed, by the dealers that profited on his work. In fact he was instrumental in destroying culture, carrying out the dictates of the Communists to cheapen and vulgarize Art: this he did. Picasso was a vain and immoral lunatic. He is reported to have been a frivolous and uncaring lecher (some even refer to him as a lover), however he was one who used and abused whoever was unfortunate enough to have known him. It is my understanding that one of his wives and one of his children committed suicide. Why? Enough said!

It is believed/assumed that about 350 individuals own one-half of all the World's riches. This is a problem that is difficult to correct. This is a situation that could not have developed without the help of government assuming the role of the protector of the lives of all people. Keep in mind most politicians are self-serving fools: more or less. The United States is a driving force however their somewhat more influential politicians are bent on a one-world socialist government, which selected Politicians will control. For the people their thinking, the Politicians thinking, will be a disaster. The one World organizers see possibilities for themselves in a manner of strange and treasonous behavior. This is a very difficult issue to contemplate.

We are imagined to be concerned for all the people in the World however many of our politicians seem not concerned for our very own Nation, Culture and People. Many Politicians, others as well, belong to secret organizations and protect each other when things grow too hot. They can be moved from one position to another to protect their cover: they work for the government for a lifetime. The people are poorly informed or they are simply not interested in what is happening: with the spectator sports they are mesmerized into lethargy over who can throw or kick a ball. There are many social and personal problems as well that we cannot consider as this is written: nevertheless, they do exist.

What follows is a result, in part, of my life and my living at this time. I have always been a man of conscience. I married my childhood sweetheart and never sought another. I have been an individual who has had few close friends and never was I part of any group, team or faction. I am truly an independent thinker. I found being alone, generally speaking, to be the only way that one can have a personal opinion and a few Ideas that are his own.

CHAPTER I

Insanity: Are we Insane or simply Stupid?

It is axiomatic that nothing lasts forever. Forever generally defined is all forward Time, that is all time from now until the end of Time, if such there be.[5] All Objectivity is limited. In addition, both Culture and Civilization are limited. All of the past known History of this World has expired however there was always another Culture or Civilization forthcoming. Each one seemed better than the last and had many more people. Not to forget, there are Biblical Implications that cannot be ignored. God is said to have created the World in seven days; **who believes this?** *Paleontologists insist that it took billions of years more or less; who is right? Recently we find scientific evidence, which gives some reasonably significant credibility to the seven-day thesis. Whether you believe God or Man makes little difference. Either way you are locked in Time, you are in a "time-surround, from which you cannot escape" and you occupy a specific amount of Space. Coincidentally and importantly you can only see what has been illuminated for you.*

---

5   **Bearden,** *Aids: Biological Warfare.* Minds space, where an Idea originates and is contained is a very illusive and strangely formed space. Much research has been and is being done on this aspect of human existence. It is understood that to some degree, mind space can be altered and engineered for the purpose of changing thought patterns (Bearden). Space is an Infinite Accommodation and is a corollary of Time. Space contains all including the Ideas which travel, in the Space from person to person. The human brain is an important part of an Idea as this is where an Idea originates: within the space between proximate neurons; within the brain. In fact, Ideas come from nothing, which is consistent with Genesis.

God, as an Idea is the most important part of Man's Destiny. The Idea of a God has been around as long as History and involves a manner of supernatural or existential presence, in some way motivational for a population. Some Scholars date history being as old as 200,000 years: others imagine a much shorter time-frame.

Heaven is where one becomes one in being with the father and is not understood by living beings: it is an existential dilemma. The most significant aspects of the driving force of humanity cannot be known. Only death provides one with an opportunity of understanding: what is Life.

Imagined needs are imposed by political and economic forces not open to correction by the common man who is in fact captured by this aspect of Destiny. Huge amounts of wealth provide cover and a means for those that do great damage to the People, the Culture and the Civilization. At present George Soros is guilty of sedition against this and other Nations although his wealth and mobility will allow him to proceed until death takes him. In collusion with some Politicians he has power over governments, which is in direct violation of our Constitution, written to protect all of the people.

Referring to the bible we are informed that there will be a last day. This is a difficult question to ponder for all that do not believe the Bible. Nevertheless, every single living person will come upon his last day as a live and mortal being. There is much dissention and doubt on the part of many regarding what, exactly, does this mean.

You are destined to an unknown future, at the end of your time you will face death:

Alone

And, in the end we are all dead! What matters if our clothes were in *"style"* or not? What does it matter if our hair was just the right color? What does it matter how many men or women we have bedded down for an instant gratification? Does our individual life really matter?

To whom does it matter?

Are we simply a small amount of flesh and bone or are we more than that? If we are simply flesh and bone, when we die we are no more. If we are more than that what part makes us more?

The Idea of a Soul has been around for a long time however only a few can imagine for certain what that is. What happens to us when we die, what happens to our Soul? Such Questions as there are may draw into attention the *Idea* that our life is, "somehow" everlasting. No one knows exactly what this means. Christians have Jesus as their Savior, he bears the weight of all sin and he has promised redemption *for some good men, not all* **however!** All are welcome but each should come of his own volition. All men do not accept Jesus as their Savior some hate him, while others ridicule the Idea of His Being.

To be redeemed one must have lived a good life <u>as a Catholic</u>: this is a Catholic, meaning universally Christian, **belief**.[6] Other Christians and those of other religions have their own ideas about this, which may or may not be correct. Keep in mind all other Christian Faiths are derived from the Catholic Faith, Universal Christianity. Other Faiths are of man's making; those are heretical, for one reason or another and are not *"complete faiths"* as is the True Catholic Faith, which comes from Christ. Beliefs are often difficult to understand: those originate slowly and are unique? Those grow in Time one idea forming from what is existent within the mind of one or many. Some beliefs have an origin in what is primitive and uninformed, given what is known today. Such beliefs cannot be considered too seriously however cannot be dismissed either, since millions of people hold to them. This is a difficult issue to approach. It is difficult for a contemporary Westerner to justify the beliefs formed of superstition and witchcraft nevertheless those do exist and can be compelling for millions of people. Importantly such beliefs co-mingle with other beliefs and we find very strange *"summations"* forming.[7] Beliefs today have a distinguishing characteristic of bringing together thoughts and ideas that have never been considered before by the common man: this is a consequence of the extent and viability of modern communication. No one is certain what will be the consequence of this phenomenon. It appears that Satan or the Devil is in control of many perverted notions held by millions of individuals. And, such notions are motivational leading to war, and various forms of brutality, which keep good men occupied

---

6   **This belief** will find great criticism from some other Christians. There have been many heretics, some of which have deserted and began a new religion. Martin Luther is prominent amongst such dissidents. However even Martin Luther maintained many Catholic tenants within his thinking: it is difficult task to abandon all that you have believed in at a former time.

7   **A summation,** in this instance, is a complex mixture of all past incidents, and is a complex combination, which is very difficult to understand. This is especially true since no one knows for certain what the important elements are, and why they are being considered. Almost all modern rhetorical considerations, meet with this problem sooner or later.

in defense of goodness. Not to forget everyone's **Idea** of what is goodness is not the same. This is a very perplexing situation.

Some, in this World, are attempting to bring all Faiths together in what presents a somewhat ecumenical understanding. It is difficult to imagine agreement where the philosophy is very distinct and, in some instances very defensive and singular. Politics are important too since they have assumed or taken on the attitudes of being a Faith.

Politics at the present moment assert a religious temperament that is a false temperament. This is blasphemy however who would make that connection? Politics should serve in the governing of the people and should be uncorrupt, remaining within decent moral and ethical understanding.[8] Nevertheless our politicians seem to be in politics for what those, as individuals might gain for themselves. Most at the higher levels are lawyers and are wealthy or become wealthy, by the world's standards as those, generally speaking, corrupt every **Idea**, which they encounter.

Keep in mind Politics at present is inimical to Religion, our politicians have insisted on a separation of Church and State. In my judgment this is a fatal flaw in our system where morality is divorced from the workings of government. It is obvious every day that many politicians are immoral pretenders attempting to do what is impossible aided only by their own conceit and self-promotion. In attempting to please everyone those lose sight of this or their main support, namely the Catholic Faith and the philosophy, which has developed from it over a period of twenty five hundred years. Many of them are fools and some are hypocrites beside. The billions being spent and squandered because of a make-believe enemy are proof of the inadequacy of the System: this is certainly not Christian. But who can and who will fix it. We send our sons to be killed by strangers whom those cannot and will never know. As we do this we reward them with higher pay and worthless medals. We send them to school so those can *"learn"* to execute and pay for more of the same. Those are taught to kill and to hate for the good of the System, which is in many ways often rotten to the core. For the sons that are killed we play a bugle over their grave and present the family with a folded flag. The men so called that fight for the munitions makers are little more than children are? They are brave and imagine they are doing the right thing. Are they? We imagine they might better be doing other things.

This brings into question, what is a good Catholic and infers certain elements that are fundamental to the Faith. Such assertion brings forth, great alarm for billions, who are not Catholic and it is therefore a difficult part of the dogma of the Catholic Church. Time has confused us and millions do not believe this to be a condition of redemption. The Catholic Faith is hierarchical and has a dogma that is unchanging. This is as it must be for the purpose of maintaining a decisive and final Faith. Madeline Albright, our former Secretary of State, "imagined" that the tens of thousands of Iraqi children killed could be considered as collateral damage. Nevertheless she mourned the passing or killing of one Jew. Why is this? Is this hypocrisy, if not what is it? Are not all men made in the image of an Infinite being: God? Apparently those such as Madeline do not understand much about the most important things. She should have been employed in a simpler task. She might have made a very good dust maid or an assistant cook.

---

8   **The Founding Fathers:** Those that wrote the Constitution which is being carefully deconstructed as this is necessary so to "meander" to a one-World government. A one-World government is an idea, which has been pressed by those that have too much authority over their fellow citizens. It is imagined, at least, most people would not choose such method, they prefer to have their own thinking included in any governing process.

Our Societies, Cultures and our Civilization have become very complex, beyond the comprehension of all except for the best or most well informed and capable people; and they are few and even those do not have perfect knowledge. Most believe what those are told to believe by strangers and by those whom they will never know, Internationalists hoping to dominate all others. And *all believe the same lies as most others believe.*

Perfect knowledge is God's knowledge. Only God knows why the wind blows and what happened, every day everywhere for all passed time. Only God understands with perfect comprehension what is in store for every single human being. Such is Godly, wisdom. Who and what is this God that can know everything? Man is able to anticipate with some clarity however does not really know what is happening. His plans never work because those are generally based on vanity and greed, which are sins and anxiety, which often forms as a neurosis. In our chosen leaders this neurosis manifests as a motivational force in the **"Will to Power,"** which is a most significant driving force in our existence. Christ admonished us that everything in this world is vanity. Often our achievements have vanity as the most significant motivation coupled with the will to power. Athletic contests the Opera shows, Racing events, and all forms of miscellaneous competition endeavor and are formed largely because of vanity. Who is first, strongest, prettiest and on and on. This has become as a national and worldly driving force. People are killed at athletic contests as they storm the Stadium so to watch a meaningless game. The economic impact is astounding with all the over-priced junk food and drinks.

Men have developed wonderful systems and have magnificent accomplishments however:
Many important men are not aware of the most significant elements of their being.
Nevertheless, they do imagine that they are; their imaginations run wild.
Men are not cognoscenti of the nature of their being, in Time.[9]
This is a tragedy however, is no less than true.
When elements such as discussed in this work are considered
It is often with great apology or humor, of a tainted sort that is motivational.
Certainly there are difficult issues to comprehend and to deal with: we will try.
At other times the issues being addressed will seem clear enough,
However significant comprehension is generally lacking

When a subject is approached with insufficient knowledge and is not well understood:
Many will have a smile and a shift to something more "pertinent" or so it would seem.
There exist forms of humor, athletics, Disneyland stuff and the spectacles.
All are forms of distraction from what is truthful:

And what is meaningful.

---

9   **Cruttenden, Walter.** *Lost Star of Myth and Time.* **In the recent past,** men have discovered the existence of other Cultures, from perhaps thousands of years ago. Archeologists are finding the remains, as artifact and implement, of ancient Civilizations that were apparently much farther developed than had been heretofore imagined. Additionally archeologists are dating the Cultures of this World as being much older than what was imagined a few years ago.

CHAPTER II

Intelligence: A Profound Intelligence Created The Universe

There is a profound Intelligence that was responsible for creating the Universe.
Who was so intelligent, so to conceive of all that is, was and will be?
We have come to call this being or entity a profound God.
Who is this intelligent God-being what is he like?
Probably not like we could imagine!

* * *

Human beings generally speaking are not too intellectually bright. Those do not consider the most serious kind of thinking in their daily lives. They are tied up in the necessities of living their life: one way or another. When those have considered the issue of God, those have woven some strange mythologies, which have persisted over long periods of time. Having a God, an all-good and creative being, those also devised his opposite, the Devil who seeks to destroy what God and Man has created. Actually this is quite simple except for the details, which have become very complex in time.

The details are as those are because of the various groups of individuals that have existed separately and have developed very different characteristics in their language and understanding of Reality. Initially the continents did divide them and those went on their own way however this is no longer true. The present emphasis on travel has determined that Humanity is all mixed up and individuals are not certain how to behave. The World has been plagued with conflict and men continue to fight for various reasons, one group against another. Some of the great Religions are antagonistic toward other religions, which gives some individuals a reason to hate others. On a more personal level we have a sustained petty bickering for no reason at all.

Imagine that if man had not entered the Universe and if we had no means for measuring all that is? What would be the scale of this universe? Would an atom be as a galaxy in size? Scale is a very important factor that is perhaps not well understood. How far away is the sun: Really?

What about velocity: How fast is fast? We had imagined that light had a speed of 186,000 miles per second. Presently we are told it might be, or could be three times that. This obviates a serious flaw in our judgment and in or technologies upon which we are now so dependent.

What about Time, this too is an invention of the human brain, albeit with some support from universal reality? In fact there are repetitive functions in the Universe that suggests a form of a clock, which man can refer to. However there are also disparate functions that appear totally random.

What is a Black hole that would attract and hold matter? Why is this necessary, for what purpose should matter be contained in such a dense state? We imagine a black hole can have a size and density billions of time greater than our sun. How is this possible?

What is electricity? Where does it come from? Why is this so?

Why is there light and darkness? Who or what causes this to be as it is?

We hear spoken of end Times. What are End Times? Are end Times mythical or will we really see some profound and unusual events. Will the World open up again and release the "fountains of the deep" as (presumably happened before?)[10]

Intelligence has been and is declining increasing the number of marginal and dumb citizens. This is a very important consideration since the number of problem solvers is not sufficient for the problems, which we face and will face later.[11] Almost all people born today survive because of the amount and quality of care, which is available to them. Even impoverished nations find help somewhere and their people do survive in greater numbers than those would have without modern technologies. Millions of dollars are spent to sustain what, in another time would not have been sustained. Dr. Pendell believed that this spells the end to our Civilization. Dr. Pendall has written a book; titled *"Sex versus Civilization"* which is well worth your time to read. It is very interesting how human biological reality functions. There are other ways to figure the future becoming of the World however to try to do so may be a futile gesture. Many individuals that have been fortunate enough to be in the *"Ruling Class"* have attempted to do this however most of their efforts and programs are simply silly. Nevertheless those pursue them with a vengeance usually centered on what can those gain personally from the deal: like Al Gore, Barack Obama our current imposter president, Dick Chaney our former make-believe vice president and dozens of others. Those are *"sucking the substance"* from this nation and its people. The only thing that will save us is that *"In the end we are all dead,"* (Shakespeare) including the thieves and opportunists.

The population problem is a religious as well as a social problem, which we presume has never been encountered before. The fact that various religions look at population as something very important places this in a special category. Keep in mind, there are religious bits in almost every argument and every defense as wall. No one knows what the outcome will be however millions expect that God will intervene:

Will God intervene?

---

10   **Brown, Walt,** *Creation: in the Beginning. Compelling Evidence for Creation and the Flood.*

11   **Pendell, Elmer PH. D**. *Sex Versus Civilization.* Noontide Press, P. O. Box 76062, Los Angeles, CA, 90005. © 1967 Dr. Elmer Pendell.

CHAPTER III

Civilization, a Complex Form of Human Extension

Seemingly, Human Acts are driven by Objectivity as well as Subjectivity

A Critique of human behavior
Based upon a peculiar understanding of distinctly formed Thought Patterns
Thoughts do form patterns and also series of patterns as those are enacted

Robert R. Fiedler © April 5, 2002
Professor Emeritus, CSLA
M. A., M. S., M. F. A.

Civilization, as we understand, is comprised of a wonderful array in respect to what is objectively, determined to be as Artifact and Implement. All that we have is an example of a technical and inventive bringing forth; in order as it were, the ideas of many men. As the Ideas combine and are refined we find ourselves benefiting from the curious combinations in thought forms and thinking thus bringing this Reality to a significantly identifiable level of containment. The actualized past can be understood *as forming a complex objectively determined multiplicity,* ***a summation of Humanities existence.*** *The known, understood and remembered* past is what we have recorded as history. Some of this is as tangible Reality and some a matter of the mind, Mythology or Metaphor.

This complex phenomenon is observed by all that are presently a witness to reality. It manifests as an *unfolding as well as enfolding* ***simultaneity of accommodation***, which is of an involving and evolving nature. It is axiomatic that any complex reality as defined above is, as a totality and is without precedent. There can only be one **NOW.** This is true because of the nature of time and space in reference to individual life, especially human life, which includes a sense of personal being, with all that this implies. All previous Civilizations underwent internal transformations, thus might be understood from a similar point of view, however none of which we are aware are/were as complex nor as extensive as the present one, which because of this profound Idiomatic is perhaps (actually, probably) doomed because of it. Precisely, the most significant elements given to function, in this present circumstance, are products of highly technical and deliberate thought, which reaches back in time for origins that are difficult to imagine. Presumably there was much disagreement and conflict in the past, which has been carried forward, *as Ideas about the past,* manifesting in what we observe presently. Such thought is based upon *precise mathematical and physical knowledge,* rapidly extended by the advent of increasingly sophisticated implementation, given to near-instant communication. Man stands presently, coincident with what we deem as profound advancement in the realm of human thought. It is evident that our implementations must be applied with carefully determined objectives in mind and with a truthfully discerning insight. It is important to understand that subjectivity ***seated in an evil intent*** can be absolutely fatal to humanity. Without "Divine Intervention" this is a certainty!

***Right now this is exactly what we have!** A few presumptuous and arrogant fools are attempting to usurp the prerogative of all humanity. Their understanding and therefore their acts are based on ancient and cabalistic forms of misunderstanding: many reject Christ as being inferior.*

Individually, we are the beneficiaries of circumstance. Certainly, at any time there have been fortunate individuals who have been gifted with a particularly generous circumstance, and this is true at the present moment as well. Presently, success is projected on the multitude as some form of entertainment, which may have questionable motivations, or a devious purpose. It should be apparent that entertainment is a combination of truth and fiction, blended for the purpose of gaining attention, so as to be able to sell tickets and products and performances. However it is certain that crucially important truths should eventually be generally known. However, the assimilation of truth for each individual may, in some instance, require many years. Actually, it is also quite certain (at least in the opinions of some) that extended investigations may be politically or otherwise *subjectively* pursued, with little or almost no meaning or justification, excepting to gain wealth for the most immediately interested parties.

An interested party, in any event, is always *subjectively* involved and thus is to some degree, self centered or generally self-concerned: Those are vain. However what is acted out or written may project, with well-reasoned intent (however, tacitly), a message behind the message. The message behind the message is often completely different, from what is imagined by the object of the effort. Importantly, Ideas advanced for consumption gain prominence, in their effectiveness, from any public exposure brought about by sensation. Music provides the most obvious sensation and can be very compelling. Importantly, all variations of human behavior can be given to some manner of expressive form, artistic and/or theatrical. Monumental productions have been developed, as never before, which exploit both the actual performance together with an ideology, all as a business venture, ***most often as a production for money.*** This brings forth the notion that money corrupts, from the long past Roman Empire, thus is carried forth the notion of bread and Circuses.

With great emphasis on subjectivity and innuendo in solicitation of gaining acceptance, for what had been heretofore considered inappropriate forms of behavior, Mass Media has given great force to the moron, the pubescent and the politically well situated celebrity. This has been accomplished mostly to the demise of profound understanding and to confuse the meaning of Virtue as being opposed to Sin. **Vice** is projected as pleasure whereas **Virtue** is most often depicted to be a laughing matter, and especially is denigrated by the silly and profane comedian. The subjectively projected nonsense, which is so apparent in our environment, is certainly important in the mind formation and consolidation of both children and adults, too preoccupied with their own circumstance to give time to serious study. As such they are easily victimized. They are immured without understanding what is, in fact, happening to them. Astoundingly, the salaries paid to media personalities is outrageous compared to those who, in fact, offer much more for truthfully reasoned and honestly pursued endeavor.

All forms of acting, rhetoric, versification, elocution and artistic production, involving use of language, have an element of *subjectivity,* which is forceful, as it is evident. Actually, *the imposition of one's self* is what makes any production or work of literary merit especially meaningful, given to *subjectively* peculiar understanding, however by innuendo much can be implied tacitly, which will affect the way the work is projected and understood, ultimately its effect on others. Tangentially, this ultimate effect on others is what is crucial to our interest and calls forth, that is beacons, some attendant understanding. Thus, we mention the current interest in probing, with intent to stimulate and/or modify the individual, as well as the collective mind. Furthermore, one must consider the notion, formulated by unknown *subjectively interested others,* of behavioral modification, given to a political and social purpose. This brings to attention the importance of *Reasoned Motive.* However, all motivations are not certainly honorable. *Subjectively* formed motivation directed toward a negative consequence, which it will engender, is a hallmark of our present complex circumstance. This touches upon the notion of a salesman's mentality, with an emphasis on economics. What's in it for me?

Almost all effort is expended toward gaining enough to live on for one's self and one's family, where a legitimate family does exist. There was a certain amount of decency, in reference to responsibility, and respect due a man for providing for his family. At present, in the United States, some other places as well *"persons"* work for the salary, fees, stipends and or benefits that go with the position. There is great interest in *legality* and virtually none in *humility,* prudence, decency and, generally, *morality.* This is a tragedy that is being deliberately encouraged by those with the most power, and the most money, determined to enslave the rest in a manner of sociological prison. Their object is apparently to destroy Christianity, the creditability of Jesus Christ and, for some, the Caucasian race. Those are virtual enemies of what is held dear to millions perhaps billions of people. Those draw their myopic Ideas from an *Ancient and Tribal* past.

Sex is important and cannot be denied. Sex must be limited to marriage and the begetting of children and the sustaining of a family. Sex is not entertainment although it is pleasurable: for a reason. The reason is to sustain the human race: it is absolutely essential. Some Catholics have large families, which seems like a good Idea, to those that have a large family. Nevertheless there is the fact that the world is growing at an alarming rate. The population has ballooned from one billion to six billion since 1840, within a century and one half.[12] By 1930, *a mere 90 years,* there were about two billion people in the world. In 1961 there were three billion people in the world: **in *just 31 years. Fifteen years*** later there were four billion people; *eleven years* later there were five billion people. Presently, there are six billion plus several hundred million. This must not and cannot continue.

Catholic people must be educated and some should be encouraged to have fewer children thus to slow the advance in numbers. Responsible parents will do this as has been proven in many places, especially Europe. Illegitimacy must be strongly discouraged, as must be the disgusting habits of some of the movers and shakers in this world. Men that boast of their disgusting habits of fornication should be encouraged to "shut up" and should be ridiculed for such uncivilized behavior. Men should not take advantage of pretty young girls who are too young to be mothers. The Law must effect serious punishment on any that would do this. There are cultural and religious elements involved here that will be difficult to supplant nevertheless such habits must be better understood and curtailed for humanity and the future of the human race. The subject is too broad for this writing however is it very significant in effect.

---

12 **Pendell, Elmer PH. D**. *Sex Versus Civilization.* Noontide Press, P. O. Box 76062, Los Angeles, CA, 90005. © 1967 Dr. Elmer Pendell. Pps. 12 & 13. "Our problem becomes more formidable with the shrinking of time in which the billions are added: 90 years; 31 years; 15 years; 11 years; 9 years." This cannot continue starvation will help to solve the problem!

Some persons in a commanding or seemingly opportune setting are able to bilk millions some even billions from a malignant form of <u>*Democracy become as Socialism in service of* **Greed.**</u> **Greed** is the most obviously operative of the *seven deadly sins.* There is little attention given by the really rich and successful to the needs of the little persons, the ones that do all of the service and otherwise necessary jobs, which provide the millions and billions for the fortunate few that, manipulate at the top. And, there are very few indeed. Some of the more fortunate do engage in charity, which those (milk) for tax refunds. Nevertheless next to the cost of a fifty million-dollar yacht their efforts are marginal at best. Those do receive great acclaim for their efforts, which is certainly somewhat reasonable. The Person is being redefined by sociologists, psychologists and government usurpation. Notions concerning the Occult figure quite prominently in their plan of divide and conquer. Most individuals will value their liberty and the freedom to be as they would like to be, beginning with haircuts and dress and working toward a more complex and often misunderstood "***kind***' of being. Today's ***"person"*** seems very confused concerning what, who and how they are and how they should act. Those are taught to *"**Act**"* as those engage in one performance after another. A form of Sociological Engineering has deliberately confused today's youth. The engineering works for [the] System, which almost no one understands, doing what no sane man would do.

In all instances of subjective as well as objective imposition the past gives impetus to the present as the unknown future is being beckoned, becoming (in time) a newly formed reality as part of the construct of an ongoing Civilization. In many, perhaps most instances the objectively defined implementations, especially those, which utilize the new electronic forms of technology, are placed in the service of self-interest, which in profoundly significant negative instances will ultimately prove fatal for millions.[13] In fact, this is most likely what will destroy the Civilization and introduce a New Dark Age. The New Dark Age is not understood in advance of its becoming and will be a surprise, placing billions in desperation. Those who are the imagined leaders will, very likely in effect, destroy most of what has been more wisely nurtured. Those are presumptuous fools and shallow minded nitwits.

The most obvious of these appear in the distribution of *pornography* and the mass appeal of *gambling,* both of which, for many, become an addiction. Shame and self-restraint have been abandoned by clever use of words in service of self-interest using the technologies of communication. Communication should be considered more intelligently and should not be simply babbling on the phone or over the airways.

The computer and the Internet provide the ultimate form of communication and distribution of information, in an implementation, which is marvelously *objective* in complexity and formidable as a means of communication. *Subjectively formed notions,* whether seated in truth or not, are widely available. For the layman, the mechanics of the computer, combined with the intrigue of searching for some personal satisfaction, make the computer a wonderful therapy for the curious, however the ill advised may be *subjectively* assaulted by what is available. The accountant and the money manager find the dependability and *objectivity* of this implementation to be of ultimate perfection, in the accounts receivable departments and in the offices of big government.

---

13   ***The way War becomes*** from the encouragement of unknown others is an example. War always has elements of secrecy and intrigue, for incorrectly reasoned objectives. War is always sinful and destroys the lives of the victims one way or another.

The courts and the airways are evidence of the theatrical nature, which has been given to *"revised notions"* of historic events, all for interested viewing by a population of poorly informed spectators, with nothing better to do than watch in an attentive however stupefied silence. The extent of any significant consequence, which may be just now becoming apparent, as the result of this unforeseen and complex Problematic, is not generally understood, or is understood only in part. Indeed, truthful dialogue is restrained by the imposed expectations of political correctness, given to the direction of fools and money-grubbers. Ultimately, as in the past, the wisest and truthfully good man amongst us will be crucified. The form of the crucifixion may be different however the effect is the same. This is precisely what happened to Christ; a consequence of circumstance much as is right now, misunderstanding, usurpation and the lie.

We admonish that Civilization is, in both general and specific terms, an extension of manner, Habit and custom in a very substantial and truthfully unfolding reality. Population aggregates stem from the family, the community, the tribe, the nation-state and finally the great nation. For some, the ultimate form will be a World Order, under the rule of corrupt law, within which law Christian Morals will be abandoned in favor of Popular Opinion, driven by unknown masters of finance and the media. Men such as Donald Trump, George Soros, Clint Eastwood and Willie Nelson have too much influence on too many people. The doings and rhetoric over-comes the nearly non-existent thought and ideas of millions. Their influence is coupled with a venal, selfish and limited sense of what is truthfully significant. The notion immediately above, as inferred in the title of this critique, suggests we must begin to question just what exactly is being extended, in the domain of a *subjectively compromised reality,* when such compromise is secretly imposed. ***May we question this?*** For what manner and purpose are present nefarious impositions being pushed and for what eventuality have they been determined? Who will gain most from this endeavor?

Often we hear spoken of a New World Order. What exactly does this mean? From whence did such concept originate and who will most benefit from this, if and when it might come to be? The Idea is not new. Wealthy and influential men, including various leaders, have always wanted to rule the Civilization, or that part of which those were aware. The Idea of a Master Race is old indeed, dating from about 500 BC.[14] It is the will to power given to a means of enactment. The means of enactment in the past were dependent upon threat, fighting armies and starvation. The new form is money, finance Capitalism working against the common man. ***Money has moved from being a servant of humanity to being a controlling force,*** which can be used with impunity.

Objectively sustained thinking has afforded us with marvelous technologies, however not many can imagine what might be the ultimate outcome from all this wonderful technical advancement. In many instances, implementation appears to be far beyond what is reasoned as appropriate and much of it is developed in service of foolish and corrupt opportunism. Actually when the entire World has the technologies for rapid and seasonal mass production we will have so much stuff that it should be practically free. This raises a pertinent question: How much is too much?

Technologies based upon verifiable and well-understood complexes are very fruitful in achieving the outcome of intention. The modern airplane together with the implements for war makes this obvious. Engineers know what they are doing and are quite able to proceed with some high degree of certainty, having stood (as it were) on the shoulders of all the giants who have come before

---

14   **Mullins Eustice,** *The World Order, Our Secret Rulers*. (Pub. Ezra Pound Institute, Staunton, VA. 24401, Second Edition, 1992).

them. However, in the realms of the more philosophical, theological or eschatological formulated thinking, concerning political and moral issues in particular, given to the great variety in the thinking of humans, things are not so good. ***We are far behind where we must be,*** if we are to succeed and to sustain as an ultimately complex Civilization, with promise for a better and more enduring future.

Western people, in spite of complex communication networks, are not fully aware of the sentiments *subjectively* held, by most of the peoples of this world and we do not know exactly what their intentions might be. This is certain since all information given is not based on perfect knowledge of the truth. Information, whether truthful or not, is open to interpretation, thus it becomes subjective (given to the interpretation of the subject) in the process. Only the Catholic Church stresses the importance of absolute truth, the continuation of Tradition and perfect knowledge. The Western World, largely become as a result of Catholic thought, which appeals to Mankind, is extremely complex and somewhat evasive to the uninformed or to the heretic.

The Catholic believes all men, are made in the image of the Creator, who shares an infinite personality with His creatures. *This is a most profound **Idea*** whether or not one believes it is true. The Catholic Church is ridiculed for this understanding and conviction as being dogmatic, which it is and must be. In the terms of a Philosopher, *that which is must be as it is or it would be something else.* This applies very much to Philosophy, *as an objective discipline, the dogma is certainly essential.* Keep in mind, Science has many definite tenets (dogmas) upon which our technologies and our Civilization are built. The theologian must appeal to common sense and the Intellect to make universal Christian dogma evident, thus to be more generally accepted as belief. Theologians, prone to a too *subjective interpretation* as they succumb to vanity, are not always convincing, beside which some inspire to undermine what has been accomplished in this world. Irrespective of subjectivity, ***Truth is eternal*** and as such [IS] absolute. ***Simply put, what [IS] is ALL, that [IS].*** This is an importantly *crucial* issue, since all mankind does not believe in the same God, nor do those believe in the same way or with commensurate comprehension, albeit there can be only one Omnipotence and only one Humanity. Humanity presents a very diverse singularity; it is an ultimately complex, multi-faceted singularity. Keep in mind, a singularity can be parsed or broken into segments.

Given an understanding of the complexity of our present dilemma, it is wise to reconsider our understanding, of what is the consequence of separating Church and State. Given the nature of the present Idiomatic, this is no easy task, however there must be found (as does exist) common Tenants which, might help in the development of a consensus. Religiosity is one thing, Goodness quite something else; history is evident as proof of this. Given the Islamic Religion, which has some fine tenants, there is much which might be said about this assertion. If we expect others to develop a common understanding of what we are doing, it follows we must put in evidence some common held understandings of our own.

In the past some Religious Men, so called, did monstrous things. This was the fault of the man or men not of the institution and is why the Catholic Church, founded by Jesus Christ was determined to work from a position of perfect truth. Omnipotent Truth is Perfect Truth, the Truth of the Creator. Nevertheless, the question for some does remain **who was the Creator?** It requires that more men, all men, understand this and furthermore that those behave with this understanding as a basis for personal action, controlling all acts of personal volition.

The best Statesmen attempt to do this, to form correct and decent consensus. However they are often missing a part of the main ingredient, which has its origin in morality and the moral order, for all men, for all time: precisely the birth and life of the Man Christ, who founded the Catholic Church. Politics must include acquiescence to natural law, which preceded all forms of man-made laws. The rule of law, as presently understood is missing many of the most important dimensions, defined in the Ten Commandments! Some want to remove the Ten Commandments from the dialogue and to not consider the implications. Such as they, may be considered as immoral and possibly nefarious. Moral objectivity is based on absolutes, which are defended in reality as given to past well-understood incident. If we do not learn from the past, we will certainly repeat the same errors, which are known as such, however denied. There are moral imperatives and examples of the force of goodness, in opposition to evil. Evil becomes of *misdirected subjectivity* in respect to others, which are exploited, *mostly for profits (a few coins) given to greed*: as was the case with Judas in the time of Christ. Most of the world's leaders, so called, are not wise men; those are fools with a manner of legal or military protection. They wear medals and give speeches which, no one believes because they are often written by others who may have conflicting motives and they are therefore meaningless.

People who have very little in reference to technology, who suffer because of this, do know that we have much as a consequence of our technology. Perhaps millions imagine all what is ours could be placed in their hands. September 11, 2001 may be just a beginning, albeit a sensational one. The follow-up may be quite a surprise, for now perhaps quite beyond comprehension. How we will solve this existing dilemma will determine the future of mankind, for the next few centuries at least. Many of our Politicians seem to favor bringing many of the unfortunate people here, to our country, which may ruin our country philosophically, socially, politically and morally. The philosophic and moral Issues are profound. Since we are presumed leaders this is an unwise direction. Better to allow our country to prosper as we attempt to convert others to some of our ways. This is a difficult assignment however is not impossible if and when we are able to stop the mortal conflicts: which in fact many Western leaders favor.

It would seem prudent and wise to extend and to export our *objectively defined technological comprehension* without undue negatively subjective influence, thus to afford greater access as we set an example for goodness, which others might begin to emulate. This must be accomplished in the name of universal Christianity and acknowledged as such, which co-incidentally is named Catholicism, Universal Christianity. To a very large extent this is being accomplished at the present time, however self-interest and exigent circumstance, in many instances, often prevent positive accomplishments for those who are most in need of help. For many of the needy ignorance are the problem thus *"Proper Education"* is the solution, which would include principles ordinate to the Catholic Faith; that is the Universal Faith in Jesus Christ.

There is no other way!

*

*   *

CHAPTER IV
Light, Matter and Movement

The three listed components are each dependent of the other two.
They work in phenomenal ways which, are not always well understood.

To begin all elements exist in space and are there for something less than forever.
Forever is all future time. No one really understands what this means: we do try. Most tangible forms are limited by that same tangible nature. All forms are prone to disintegration; in Time.

This is true since all forms are wrapped in Time.

What we perceive as an object is an amalgamation of molecules whose interior elements are moving at very high velocity. The movement is so fast that all of the space within the molecule appears as being solid; the solidity is what we perceive.

There are other ideas about what is an object. For example objects are thought possibly to be composed of pure light. If this is true then all objectivity is a matter of being light which is quite phenomenal, certainly unique. This has some biblical and theological basis for God is thought, by some to be pure white light. He is the light of the world.

Light is created by the burning of matter in the stars from which it radiates in all directions. Light also contains heat which radiates along with the light. Such as this represents a manner of deep and profound thought and is not within the interest sphere of everyone. The light emanating from the stars moves with the heat until it falls upon an object thereby to make the object apparent to a viewer. This is an optical event and the light falling on the object is apparent to the senses of the human person. The human eye works synergistically, with the universal order and we are thus able to see some part of reality. There exist, mathematical equations for this phenomenon which become very complex as the distance and volume involved grows toward infinity, for example, considering a move toward infinity: (∞).

$$e^x = 1 + \frac{x}{1!} + \frac{x^2}{2!} + \frac{x^3}{3!} + \cdots, \quad -\infty < x < \infty$$

What we see will direct what we do to a considerable degree. The mathematics, are quite forbidding however, given a degree of common sense, this does not prevent one from understanding what is happening. As the light moves away from the source, when the distance is doubled we retain one fourth of the illumination. One can understand that the amount of light is tending toward nothing from the moment it leaves the source. One can imagine that the light reaching the earth from a distant star was very intense when it first left the star and has diminished greatly before reaching the earth where it is now visible. Additionally the amount of heat is diminished as well. If this were not true the earth would have burned up long ago. All of this appears to be part of a Universal plan of what we would consider a mathematically perfect order.

Considering the diminishing of light and heat from the source presents us with a real factor in the universal order of existence. There is a profound understanding in this aspect of reality. Posit a question to yourself. At what point is the light and heat completely dissipated and therefore no longer exists? Is there such a place? What happens at such place if such place does exist? Both questions seem rather obtuse however they are not. All of reality exists within a domain subject to this phenomenal and somewhat "Holy" consideration. The temperature is held to a certain mean degree at exactly the right place for the existence of life as we know it to be: any life for that matter.

This is not accidental, this is planned and brought to become by a profound and omnipotent force. This is the force of whom we call God. God is all powerful and infinite in Time and Space. God made the rules and figured out how to make them work for as long as will be necessary. No one is certain of how long that might be. Man bungles with the comprehension of this omnipotent force which he cannot understand and will never control. Men will control some small part of reality however not all of it; **never!**

Movement is significant as well. Objects move including much of which we cannot see. The movement is necessary so to maintain the proper balance within the system. Rotation, a matter of movement, is important so to achieve the exposing of all surfaces to what are necessary forces and conditions for maintaining, equilibrium in the system of things and bits of things. The things which we see are obviously apparent whereas what they are made of is not. By their outward appearance we recognize a chair, a table or a bed. The composition of the materials, that is the

$$(1+x)^n = 1 + \frac{nx}{1!} + \frac{n(n-1)x^2}{2!} + \cdots$$

Bits that combine to make them are not so apparent. The bits are of interest to researchers and those seeking deeper meaning of reality.

Movement makes the whole outward surface of an object apparent to the light and heat, that envelope it compensating for the direction and placement of the source. This too is a phenomenal and "Holy" occurrence and is the insight and working of a divine intelligence.

$$(1+x)^n = 1 + \frac{nx}{1!} + \frac{n(n-1)x^2}{2!} + \cdots G = I = \text{All that is:}$$

"God is among other things

An Idea, only a part of reality; however this Idea is the most important part."

*

*   *

CHAPTER V

Thoughts

A cold wind blows across all faces, turning each to ice.
To live and to die is to know, then finally to pay the price!

Foreboding, almost endless is the merciless, windblown sea
The silent depths of which can easily capture you and me

No manner of human strength can resist the silent depths
All joy and anger there, in darkness, is turned to silence

High above and looking down, each one seems to own the mountain
Still and awesome, the mountain is not for sale

No manner of money can buy one little piece of the sky
All Heavens above belong to Him! How many wonder why?

Perhaps, whether or not you may now agree
This you will know by and by

If you were a bird then you might fly
Yet still not possess one little piece of the sky

TIME

Time stretches like transparent rubber all across the Universe
Thence returns from whence it came

And; no two moments are the same
Adding to our sense of wonderment!

All we can see are snowflakes; falling in random places
Turn to white, all empty spaces

Then in the spring the silent snows are melting
Gone all that was white, having left no traces

NOW

Now: Time is as a moment, as an instant become, it is somehow manifest
And we perceive this as an event, from, which some consequence emanates
No matter what all acts have consequence!

Thinking can never change the consequence of Now, when such consequence
Is once free, in time/space from such event?

Nevertheless, frozen in the past, not one instant will ever last
Only consequence remains, which is what each must live with

This is, in part, the surmise, which underlies some aspects of what is called
Original sin and it relates very definitely to our possession of Free Will

Free Will, it is believed by millions, is a gift from God
Not all will believe this, however, all should at least consider that this [is] a part of reality

A belief in God, is the principal component in the thinking of millions
And, this has been true for a very ling time

Now, the future is becoming as the past, this is the great existential transformation
Whatever was is and shall be regardless of whom rules each nation

Now, Evil is working as ever before, attempts to kill all that is good
Simple as this appears to be, it is most often not understood

Understanding requires the best of a man, wherever he may be
Now, however, obviates the truths, which he may not wish to see

Sin is living in every soul, defining wherever each man may stand
It propagates in various ways often deals a treacherous hand

SIN I

_____

The Seven Deadly Sins

Avarice, Envy, Gluttony, Greed, Jealousy, Lust, Slothfulness

Sin is relentless and may seem a delight, striking hardest the young.
So often sin turns what was beautiful into a pile of dung.

The young maiden dreams as she brushes her hair,
Only to find life is full of trouble and despair.

What seemed lovely, so fine and good?
May all be taken swiftly away?

What seems so right?
At the time
May be
Simply
Lust

Envy
Is to covet
What rightfully
Belongs to another

Envy makes it impossible
To enjoy one's own possessions

Envy is part of stingy and encourages jealousy
Which, brings about indignation, sadness and despair

Longing for what is impossible, the fool imagines what can never be
Advertising has taken tight hold of this concept and works it by the season

Individuals covet what they do not need and may never appreciate
Nevertheless they march to Satan's tune in a vulgar parade

The fool is spawned and feeds on ignorance
Of this silliness, all must be aware
Much of life is simply an act
Too many have signed Satan's pact

Notwithstanding, the Comedian and the Juggler are part of life's game
However, the effects of sin are always the same

Envy is handmaiden to **greed,** bringing misery to every nation they play hand in hand
Wars are fought and millions are killed with little or no insightful reason, blood covers the land
Jealousy too, will have its sad effects, mostly on they that presumably lead the band

SIN II

_____

Avarice and **anger,** becoming as rage, rest heavily on the shoulders of an unfortunate jealousy
Causing pain simultaneously to both perpetrator and victim
Avarice is important in mortal conflict
As it reinforces aggression
Against another
Gives reason
Where
None
May
Be
*

Gluttony and slothfulness go hand and hand, like you know, each supporting the other kind
Then food and laziness combine to wreck havoc on body and mind
And together they suffer an intermittent agony
From growing large and reducing
Looking in the mirror
At self grown fat
And older
Too
And
Lazy will
Not accomplish much
Rest and sleep are your good friends
As you imagine that all is not what it should be
Nevertheless you must never do what is justly required of you
Rather just complain and let another do your share like mommy once would do
Who then might build this world, as must-need is, if there were too many more just like you?

Sin seems as so much fun and has placed goodness on the run, in [the] land of make-believe
And so much of what is, in truth, is sinful but viewed as harmless entertainment
And when so many are involved, it is impossible to change the game
The corruption of our youth has given sin another name
Which, no doubt, provides cover in advance?
So, most everyone will take a chance
Especially sex is viewed as fun
Which certainly it is
And the lecher
Will always
To get
His

When one considers sin, as being customary, it is difficult to understand why it is considered as evil.
Sin when multiplied is never imagined as sin. It soon becomes a custom; and, sinful ways abound.
Everyone is doing it, so they say, influencing young and old. Then anyone can *"do it"* any way.
When there are no rules and everyone has the tools, then the orgy will begin.
And this is exactly when Satan and Lucifer will step in!

Robert R. Fiedler © 5-3-2005

CHAPTER VI

Thinking

One can imagine, possibly assume, that no one in this World
Could have a truthfully comprehensive grasp of what we call Reality.
Such comprehensive thought requires a certainly Omnipotent [One].

That [One] is whom many call God,
The Creator of all, that is seen and unseen.

Whether one believes in God or not is quite unimportant,
The fact remains, God is a persisting Idea and as such it is imagined
He is able to understand all that is, was or will be: past present and future.
Keep in mind, what any man or woman THINKS is irrelevant in the infinite and
Real complex of what we perceive and understand as our present REALITY.
Some imagine knowing so much, how everyone should live and behave.

They are generally wrong
In fact those are FOOLS.
Those are narrow-minded, vain and inept in their thinking.
Nevertheless many of them have become unimaginably wealthy.

Ideas, which emanate from Socialism and Communism,
All forms of Collectivist thinking are the mortal enemies of humanity.
Such thinking will lead the World into accepting a one-World Government.
This is a very unworkable plan designed to impoverish most of Humanity.
In such plan there will be no room for a Divinity, no room for our God.
This will be a Communist Utopia, everyone will do as expected:
Or face serious consequences; they will be serious!

People believe what they are told to believe by their leaders.
The leaders are mostly simple-minded fools, but they do have the power.
Communism implies communal living sharing the wife and kids with others.
This is **an Ideal** that has persisted over a long period of time; it will continue.
It is now possible to see how this can be done with words, not guns.
Guns will only be used against the more primitive people;
Who are not well indoctrinated, into the System?
For a short period before total chaos;
An ancient religion will prevail:

There are remnants of cabalistic Jewish-Zionist, Marxist and some English thinking
Such Ideas have captured Western Civilization and have poisoned the minds of youth:
Such thinking may form as the WILL TO DOMINATE all others.

Are we being reasonable?

In spite of the mountains of written material and the inconsistent musings of our leaders, the above assertion stands as a certainty. This is true because of the nature and substance of a great Universe and a Civilization, which is always in a state of flux, receiving and giving simultaneously, as it is destined "To be" or not to be. There are simply too may variables and too many points of view for anyone to imagine that what they are doing is absolutely correct. One must consider the nature and substance of all the information. Additionally one must be truthfully informed, **[Who]** *is doing the thinking* and **Why?** Who is doing the thinking calls to question the level of intelligence and the thoughts already contained in such, as a thinking or thoughtful mind. Many of the World's leaders, as we understand them to be (?) have been crude Dolts that enjoy taking advantage of helpless victims. The worst present form of such ignorance, intransigence or insolence is in the encouragement of children to do there fighting. *Those haven't the guts to stand up against their "presumed" enemy.*

The children are sacrificed to the dumb and stupid reasoning of somewhat perverted adults.

What does this mean? Why?

Why one is assertive one way or another is tied to intent, which may or may not be broadly known.[15] Intent is very important since outcomes are presumed in advance and carefully pursued. When the intentions are hidden and are not widely known, as is so often the case, such efforts can be deemed as being ***secretive or conspiratorial.*** The call is for *"Transparency,"* which is the wrong word *it is a euphemism* to confuse the People. As such it means nothing! What is needed is simply honesty, decency, truthfulness and fair-minded endeavor, all considered from a Christian, or Christ inspired point of view.

For those who do not believe in Christ, just consider the **Ideas** without the person and do not confuse Christ's **Ideas** with the many schismatic religious ideas that plague humanity. With a multitude of dispositions, different levels of knowing, the various forms that the intellect may take and with innumerable beliefs it becomes necessary to call on Divine intervention, which is not necessarily understood or appreciated and may not be apparent, especially so to unbelievers. And, such intervention may not always be forthcoming in the future. Many deny the existence of a Divinity and there are many interpretations of what is Divine. Certainly, evil men would call Satan divine.

Initially, where do thoughts come from and how are those thoughts developed? What motivates or causes people to think?

---

15 **Intent is not always clearly understood** even by those that are *"Imagined to be Somehow"* in control of emerging circumstances. The reason for this is because of the large numbers of *"Near Truths"* that may have been encouraged or overlooked in setting up the **DEAL.** This is understandable when one considers all of the "seemingly" necessary polemics, which may accompany the "Dialectics" of the politically inclined Movers and Shakers, given any circumstance. This introduces a new dilemma. How does a Bantu tribesman understand the nature of the affairs "thrown his way" for his understandably naive manner of being? One might imagine things are bad, at this very moment, and are becoming even (worse). Where are the wise men leading us? Who are the wise men? Why are those considered wise? *Keep in mind Thoughts do have form as well as substance* and those originate from SPACE! We are living in that SPACE, which includes and holds all that is!

Consider all of the emphasis placed on what is imagined to be correct. **First** there is the information, which may or may not coincide with the *known and understood truth.* Communication is simply an exchange of Information, which may be true or false or a bit of each *for the effect it might have on the Recipient.* At best, such exchange or deliverance is difficult because of the nature and intent of the provider as well as those who receive the information. Basic Intelligence and the ability to comprehend are immediately obvious. Nevertheless there are innumerable discrepancies. We have *heard "Oh what a terrible web we weave when first we practice to deceive"* uttered by no less than Shakespeare. This statement underlies the reality of all present and past political, ethical, religious and all other thought forms. Let us consider the reality of this assertion.

Thoughts do have form. The form of a thought is related to the objective desired and to who is doing the thinking and also to the purpose and direction, which is the object of such thinking. All related elements are tempered by the level of intelligence and to what means are available in attaining one or another outcome from thinking. Keep in mind; all thoughts are inter-related, each to all others being brought into the system. Given any such [System], *certainly a very complex abstraction,* it must be understood that each individual will not have all of the details or all of the necessary intellectual components required to participate in the unfolding consequence of that same dialogue, which includes certain elements. This is most unfortunate however, is part of nearly all structured literary encounters. Study should provide the necessary restraint on all thought systems. What is being considered, at this point is simply the meaning and intent of words and the honesty and reasoning which supports the veracity of such intention (In fact, this is Philosophy). All Philosophies are *"thought Systems"* thus the entire system should be understood. This forms a difficult impediment in most thinking, which is nearly impossible to deal with.

Second, For hundreds, perhaps thousands of years, men have created mythologies and stories of various kinds that have become accepted as the truth or something near the truth.[16] In each instance we imagine that the originator had something "in *his/her* mind" that gave the reason for what he did or the object and reason for his understanding. We may or may not know exactly what the reasons for past acts and beliefs were. *Many assume* what were motives or goals *and act as though their assumptions were correct.* **All understanding is** personal although there are some or many that may agree generally in the substance of a given understanding. Such consensus leads to the promotion and promulgation of one or another unique mythology. Mythology becomes embedded in 'Tradition" and may remain for centuries. As such, for some the Mythology is an important part of "their' Tradition and Culture. Primitive people are *"thought, by some, to be"* more in tune with their mythologies, which may or may not be a reasonable assumption. There are many mythologies forming at this moment whereabouts *the seminal information is slanted in favor of a desired objective.* War, especially, begets a form of mythology, which in turn is used to motivate further killing or to engender a feeling of hatred, at least for the moment, and nationalism or even heroism.[17] None of this is good! When the player in a mythology is known and well understood,

---

16 **Every act** of every man adds a small bit to what is the truth. Most of this has very little consequence however some acts are significant and add immensely for good or for evil to what we know and understand. Be that as it may, the Truth is Reality, without censure or promotion. **Reality** [IS] Truth.

17 **Keep in mind** the history of War, therefore to a large extent any mythology, is generally written by the victor. The looser is given little opportunity to express an opinion, if any, so the history will favor the position and motives of the winner. Of itself, this fact (alone) is responsible for the near-universal misunderstanding of our present political and social environment.

such as a son or father, then the form of the mythology has a more pertinent meaning. When one, well known, is killed or maimed the meaning is probably made clearer, by that fact. When the mythology is the work of clever interlopers, lunatics, traitors and frauds the Mythology is more difficult to comprehend however, is no less effective. Indeed, the effect of a carefully structured mythology, which is promoted, for example by mass media, may be profound in its effect on a given population. "We the People" is *an abstraction* that only has a definite meaning pertinent to the context of a particular circumstance.

To repeat **"We the People"** is an abstraction that only has a definite meaning pertinent to the context of circumstance. Keeps in mind there are many forms of "We the People" which have been encouraged for one or another purpose, usually with some political intention in mind, often an invention based on a slogan or a form of coercive intent. Keep in mind also that an understanding of "We as a People" can be structured from outside the Group that considers itself as such. *We the People are a euphemism, so to cover present **Ideas** and procedures for, which popular support is vital and necessary.* Mobs cry, "We the People" without any understanding of what are "We the People."

It is difficult to give that, which is secretly contrived a definite meaning since it is a form of thought substance not easily accessed. Secrecy, in such instance serves the objective of the perpetrators even as it confuses whom we call the People or the Public. "Secret knowledge is the basis of all power. Your source of information depends upon who you are and what position you hold in Society."[18] With mass communication this could be changed however even mass communication suffers from all the same contrivances as were apparent before. Most forms of communication and most thought forms have unknown elements, which must be given some creditability. The People or the Public is left wanting as the confusion mounts, in Time, presumably aiding the beneficiaries of the mythology, *which at this point becomes as a Hoax.*

The understanding, which insists that six million Jews were "deliberately killed for political purposes" during the Second World War, is a good current example; there are others as well. This is no joke; it has affected the thinking and the thought substance of millions of individuals, which thought substance, is variously intermingled within the minds of the People. Certainly millions of individuals were killed during the Second World War, Christians, Jews, Moslems, Atheists, others as well. No one, no single person, knows exactly how many, or exactly how each was killed. Because of the extreme conviction of the perpetrators of the Myth of six million, this is a very difficult subject to approach and it is not our intention to deal with the details. Others are better qualified than we are. We state this only as an example of what *may be* a current mythology, *which has been promoted for political and financial reasons.*[19] Most of the evidence, which denies the number six-million and which claims a number which is much smaller, is suppressed because of misunderstanding or because there is a need to keep the mythology of six million alive. The

---

18   **Jacobsen, Steven,** *Mind Control in the United States,* With an Introduction by Antony Sutton. Critique Publishing, P. O. Box 1145, Santa Rosa, CA 95406. ISBN #0-911485-00-7. LC #85-70431.

19   **Poncins, Vicomte Leon De,** *Judaism and the Vatacan.* Translated from the French by Timothy Tindal-Robertson. 1967. Reprinted 1985 and 1999. Pg. 51. "At the end of the Second World War, Germany was condemned to pay to the State of Israel in compensation for the wrongs she had done to German and foreign Jews indemnities amounting to 2,000,000 marks a year, and these payments, which have been made regularly, have contributed considerably to the budget of Israel." **ALSO:** see footnote 1, page 51 for further details. Such payment must be a part of the "Jewish equation."

reasons for sustaining such as this Mythology are secret in fact may be considered as *conspiratorial,* in that those are promoted as part of what is considered by some to be a Hoax? The evidence perhaps false has been promoted relentlessly and the Myth is building in the minds of a large segment of the World's population.[20] Some others do imagine that there is much exaggeration in the claim that specifies six million and those deny that number for various reasons.[21]Their reasoning and account of the details is subverted or made to appear foolish by those in charge of circumstance. In fact, some of those who were presumably a part of this misunderstanding had only a minimal experience with the subject which, they perhaps did not completely understand. This is not an unreasonable assumption!

Third, Ideas and thought forms are altered by new information given and by new facts in the mind of each individual that is open to receiving such information. Individually we process information, which may or may not be truthful, in reference to what is already within our mind. *Individual thoughts originate between the ends of proximate neurons* an evasive process, no doubt, nevertheless functional. Research is being done on this and we cannot comment at this time except to suggest that those thoughts originate apparently in space and from nothing. *This has a Biblical Connotation that goes directly to Genesis,* and we infer that no one [can] understand this. There are some things, such as this, that we cannot know and must accept on Faith. The principle philosophy driving Faith of the Western Civilization has been Catholicism, which unfortunately millions have chosen to abandon, searching for a Faith that suits their own incorrect behavior and often-bad taste. Any Faith which is chosen will be, at best, incomplete.

The Catholic Faith as enumerated by Christ, the Savior, has been and is being carefully deformed, in the minds of the people, altered in its Liturgy, Vestments and Architectural wonders. The Alter the communion rail, the tabernacle is missing or changed. Who watches over this and guides the decisions? It may be a Committee that wishes to include all points of view. It may be an ecumenical group that hopes to change the nature and structure of a divinely revealed Faith. This is a complex Issue, which must be better understood. Largely the administrative personnel, including the Popes that have been commissioned to guard the Faith are accomplishing the destruction of the Catholic Faith. Beginning with Pope John XXIII who is known to have worn an ephod,[22] beneath "his act"; was Pope John XXIII really a Jewish Priest posing as the Pope of the Catholic Church? There have been a number of anti-Popes during the history of the Catholic Church. It is understood that Pope John XXIII was a Mason and did attend Masonic meetings in civilian clothing.[23] Pope Paul VI was also heretical and had a long list of blasphemous and improper acts.[24] Pope John Paul II was an ecumenicist and included many other forms of worship to be a part of his Papacy. Each time he embraced another form of worship he gave up something

---

20 Some believe the number of six million was first used in about 1939 and referred to all of the Jews in Europe, at that time. Nevertheless, the number has been defended and is not considered by the perpetrators to be rather exact. Who knows if this is true? Keep in mind large numbers (?) of Jews did emigrate to the United States and other places as well.

21 **Butz, Arthur R.** *The Myth of Six Million.* The Noontide Press, PO Box 76062. Los Angeles, CA. © 1976 A. R. Butz. ISBN 0-911038. LC # 77-78964.

22 **The Ephod** is "a richly embroidered outer vestment worn by Jewish priests in ancient times."(Webster)

23 **Most Holy Family Monastery,** *A Voice Crying in the Wilderness,* Issues 1-2-3-4. 4425 Schneider Road, Filmier, N. Y. 14735

24 **See Tract on Pope Paul VI** from Most Holy Family Monastery.

from his own. Many of the Churches enemies supported his nefarious ways. Just now he is being considered, by some, for Sainthood. Pope Benedict VI is the fifth Pope to deny certain aspects of the Faith. He is in a very vulnerable position because of the divergent views between, which he must carefully thread his way. He has a brilliant mind however, what is his reasoning, what are his objectives? If the Catholic Faith is destined to be the Universal Faith how might this be best accomplished? Certainly not by giving up the basic tenants of the true Catholic Faith

It is easy to understand that when one is able to assert influence at the highest level of the papacy the destruction of the Church becomes, for a time, as an eminent threat. This provides for the narrow road, over which each must travel, to attain Heaven. Good people must object to the blasphemy and hypocrisy within the Vatican and insist that proper steps be taken to reconstitute the original form which, was that Institution founded by Christ. In disposition, philosophy and objectives the Church must remain as Christ and God intended, with the guidance of the Holy Ghost, spirit of Christianity. The Popes are the leaders of the flock. Are those leading in the proper direction? The attacks upon and negligence within the Catholic Church threaten the Civilization and all Cultures within. *The Catholic Church is the Christian basis for our FOREVER!* If the Church were to fall, the Civilization and Culture, which is Christianity will fall with it. Certainly this is the hope of the Anti Christ, whomsoever he/she may be? Actually, there are many Anti Christ those are everywhere apparent.

The Catholic Church is opposed too much of what is understood as the New World Order. The Council on Foreign Relations, The Bilderburgers, The Club of Rome, Cecil Rhodes Round Table groups, The World Bank, all subversive groups and conspiracies some present Governments and any of the sin and thievery, deceit and fraud that those may represent. The Church opposes all forms of political secrecy, cheating, lying, murder and all of the sinful ways of all men, *not some but ALL.* The Theology and methods are God given designed to create a perfect society. God did hope and continues to hope that men will reach the highest level of attainment, which is *Angelic* and become one in being with Him, forever. Toward this end man has been given Free will so to become perfect of his own volition. Personal volition, well directed, is perhaps the greatest asset on the way to Heaven. If you do not believe in God consider the programs without the figure of God as head, those are well conceived and have brought millions to understanding about good ness and life. Those are essential to the smooth workings of the Civilization. They have replaced much of the superstition and witchcraft of the past with learned and inspired understanding without which, we would be certainly doomed; now and forever. In a practical sense the Catholic Church has aided in the development of Science, Industry, matters of Procedure, Hospitals, Schools, Social accommodation and a myriad of related elements and functions.

Fourth, it is known that the Catholic Faith can provide a cogent Philosophy, finished and decisive to guide Civilization.[25] One cannot add to or subtract from this maturely developed Philosophy; *alterations cannot improve on what is perfect in its being.* We assume that the Philosophy of Catholicism is perfect and is God given in the Ten Commandments. We acknowledge the Crucifixion of Christ, His placement in the tomb, His resurrection into Heaven and that he is

---

25 *Actually the Philosophy,* which supports as it defends Catholicism, is right from the mind of Jesus. It is direct, straightforward and clear, from the mouth of; whom millions believe was the Son of God. It is most unfortunate that it has been made to appear so elaborate and difficult. What exists is as a diagram of the defense of the Church against all that are not strong enough so to accept perfection offered by our Lord. The living, often have difficulty in accepting the perfection of the Lord and Master: Creator of all that is seen and unseen.

seated at the right Hand of the Father. We acknowledge the Holy Spirit who is one in being with the Father and the Son. We do not believe there are better "ways to Heaven" than Catholicism. *In fact Catholicism with Baptism and the Sacraments is the only way.* Heaven is a universal, meaning a Catholic Place; to repeat Heaven is a Universal Place: all are welcome and may join of their own volition. Not all believe this and in our judgement they are in peril of damnation. Their peril is primarily of their own concern as the result of their own free will however; our concern is that they may have caused the ruination of someone else, especially youth. The last five Popes have found themselves, one way or another, to be in the position of leading their followers to damnation. Populations and individuals are interconnected in various ways, which are not always known and less often understood for the effects that those have.

God as Father is an Idea, shared by millions, *which has its origin in linguistics.* The Father of the Universe is the Progenitor of the Universe, meaning **[He]** created the Universe by **"His"** Omnipotent Will. *This is not only interesting this is profound thought with the most eminent consequences.* Christ, the Lord was a real Person; he lived and breathed and ate and slept, just like everyone does. For *political reasoning* He was crucified, died and was buried. Thereafter, it is **[believed],** He ascended into Heaven. This **Fact** is an important part of our Reality, perhaps the most important part? The Holy Spirit proceeds from the Father and Son and helps in making the right things happen. The **Idea** is that such Spirit permeates all space, is invisible and is ethereal in its being. Since it is in all space it touches every human being, every day. Furthermore, the **Idea** continues and is that the three persons form the Trinity, Father, Son and Holy Spirit.

No one knows personally the individuals that killed Christ however some are inclined to blame all Jews. Undoubtedly there were Jews involved however those are dead and the content of their minds died with them. Nevertheless their thoughts as ***"Ideas" do remain as part of our current collective thought content.*** Following, what Christ has commanded, those are forgiven; we did not forget what they did however we do not blame other Jews for their blasphemous behavior two thousand years ago. To do so would be unfair and makes little sense two thousand years after the fact. However the presence of Christ and his Crucifixion has set the tenor for all that has happened in much of the World since then.

In the Talmud there are ravings about who was this Jesus. This too is wrong nevertheless this does influence people touched upon one way or another and is generally harmful to the living, becoming as an extension of a distantly born cabalistic and evilly inspired mythology. The mythology lives in the minds of individuals and prompts further probably unnecessary and perhaps incorrect action. This is difficult to access and more difficult to correct. Nevertheless this is part of the collective thought process and is continuous: evil begets evil whereas good begets good.

We acknowledge that everyone does not believe what is in the above paragraph. There are unbelievers and those that have been given to another Faith. Other Faiths are lacking or those are not based on so thorough a Philosophy, some are antagonistic others are too worldly or Pagan-like in their suppositions. The Jewish philosophy is old and very complex however contains much that *should be forgotten or at least more rationally and correctly understood.* Many Jews attempt to do this. Our God Commands, that we should love those that hate us, so then to obviate their position, which may be wrong. Forgiveness leads to love and understanding whereas to hold a grudge leads to contempt, ill will and ultimately to War. ***War is a form of collective insanity,*** at present driven by astounding technologies; ***the processes are Evil in action, they are the works of the Devil and are unjustifiable.*** War is economically profitable for those that produce the implements and materials necessary to engage in conflict. All this varies in time and placement.

Certainly if one kills your father, your son, husband or wife you have been given reason to hate them, nevertheless this is wrong and will incur more of the same in a never ending spiral leading to Hell and damnation by all who follow this path.

The Islamic faith, at this time, is in the ascendancy and we mention it because it has practitioners that are zealots, killing themselves along with their victims, so they may go to Paradise. This is a foolish and **childish misunderstanding.** If Allah demands this from his followers He is not as our God, who demands goodness and good works rather than evil and killing? We understand that the People of Islam are just as we are except for some of their **Ideas,** which are decisively functional in promoting their behavior. This is one proof that confirms that Ideas are what separate men. A Sin is always a Sin no matter who commits it. The Catholic Church understands this and that reason is enough to accept the universality of its presence. ***Catholicism is for all men for all Time:***

From NOW till ETERNITY.

Different personalities express themselves in variously different ways. Some men are anxious and volatile, while some others are patient and forbearing, such traits determine the nature of one's behavior. Good personal traits can be learned, formed in the mind and are beneficial to others as well as to the self. If leadership is anxious and volatile their acts will be determined thereby and this will lead to catastrophe whereas the reverse is also true both patience and forbearance are Virtues. ***Virtue is the opposite of Sin.*** The virtues must be more generally understood as leading to the determination of a particular consequence and should be mindfully taught in School as well as in the home. Consequence is effective in determining what happens to a People! Keep in mind Sin begets Sin whereas Virtue begets positive and fair consequence.
Sometimes the behavior of some Individuals is perverse or aggressive, as is that of the homosexual. Such as those *do not fully understand what a Faith is* and why it is so important. Without the proper and correct understanding of Faith the World is certainly doomed. Homosexuals are duped and are being *used to support certain political and economic programs* within the community. Such programs are transient however the damage done to the homosexual is permanent, *perhaps eternal.* Homosexuals will not necessarily agree with this however, if they are able, those should consider the meaning of the assertion.

Fifth, sometimes the believer because modern Civilization includes some of each of the above listed Beliefs and many others beside the World is at a point of complete confusion, ultimately dissolution. Actually we have been here for quite some time although not knowingly so by the People of the World. The separation of peoples by being placed on different Continents has protected the human race from becoming too much like the Tower of Babble. However at the present time with the becoming of air travel peoples are migrating in astounding numbers. Some do so of their own volition while *others are moved to serve political objectives.* Those moved for political reasons are moved for what appears to be a part of a worldwide Conspiracy to destroy the Western Soul, to destroy Catholicism? With Television, the Radio and the Internet **Ideas** are travelling much more quickly than before.

In the United States there are large numbers of aliens that have been brought here to satisfy their alleged needs for political asylum. *This is made to appear as a good idea by the brainwashing techniques of the establishment:* even various churches are involved for one reason or another. Individuals imagined to be threatened by their own people are seemingly protected. In this instance the establishment appeals to Christian compassion: which proves the delusional and hypocritical nature of the elite that have captured so much of the World. In some instances, for a small number of mortally threatened individuals, this may be a good idea however when whole communities are involved it is not?[26] It would be better to solve problems where they originate rather than confuse everyone with migrations of different kinds of people to unknown perhaps unfriendly places. Atheistic Politicians delight in promoting this sort of migration as part of the process to destroy Catholic Christianity and the Western Civilization in general.[27] Such movement, one way or another is underwritten by great wealth.

This brings us to the **Sixth** consideration. There is too much money being controlled by too few people.[28] We are not speaking about the simply rich, who have made their money honestly from some endeavor. We are speaking of *the rich that conspire with the Government* to rob the majority of the People, one way or another. We are speaking of our Federal Reserve System, which is not Federal and has no real reserves, which can print and issue currency at will, without reason or need, except as politically contrived. We are speaking of Tax Exempt Foundations that are given extraordinary privilege in tax Law and Corporate Syndication's that virtually control all commerce. We are speaking of the outrageous fees and commissions, bonuses and similar rewards paid to some advantaged players, that comprise a select group with the proper *"attitude and connection."* In the Law these same People are given a right to excessive behavior even as others are taxed to death on everything they do. Tax Exempt Foundations, enjoy an existence in perpetuity, which guarantees their survival to do great mischief and provide a safe haven for the great wealth of individuals. Those are an important part, of the slow nevertheless certain take over of the Civilization. All this is done legally in the light of a somewhat perverse day.

If we open our venue to a World-wide scheme we find many moments of despair, it is common that individuals disappear. The vitality of youth is a commodity that has preference in the minds and hearts of the too wealthy reprobates that suck on the system: certainly not all wealthy individuals are hypocrites, many are profoundly decent. Children are kidnapped and sold into a form of slavery or for use by the rich as sex objects: some of such perverts have been Americans. Pretty young women are kidnapped *for their beauty and for their crotch* and are transported for work in brothels and bordellos. The rich and demented take complete advantage of another human being for a few moments of tainted pleasure. Trafficking in human beings is a lucrative business and is responsible for untold misery. Those that engage in such business must be caught and should be prosecuted to the full extent of the law, including capital punishment where appropriate. International Law, should make catching such as would destroy the lives of others a top priority.

---

26 It is the understanding of some men of science that the food one eats should be grown or originate within one-hundred miles of where one was born. This suggests that one should remain near to their birthplace. If this is true, then the world will suffer from the movement of individuals. Apparently such suffering is not well understood however the problems of Race may be a part of this suffering. Only God would understand this.

27 Keep in mind; many of our Politicians are under a sworn oath which supersedes their "oath of office," which is a secondary oath. We have no idea of what this means however mention it as a part of the TRUTH.

28 It is believed (or imagined) that about 350 individuals control about one half the wealth of this world. Why would anyone want so much if those did not have some sinister plan as a motivation?

This is precisely why we do need a legal system based on the Ten Commandments, which is a Catholic system, meaning universally defensible, for all people for all time. We have this however do not practice what it dictates. The ancient habits and customs of selling young men and women into slavery must be stopped. Men must be taught the Virtues, self-control and patience and must be guided away from what is lustful and debilitating. These are broad statements nevertheless there are many indications that they are true. What we witness on a broad spectrum is the <u>War between Good and Evil between Lucifer as the Devil and God as Divine Master.</u> On the surface this seems easy to understand however considered more deeply we lose most. <u>This is the battle of Armageddon; the battle of the Apocalypse,</u> the entire Human race is involved one way or another. The battle is slow but continuous and captures or loses one Soul at a time rising toward Heaven or falling toward Hell. The battle is both real, in the habits and manners of the people and mythological, in the writings of Saints and Martyrs.

Tangentially, this is the Show that must go on and will continue until the end of Time. We imagine from calculations that the earth spun faster in the past, which would change the nature of Time, as we perceive it.[29] This is esoteric information however is probably true, generally speaking, according to some of the calculations, which have been made and, which we have observed. In terms of what is Timely this is important and should be considered along with the forgoing paragraphs? If the rotation of the Earth is slowing this would suggest that at some point in Time it will stop, which would mean that a day would be forever, infinite. This is a speculation worth your contemplation.

The **Seventh** consideration is one's placement in the scheme of thing. Our Civilization with its complex of Institutions is vulnerable to deceit and fraud. Because Institutions are large and balance sheets are very complex there are many places where one might hide from detection, especially when one is an **Insider**. "What you know and the reliability of what you know determines everything that happens to you. Therefore it is only in your best interest to seek and know Truth, no matter how unpleasant it may be. No real progress can be made by man as an individual or Man as a race unless it is built on the solid foundation of ***Truth and Justice*** (This author's bold italics)."[30]

We imagine Bernie Madoff to have been an insider and must have been profoundly "clever" in having stolen about sixty five billion dollars, from investors, before being discovered. (Clever is not goodness or is clever wise. More often Clever is Evil in disguise). He is perhaps the biggest thief in a world of thieves. Being positioned as he was gave him the opportunity to defraud and cheat everyone with whom he did business: and he was a Jew, which spreads hatred generally for Jews. This is unfortunate however no less true. All Jews are not thieves; Bernie Madoff became a thief because of his position and because of his thinking and not because he was a Jew. A good man will forgive him as was taught by Christ, the first Catholic, however he should return the money, at least as much as he still has.

The Jew is an interesting person having been excluded from participation in some forms of commerce for religious reasons; nevertheless he was allowed to lend money at interest. At first the lending was small however as Civilization and Cultures became greater so too did the

29 **Brown, Walt Ph.D.** *In the Beginning, Compelling Evidence for Creation and the Flood.* ISBN #1.878026.08-9. Printed in Hong Kong

30 **Jacobsen, Steven** <u>*Mind Control in the United States.*</u> Critique Publishing, P. O. Box 11451, Santa Rosa, CA 95406. ISBN 0-911485-00-7. Library of Congress 85-70431.

lending, especially to Governments. The Jew being intelligent took advantage of one of the few opportunities that he had and because he was prudent and thrifty he did succeed. He became a Banker to Princes and Kings, ultimately to many governments and much of the world as well.[31] Some people condemn Jews for what they did however they were lending money to gentiles that hoped to kill one another or someone with whom they did disagree. Both may have been wrong the Jew for practicing usury and the Gentile for killing his brother. Each needed the other to do what was done in the forming of the Civilization and the Cultures within.[32] ***This formation was an incorrect formation and continues to this day.*** All this is History however, the memory is aware of what happened and many are not willing to forgive and to forget. Such memories are latent in the minds of millions and do influence their thinking *(process)*.[33] No one, except a God, can imagine how these thoughts will surface or what the consequences will be?

Eigth, the fiscal and monetary contrivance of the present time is astounding and unwholesome for the world in general. In seeking new ways we are aware that, fewer and fewer individuals are part of the monetary equation. Prominent amongst those are 33rd Degree Masons whom have been chosen for this "Honor," being a 33rd Degree Mason is an Honor amongst Masons. For example the day after the bombing of Hiroshima and Nagasaki President Truman was given to this Honor. We have wondered why? Probably even he wasn't certain of why? If he was then, he shares greatly in the responsibility for what happened. Human beings cannot be honestly considered as **collateral damage,** every human being must be respected for his human value! We are led to believe Truman was a small town boy and would never do anything wrong. Is this a truthful understanding of the man who might or would approve of such devastating brutality? We think not. Keep in mind we were bombing women and children and both cities were said to be unarmed.

Thirty-third Degree Masons are very prominent in our Government and have been since the founding of the Republic more than two hundred years ago. On wonders at the value of their Oath of "defending the Constitution," does it have any value at all? What is the meaning of their "seemingly" curious mutterings? Are such mutterings meaningful or are those just for the effect that those might have?

The **Ninth** consideration is Family and friendships. Certain families are prominent and have been so for a very long time actually for centuries: for example the Windsor's or the Delano's. They form an aristocracy based on wealth rather than blood, and they have replaced the Order of Kingship. From the tenth or twelfth century and before, we have had noblemen and Kings, rulers of the masses. Those were warriors and lived in castles, surrounded by a moat. From such places those could defend themselves better than a man on the ground.

---

31   **Corti, Count Egon Caesar.** *The Rise of the House of Rothschild.* Western Islands, Publisher, Belmont, MS.

32   This is an example or form of interconnectedness that is typical of our Civilization. 02178 © 1928 Cosmopolitan Book Corporation. © 1972 Western Islands Edition.

33   ***Thinking is a process,*** continuous, enfolding and out folding simultaneously. As such thoughts are very complex: they are ethereal complexes: emanating from nothing between proximate neurons within the brain. This is consistent with the meaning of genesis given a complex and profound understanding of both Theology and Neuron Biology.

Attendant to Kingship the lawyers were building a legal network derived from an historic past. The past was gone however the **Ideas** remained and were promoted from century to century. We heard spoken of an ancient landed aristocracy that held the peasants in contempt. This may or may not have been true the way that we understand it, nevertheless all that remains of the thinking is as an **Idea,** a story of sorts, which may or may not be true. With present technologies and Disney it can be imagined, at least, that many are confused between history and story-telling. We have the remainder, truthful or not, of what may have happened until this moment in time. Who wrote Harry Potter Stories is promoting a false and romantically ideal story of the past. Since more youngsters read Harry Potter books and see the movies than might pick up something historically truthful one wonders what will be the consequence. The present is an unfolding/ enfolding phenomenal **NOW.** At present the numbers of people is staggering, in some places, whereas in some other places large tracts of land are barren and uninhabited. Crowded places are congenial to vice and corruption and are becoming worse as more individuals become addicted to the profits and false benefit of vice and corruption. Unfortunately, in such case, the future will mirror the past and become even more terrible for millions.

Most of what modern Americans know they have found in the Newspapers and from reading various books and articles. Therefore what those have is as another man's **Idea** about existence. Tourists go from place to place looking for what is historically unique or just interesting. Those gape or gawk at the many wonders, which they find in all the different places. The Ancient Ruins, the Taj Mahal, Great Cathedrals, the Great Wall of China, Narrow city Streets, Giant Water falls, crowded Market Places, Tombs, Beautiful Mountains, the Grand Canyon, and the Pyramids: see any Travel Brochure and you get the picture. Tourists view the creme de la creme from each of the long gone civilizations and cultures.

The Entrepreneur responds by taking fragments, which can be easily duplicated to provide replicas, making them in plastic or some plaster-like material, which can be covered with false gold and sold cheaply. Our homes and especially the garages are full of this stuff, **STUFF,** actually **JUNK,** bought for the effect it might have or for the Style it may display. In a sense this is decadence however who ever thinks of this? We all wonder and ask the question, why? Why does one wish for a gold colored monkey or a symbol of some primitive religion on his fireplace mantle, on his walls? Why not seek a work of art by a contemporary that has spent four or five years studying the subject?

Crowded places breed crimes of various kinds and forms of vice. Vice becomes as a business the only business, involving Sin that functions with the lights on. This **Type** of vice has spawned many *"Do-gooder"* groups to spring into action with appeals for the homeless, the hungry, the destitute and the raped! The Blind, the physically impaired and the many variations all have their own spots from which to beg for your help.

Lotteries and gambling are predominant forms of what is called entertainment. People flock to gaming parlors to give their money to racketeers and thieves that wear a pin striped suite and a bright colored silk tie as those imagine themselves to be successful. The hoodlums pay more for a single tie than most men pay for a suite of clothing. Some of the purveyors are average citizens thus to cover for Organized Crime. Sporting events are set up for the eager participation of fools and the curious spectators. Millions have nothing to do, thus sit someplace watching another do something, anything: play football or baseball: Hit a golf ball or tennis ball: watch simple men drive a car around in circles: Gamble with cards or dice. All this is meaningless, except for the money and [It] is recreation for simple-minded participation. This is not meant to insult anyone except look around and see how much one will spend for a ticket to some spectacle to be viewed while wearing the cheapest clothes he can find.

Prostitution is encouraged by weak mined men that will give a young woman a few coins for a chance to *invade her intimate place whereabouts the future of Humanity is depending.* The young are easily enticed by the elders with a wallet full of bills and a corrupt soul. Most youth today are interested in simple body movements, athletics and such; those are not properly encouraged in things of the mind the most important things. Who cares? Who understands? How might we escape from such enticement? Jesus has the way, yet many scorn the belief that will set them free. The Catholic Church, as originally formed, holds the Keys to the kingdom of Heaven even though many in the clergy during the twenty past centuries have made terrible mistakes. Many laymen have attempted to change the divine nature of the Church and have forsaken the holy and sacred mission. No living man is as wise as Christ is, and no other Church has all the answers. The Catholic Church provides a complete theology and an attendant philosophy given by Christ and carried forward by Saints and Martyrs unchanged for over two thousand years.

Most of what happens in this world is good:
Nevertheless evil seems to have the greatest economic impact:
War, gambling, thievery extortion to name some of the misadventures are all Evils.
As individuals we must strive to be perfect in every way:
We must not corrupt others with our own poor examples.
All the problems in this world are the consequence of individual actions.
Indeed, to correct the nature of one's own actions is to save this world.

For all future generations:
And for our children:
For the children:
Everywhere.

To begin, simply be good!

*

*   *

Chapter VII

Cellular Function and Human Attitude

Your Cells are perfect. You should try to be perfect too.

_____

There are many different kinds of Cells:
Body cells, communist cells, prison cells and fuel cells
What follows touches, to some degree upon each one of them?
The present complexities, which are encountered demand that we do
Reality is so vast in scope it demands comprehension of inordinate complexity
Thus are developed interrelationships, forming a meaningfully operative paradigm
We attempt to encourage pertinent understanding, by forming cross-disciplinary concepts
The Paradigm that forms in your mind, your ideas and attitude make you who you are!
Do not underestimate the degree of intensity and control enacted by attitude.
Attitude will control all of your thoughts and actions.
It is obviated by your personality

At The Dawn of Time humanity, as we know it, did not exist. Nevertheless in the beginning was the [Word]. No one remembers the dawn of time, as humanly perceived, however there are those who do imagine. Recently, given the presence of photography a rather new discovery, much of this imagination has been given to the production of movie and television spectacles, with imagined creatures and mechanically deformed parodies of humanness. Such grotesqueries entertain as they <u>deform and mystify the minds of millions</u> (mostly children and immature adults) who, in darkened places, spend their time watching the over-advertised fantasies. Nevertheless, there are truthful elements in even the most fantastic theatrical productions, which lend credibility to what is being portrayed. In a sense, many of such productions are propaganda in support of political and religious reasoning, forces and objectives, not truthfully understood, which have been and are deliberately or inadvertently hidden from most of humanity.[34] "… (The) first principle of mind control is distraction. The most effective way to conquer a man is to capture his mind. Control a man's mind and you control his body."[35] (This is most obvious in the formation of an army: *author's comment.*) The most obvious objective, of course, is to make money or gain the power of some advantage, money supports human intent, which is the means for carrying on a form of complex Commerce: and Money encourages and supports expression of ***"The will to power."***

_____

34 ***Thinking*** is a complex continuum, which can be quite evasive as to origin and reasoning supporting any thought. As we live thoughts commingle as new Ideas enter and some others are modified or fall into the subconscious. Nevertheless when placed together thinking and thought content controls our actions and aspirations. It can be no other way? In the beginning was the word. The past bears on the present and is functional in respect to the quality and complexity if the Ideas which we entertain at a [NOW] moment. Every living being is living NOW: in NOW time! Thereafter thoughts as **[Ideas]** are altered by various impositions in a never ending, individually inspired waking or thoughtful individual consciousness.

35 **Jacobsen, Steven,** w/introduction by Antony Sutton. <u>Mind Control in the United States.</u> Critique Publishing, P. O. Box 11451, Santa Rosa, CA 95406. ISBN 0-911485-00-7. LC # 85-70431. Pg. 3-4.

Robert R. Fiedler

"Newspeak" (*Boldface type by this author)* redefines words that at one time had universal meaning, making it more and more difficult and ultimately impossible for people to communicate thoughts not sanctioned by the government, a ruling elite. Traditional definitions are eliminated while new meanings are repeated over and over again until accepted. Language is used to conceal truth and dignify absurdities."[36] The most obvious case of such distortion is in the meaning of such words as marriage, homosexuality and murder. The word Marriage meant the conjugal union of one man and one woman, it was holy and permanent and indissoluble except in "very" rare circumstances and, importantly it was defended in the Law of the Land. *At present the definition is an absurdity and, for millions, defies both logic and wisdom.* Homosexuality was considered as being abnormal, by some a mental illness by others and by the Catholic and Christian Church a mortal Sin. Homosexuality is now being "pushed" as another choice so to complete an unusual *understanding of* the charade, which *"somehow (?)"* will alter what is meant by vulgarity and Sin. Murder is now considered a legitimate choice when having a baby is a bit inconvenient. The alteration of meaning is being perpetrated and pressed by the United Nations and by our government, which is near-completely divorced from the morality of the Western Civilization and from the People. *Our government is under the control of an international cabal of socialist and Marxist Zealots intent on subverting our wealth, which those have already done, to further their questionable objectives.* Every Issue is turned to their advantage by a controlled media. Our government is controlled by an alien disposition, which despises Christianity and especially so Catholicism. Our government, knowingly or inadvertently, has become a champion for all manner of evil doing and for the destruction of the Western Philosophy as seated in language.

The hypocrites that we elect, most of them must be hypocrites to be elected, have an improper understanding of what they are doing. They are often directed secretly by unknown others that use them for a nefarious purpose, which they do not and cannot possibly comprehend. *Has this been planned by some unknown or sinister force?* Is this the work of Satan? Or is it known and understood however implemented by this once free and prosperous nation? *Who holds and controls this means of destruction?*

The above notion and understanding is not difficult to comprehend. Russia in1912 to 1917 was in the same position as is the United States right now; it was ruled by a very kind and decent Christian monarch.[37] The Monarch did make mistakes the most important forced upon him by sinister and covert forces. Nevertheless a quasi-Criminal Syndicate that assumed control of the money and the news of events commandeered it. The present flux is so complicated that almost no one can understand what is happening and why? Those that do understand are who are working to gain control of the country, the land and the wealth that has been accumulated over the past 300 years. *All such individuals represent evil of the worst kind.* There are some good and decent, honest and forthright individuals in the mix, however with control of the news and communications under an alien leadership; the enemy has the advantage. This is a wide reaching however subtle predicament that the good amongst our leaders must face. The people must be made over as serfs to serve the ruling elite: this is happening. Look at the manners, habits, customs and dress, the flagrant attitudes and the idiotic music, which turns them on, and you have the proof that this has and is happening. *Our nation is doomed consumed by ignorance and lack*

---

36 **Jacobsen, Steven,** Ibid, Pg. 19.

37 **Wilton, Robert,** *The Last of the Romanovs, How Tsar Nicholas II and Russia's Imperial Family were Murdered.* Copyright © 1993, the Institute for Historical Review. First British Edition, pub. 1920 in London by T. Butterworth. First U. S. Edition published 1920, in New York by George H. Dorn. French Edition, pub. Paris 1921. Russian.

of discipline and courtesy. The fools imagine this as a form of freedom. The casual dress and manners and the "shacking up" that is so prevalent tells you the people have lost their dignity. Soon those will lose their soul? Alien brutes, with no compassion, decency or concern for their fellow man will darken their presence?

Given the mundane and ordinary affairs of most people money *should have functioned* properly to the advantage of everyone. Thus men would be able to trade fairly and honestly with other men. However there are thieves that covet what others may have. Initially, there were some men that were stronger or more-clever than others and some men that were successful and became wealthy were thieves. Those became the nobility and presided, then ruled others and eventually those became Kings and Lords. Those began making rules and laws that all other need obey, which laws naturally favored those that made them. The Kings collected what those called a Tax, for the good of the people whom those did protect from other Kings. People began to expect such protection and, indeed, demanded it. Parallels to the Kings were the moneychangers. Each king had his own money minted by the Crown, which had to be exchanged with other money to carry on the commerce. The money changers sensed opportunity in making such exchanges and those would extract a small token sum with each trade. As time progressed and circumstances unfolded the moneychangers found the best exchanges, the most profitable and enduring, could be made with the Governments from which those would exact a small token on each of innumerable exchanges. Those called such tokens Fees or interest and would take a pledge of property to cover the unforeseen event of foreclosure. *The details are less important than the concept.*

*The invention of money was one of the most significant of human inventions
And will become, as it is becoming, the means to control all humanity.
Most individuals are confused by the smoke and mirrors installed to confuse them.
The smoke and mirrors are the work of the advisors, presently, appointed not elected.*

One of the most persistent "Political Ideas" is that of a Master Race, which dates from about 500BC and even before, persisting to this day.[38] It is carried as a *Cabalistic thought form* by a few individuals that believe those be special and should control and rule over all others, which is the ultimate form of Vanity, *a Mortal Sin.* Such thinking has driven thoughtless men to imagine what is simply not true. Those imagine everyone in the world is like an animal and has no significant intelligence of their own, therefore should be treated as such. Their struggles have met with great resistance and there has been War and fighting in an attempt to control others who resist knowingly and unknowingly what has been planned, by the few, for the many of the human Race. Right now those same thoughtless men are in a position of controlling tremendous wealth and have always been successful in business and trade and seek to implement the becoming of a World Order, which those will control, with the power of the purse. *Gold may be, probably will be an important factor.* Actually *their thinking forms as a preposterous notion;* nevertheless already much has been accomplished so as to make this happen. A wealthy few continue in this vain pursuit. When the wealthy few are deceased there will be more, *with familial and political connections* to replace them.[39] To repeat, Money was invented as a means to conduct orderly trade and commerce however has become the primary object of Greed, *a Mortal Sin!* Some men strive

---

38 **Mullins, Eustice.** *The World Order, Our Secret Rulers.* Second Edition, 1992. LC# 84-082357.

39 **Franklin Roosevelt,** for example, our former *Socialist President,* could trace his beginnings all the way to the Actii in Rome and was related to several of the former presidents by blood. He was a prime example of an insider and of the hypocrite.

for money since it affords the opportunity for obtaining [**Ultimate Power over others**]. It places one in a very advantagious position, so to have power over others.

This is not a new **"Idea"** however it is compelling and works very well to incite and encourage ***the Sin of Greed.*** We have obviated that Greed is a mortal Sin and as such is always very destructive. Individuals form personalities and respond to both needs and desires. Some individuals have a conscience that forbids wrongdoing, whereas others do not carry any restraint on personal action. Furthermore individuals do influence each other in their behaviors and actions. This is why we have so many interesting varieties of humanness, which expresses itself in manners, habits and custom so to form [**A**] Tradition. Tradition is variously divided and therefore one Tradition stands in opposition, or is distinct from, other Traditions. Tradition, especially including the Tradition of Language, encourages the formation of one or another manner of thought form, some of which are complex and others more primitive. Thinking is a complex cellular function that is thought to occur *between proximate neurons in the brain.* Within the thought form exists names and understandings about the world, the family, religion and sex to mention those most obvious. This is a very complex, individually entertained phenomenon nevertheless can be considered from a fundamental point of understanding. Imagine that each person is distinct in their past experiences however there are similarities which given a group will tend to form a Tradition. Political encouragement is one of such similarities and is the object of various forms of propaganda, which is often nefarious and keeps the people of the World divided. This is *commonly understood* however **not deeply understood**, which is part of the problem.

At present, in the West, America in particular, the perversion of sex has become a dominant theme in the thought forms of a maliciously functioning group of immature and mostly dissatisfied adults. Stupidly immature males lead the way since those can easily subdue and take advantage of the weaker sex, the females, especially so when the females are drunk or have been doped up. However the girls did learn a bit from the men and *a few are just as silly, evil and mentally deformed as the males.* Women become mothers so those have a different "slant" on circumstance. Importantly those must care for the babies and children unless those choose to murder them. Many "dear mommies" have done this, which makes a monumental problem for the mommies and society in general. The followers of Sigmund Freud are always there to help with silly programs that avoid any truthful understanding and admission of reality. Those "wallow" in *"togetherness, closure and lamentation"* however don't understand what is being done and sex feels so good. **Just do it!** A woman can easily find a man with a hardened stick and let him push it in her. You know where as well as I do!

Variations in thought forms, causes some individuals to become aggressive. Such variations coupled with different language structures, is the principal reason for one person not understanding another. A lack of understanding causes conflict, the ultimate and most destructive form of which is War. Evil men know that Wars can be staged and can be used to manipulate people toward one or another outcome, which will have political meaning and social implication. Life has always been this way! In the recent past much of the strength has been in the hands of those that despise Christianity, especially Catholicism, and are beholden to the works of Lucifer, Satan or the Devil. Whether you believe that such evil creatures exist or are just mythological figures make little difference, the effect is the same. Your individual beliefs are simply irrelevant, *face it,* what you think is simply of no importance in the greater context of existence! The works of Lucifer, Satan and the Devil are contrary to the best interests of society in general and certainly to the individual person. The abstract interfacing of this phenomenon with the workings of known and understood reality, are difficult to comprehend given the complex structure of the totality. Who are Lucifer, Satan and the Devil? Who believes that they exist? Are Lucifer, Satan and the Devil simply spirit forms, which takes over and control the individual person? In fact those are Ideas that motivate some to outrageous acts of violence and crime against other human beings. They (may) be mythological however become very real in the minds of perverts and those seeking some form of perverse self gratification.

More men should understand this however they do not. Because *men do not understand* what is being done and why, they continue in needless conflict, encouraged by those who will profit most from the conflict. Existence has become monstrous as nations prepare to attack other nations so to promote **"Peace,"** which is the more natural state of being, certainly more desirable. Billions of dollars are made fighting War in preparation for that final everlasting Peace. World Wars I and II plus the carnage leading up to World War III are typical examples of the promotion of Peace. The whole World is confused and complacent in sending their sons to be butchered by the assumed enemies and those are numerous, *more are discovered every day.* More must be discovered every day so as to "keep the ball rolling." All of this is presumption however few realize how those are being conned, robbed and many will die for this *"Walk on the wild and evil side."*

Imagination, notwithstanding, because of a peculiar and profound form of spousal union, every individual human being exists, destined to live a peculiar and phenomenal [time/space centered] life. (See what this author has written on Time and Space). Furthermore, "All humans, other life-organisms as well, are dependent upon a subtle vital force which creates **synergism** *via a unique structural organization of molecular components."* (Gerber MD) This vital force has origin in a multi-dimensional reality. Furthermore, molecules are *cells* with a specific nature and function, as are all of the *cells* in the human body, or any other living organism. Presently, what is called an Einsteinian understanding of reality is replacing one founded on Newtonian principles. This is a significant although quite subtle shift in the paradigm, which determines much of advanced thinking. A simplified and abbreviated species of such understanding is finding its way into the common consciousness of millions of human beings. However the means for accomplishing this are not well understood and that adds "somewhat" to the general misunderstanding. "The Newtonian mechanistic viewpoint of life is only an approximation of reality. Pharmacological and surgical approaches are incomplete because those often do ignore the vital forces, which animate and breathe life into the bio-machinery of living systems. — All organisms are dependent upon a subtle vital force, which creates **synergism** via a unique structural organization of molecular components. Because of this synergism the living whole is greater than the sum of its parts."[40] We now have a microscope, the Rife Microscope invented by Royal Rife, about 100 years ago, that can view sixteen inter-nested levels of reality and can view down to evanescence. Evanescence can be understood as being a form of mind-space, which everyone has however few understand what this means and most are not aware of its existence. This microscope will alter how we understand life to be and the possibilities for understanding are profound.

Whatever did happen in the distant past was resolved, in time, thus to develop a *Vector Sum* leading up to and producing such conditions for the living so as to be as they are just now.[41] Present

---

40   **Gerber, Richard, M. D.** *Vibrational Medicine.* The #1 Handbook of Subtle-Energy Therapies. Third. Edition, ISBN 1-879181-58-4 (pbk.) © Richard Gerber 2001.

41   **Moments are exactly as they must be for every single living being.** The past accumulates to form the present. Thus, each individual is beholden to a small segment of the past and is *a manifestation of a spiritual accumulation,* moving toward an unknown future. Each person commands a role, as the product of God-given free will, in the apperception *[the mind being conscious of its consciousness]*

Robert R. Fiedler

time, as humanly perceived, is the product of a phenomenally complex accumulation. *Present time absorbs the future as it leaves the past in the wake of Tradition and Historicity.* Present Time is a summation of *hundreds of trillions of prior bits of experience* brought forward to the present moment, to NOW time. In future-Time human beings will be and think somewhat differently from what those think and do at present. Living beings *change or progress*, more or less (by degree), in their understanding of circumstance and in their actions. Especially the very young are *persons* receptive to change, knowing not much of a past or of Tradition. The mechanistic view of Newton, still harbored in the minds of many, determined humans as being *machine-like.* Books have been written in which the human is imagined as a beautiful machine, which is a peculiarly backward, nevertheless (for some) a functional and useful understanding.[42] Tradition is an outgrowth of the acceptance of certain manners, habits and customs by large numbers of individuals over a long period of time, thus forms a basis of support for the present in the embodiment of myth, story, lore or the Intellect. We have come to understand this and other processes as some form/manner of evolution.[43] Understand that evolution can tend toward the betterment or the destruction of an existing order. From this understanding, among other things, has arisen the political notion of conservative, liberal and moderate as they apply to political action, aimed at inspiring sociological response. The "madness of crowds" is one example of a force, which might be harnessed in service of political opportunism. In an age of political assertion, one's point of view can be identified as for or against certain programs. This is mentioned because many medical procedures and the programs, which have placed them in prominent position, are often politically inspired, thereafter defended *legally by unknowing Politicians* as proper and just. No idea stands alone! However, it is important to understand that the primary cellular functions are irrespective of human thinking about them: or any thinking for that matter. ***Nevertheless cellular functions are inveighed***

---

concerning each and every moment in order of occurrence. **The order of occurrence** determines the *structure of a syntactical paradigm and engenders the probabilities for a pertinently particular response*. Each individual responds, in a unique way, such determined by the complexities inherent in a singular individual being, made in the image of an infinite Being. The Infinite Being we define as God. Metaphysically, a human person, being a singularity, is an essential element in completing the All as [the] totality, or whatever is existent. Each and every being and the singularly possessed soul of that being, is at once beholden to and respected by ***God within whose infinite image every individual becomes as one.***

42　**The Medical Profession** includes many Practitioners, present and past that imagine a human person can be repaired like a machine, remove and replace parts and **[It]** is as good as new. No animal has unnecessary parts they are all necessary, each and every one, however we may not understand *how are they necessary* or *exactly what they do?*

43　**Evolution, 1.** an unfolding, opening out, or working out; process of development, formation or growth. **2.** A result or product of this; thing evolved. **3.** a) a movement that is part of a series or pattern. b) a pattern produced, or seemingly produced, by such a series of movements; as, the *evolutions* of fancy skater. **4.** A setting free; giving off; emission or disengaging. **5.** In *biology*, a) the development of a species, organism or organ from its original or rudimentary state to its present or completed state; phylogeny or ontogeny. b) the obsolete theory that the germ cell contains the fully developed individual in miniature form; theory of pre-formation. c) the theory, now generally accepted, that all species of plants and animals developed from earlier forms by hereditary transmission of slight variations in successive generations. **6.** In mathematics, a) the extracting of the root from a given power: opposed to *involution*, b) the development of a curve from which an involutes can be formed. **7.** In *military & naval usage*, any of various movements or maneuvers by which troops, ships, etc., change formation.

38

upon and disturbed by thought forms, which encroach on the mind space of individuals. Keep in mind that in 1900 one adult person in twenty (approximately) was imagined to die from cancer. At present the estimates are (approximations). One, of every two adults will die of cancer. Why is this?

Past, Present and Future: "Strange as it may seem, every cell in your body is host to visitors from another time and place. It is believed by some medical Practitioners that the **mitochondria,** the energy-producing factories in each and every one of your cells, are descendants of independent, force-giving organisms. Those imagine this because mitochondria have their own unique DNA, or genetic code, separate and distinct from cellular DNA. Long ago they developed a symbiotic relationship with the ancient ancestors of animal cells and eventually became a part of them. Lucky for us, since it is believed that the mitochondria provide ninety percent of the energy that fuels the cellular activity and keeps us alive. It is easily seen how important well-functioning mitochondria are to our health and well being. In fact, one of the most intriguing theories of aging focuses on the mitochondria. As the machinery of these energy producers slows down, so too do the cells and organs in which, those reside. Protecting your mitochondria "from degenerative damage, may actually slow aging at its very source."[44] "The DNA in a human cell is extremely minute. Probably less than 50,000,000,000 people have lived on earth. If so one copy of the DNA of every human who ever lived - enough to define the physical characteristics of all those people in excruciating and microscopic detail *would weigh less than the weight of one aspirin.*"[45]

To have and to have not: As an individual you are aware of many various opportunities, some of which you may choose. When choosing between one and another of such opportunities it is very important that you choose correctly. Correct choices have been made known, by those that have lived before you and are known by the consequence, following any correct choice, which they have made. Such understanding is seated in *Tradition.* Also, the consequence of incorrect choices is apparent in the understanding of the various forms of misery, which have plagued individuals and communities as a result of this. We are told, in lore, that history repeats itself. Also, if one cannot learn by the mistakes of others they will be repeated over and over and over. If we look around we see that both assumptions are quite true. As individuals we have a functional intelligence, which should obviate things for us; *however we are also emotional and tend to let feelings dominate where reason should be employed.* If we make the wrong choices, early in life, we will suffer the consequences for a lifetime.

One must be very careful in the instance, of which is called **Love.** The present scene is full of hypocrisy where an imaginary love is concerned. There are also hypocrites that express what those imagine as love, without any form of attachment. In fact, Love provides a vital and permanent attachment, is the welding of two souls and *is a lasting emotional state.* With the casual attitude, which many have regarding sexual encounters one is well advised to be cautious in giving away what should bind husband to wife and wife to husband for a life time? The fulfillment provided by decently and wholesomely inspired Love is life's greatest joy and should be considered as having the greatest importance. Whom one loves and marries becomes the most important person in the world. It must be understood that truthful love is not merely sexual gratification however is much more than that.

---

44   **Whittaker, Julian, M. D.** *It's the Real Thing.* (Health and Healing, August 2002, Vol. 12, No. 8). p. 4.

45   **Brown, Walt.** *In the Beginning, Compelling Evidence for Creation and the Flood.* 7th. Edition, pg. 62 2001. © Walt Brown. Center for Scientific Creation. 5612 N. 20th Place. Phoenix, Arizona 85016. LC# 98-072389. ISBN 1-878026-08-9.

In our Public Schools we teach our children just the opposite of what is truthful. A correct form of Truth should be known and understood by every youngster. Our programs in sex education are the cause of endless maladies for millions of youngsters who "could and should" know better. The Programs are an abomination. Beside this those are politically motivated and plagued with all of the bureaucratic "Bullshit" of Public education. We teach them that sex is some kind of game for sensual gratification and fun. Just do it! Do it with whomever you can get to lie down with you! After all, sex is no big deal. Talk about the development of ignorance and whatever goes with it. This is certainly a form of learned Ignorance (Nicolas of Cusa) a disgraceful and malicious malady.

At the cellular level, each and every cell is *determined to function adequately* so as to protect the health of the individual organism from disease. Cells receive and reject what is in the bloodstream, for better or worse. If the cells have the proper nourishment they will function well combining in well functioning organs and systems. If they do not receive what is required to *live well* they become stressed, malfunction and eventually die. They will be replaced however such replacement must be of a beneficial nature. If not the new cells will also become stressed with knowable consequence, open to understanding by others. In the instance of the cell and the whole person, the inputs must be properly determined or the cell and the person will suffer trauma; such trauma may be or can be fatal, physically, spiritual and morally. In all instance at all levels we speak of both good and evil Possibilities. Where damage has been physical it can be known, understood and repaired. Spiritual and moral damage, are not seen, may be misunderstood and are difficult to assess and more difficult to repair. Spiritual damage is difficult to assess because there are so many varieties of spiritual understanding such to confuse those that might/could help and the signs and symptoms are often obscure.

Spirituality is a part of Religious thinking and involves the Soul of each person, which at present presents a nearly impossible challenge, because of the variety and shallowness of much of such thinking. Moral damage is equally difficult to access because of the politicized and imagined nature of Freedom. Consenting adult laws confuse everyone and add to the number of sinful activities, governmentally sanctioned (even promoted), which are tolerated and will plague the family and the nation for years to come. Adding to the problem is that much of what is immoral is also pleasurable, to the senses, and provides a feeling of accomplishment for those involved. It is difficult to tell another what those should do. Those that make an income from such endeavors often become part of the problem causing, more harm than good. More could be said however, we will defer to the reader's own experience.

Babies are perfect human beings. The reader is encouraged to *imagine that all babies are perfect creatures*, made in the image of God. Therefore, *it is of ultimate importance that babies are allowed the right to be born!* After all this is a human right, no doubt the most important human right. For the Dead there are no human rights. Furthermore, it might be understood that God is the Creator of the Universe and *the reader is encouraged to imagine this* as well. Certainly not everyone believes this, however it is one belief that is shared by hundreds of millions of people and is worth considering, regardless of personal disagreement. It would be best if all shared a common Faith so that understanding might be enhanced. Since this is perhaps not possible, at this time, one must maintain a position of objective tolerance for others.[46] This Notion can and must be held

---

46   **Heaven** is imagined by millions to be a perfect place. It is imagined to place one in a particularly angelic-like place, rid of all the problems found on this earth. It is that place imagined to be inhabited by the souls of the deceased. It is spiritual and infinite in duration. Such imaginings form part of

without any religious connotation by unbelievers. Since [IT] does exist, it is obvious that the Universe was [somehow] created. When one is not able to accept that this is true, it is up to that same "doubting Thomas" to prove otherwise. *Such proof might be difficult to obtain.* Confusion, in the meaning of words might enable some, with a clever tongue or pen to convince others that all that exists is in the imagination, they suppose that our perceived reality is simply nonsense. Reality, past and present is not an imaginary continuum. There are babies, perfect human beings who become real players and determine real events.

The psychological self, which includes the working mind of the individual does interpret and is somehow involved in accepting or rejecting every actual circumstance, involving life and death. For the individual, pertinent perception is requisite for intelligent participation. Nevertheless perception is only a part of any human presence. For example, a blind Man is not capable of visual perception therefore does not see as others see, however he is still a man. Why? In truth, what is it that makes him a man and not a monkey or a different Creature?

Many labor with the question, why am I? Or why is this [what is] so? The answer to such questioning is quite simple; nobody really knows! However, the Catholic believes the primary role is to love and to serve God. Nevertheless, the first question is especially pertinent in a period of self-centeredness, with an over emphasis on the importance of the self in respect to others. Such notions are almost always related to monetary wealth, gained one way or another: not always noble, kind and good. It may be presumed, encouraged and politically protected, that a form of self-centeredness is a dominant driving force at this time in history, when self-centeredness (as a notion of individual assertion) has been promoted by mass media and reinforced by a philosophically and morally illiterate population. What is known as "super" something is a matter of personal striving and as a consequence of excessive vanity, often managed by entrepreneurial greed? *The Catholic Church considers both Vanity and Greed, to be Mortal Sins.* This notion relates to Democracy, generally and to what we have named situational ethics.[47] The paradigm is quite complex, however does exist, apparent to those that are concerned enough for objective inquiry. To state that things were always this way is not enough. *Beside which such statement is incorrect!* All consequence can be attributed to some form of motivation whether one likes it or not makes little difference on certainly determined human consequence, which occurs as the product of the complexity of human involvement, leading up to said consequence. The issue of

---

the basis for much, actually most, religious thinking. One must die to completely understand this. Christians believe in a spiritual hereafter, which is dependent upon one's behavior in this temporal (temporary) or real life.

47   *Situational Ethics puts the cart before the horse* to use a descriptive Metaphor. Those who implore situational ethics have no absolute moral imperative. They imagine one or another Idea for the purpose of obtaining support, for a desired objective or goal, often with political implication. Such thinking is both *selfish,* without any concern for those who are not aware of such deception, and *formless,* in reference to being outside of generally accepted procedures. In such instance an understood Form, concerning both word and deed, is what we understand as Tradition. Thus we are aided in determining proper acts and behavior so as not to insult another who shares the same understandings. Understanding is what engenders life's expectation, one way or another. However, when a blatant lack of consideration is excused as being an acceptable expedient, at least for the benefit of the perpetrator, there is trouble on the way. This is especially true where illicit sex is involved, whereabouts one believes and is thus *deceived or 'taken in"* by *another* because of a lie. The liar calls this clever or smart. To lie to whom you pretend to love is an immoral abomination with the most serious consequences.

a casual attitude or nature has been considered elsewhere and we suggest here, now to reinforce the understanding, that *a casual attitude is an important ingredient in an uncaring and self-centered disposition and an important factor in the above-implied paradigm.*

Let's examine how the self-centered express them, in a historical context. The Boer War was encouraged and began under the influence of **Lord Alfred Milliner**, a Rothschild agent. Milliner was a Lord, which one can imagine gave him an *unearned (?) feeling of superiority.* The Rothschild's were, quite likely, the richest family in Europe, which certainly gave them the impression of being superior. Economically they were superior. What does this mean, truthfully? It matters not that their wealth was a profit from the "slings and arrows of outrageous fortune," which those meted on others that had given them so much. <u>Those were profiteers, feeding on the governments run by weak and hypocritical men.</u> Those profited from many forms of vice, all the while believing they were smarter than those that saw their endeavors as sinful were. **In fact those were social maggots sucking up the wealth of Nations.** After illegally annexing the Transval in 1881, the British were defeated at Majuba, turned back by Paul Kruger. In 1889 gold and diamonds were discovered in South Africa, shortly thereafter the Rothschilds brought 400,000 British troops from England to defeat 30,000 farmers who were decent hard working people. **The British fought a scorched earth, no prisoners taken conflict.** Those destroyed what the Boors had built with the sweat and labor of their humble humanness. Considering this, who were the noblemen? Who was most deserving of respect and income from their endeavor? **The concentration camps were begun there,** men, women and children died by thousands in the heat and pestilence of such places.[48] Did the World build a memorial in their honor or simply throw them in a trench? The same tactics were employed in Russia to destroy, what is believed to have been 66,000,000 Russians between 1917 an 1967. Who, now living can be certain of this number? **Vain and proud men did this,** for money and power. Those were following a cabalistic notion set in motion over two thousand years ago. Those wish now to be excused from all their mischief. Keep in mind the vain and powerful will be just as dead and just as cold as those that were thrown in the trenches by those same vain and powerful. The gold and diamonds extracted from South Africa became the seed money for Cecil Rhodes diamond Empire, which has been the model for subsequent Foundation type holdings. In this writers view Foundations should be more carefully supervised so as not to become the monstrosities that those are. Perhaps many should be eliminated!

**There is no honor in receiving a Rhodes, Scholarship.
Such scholarship places one under the influence of a dead thief.**

Where/ When? Where we were born and with whom we associate, especially in our earlier years of development determine much of what will happen later.[49] *Familial continuity is largely a product of* motherly love, which engenders the attitudinal development of children, who will develop similar

---

48   **Mullins, Eustice,** <u>*The World Order, Our Secret Rulers*</u>. Second Ed. 1992, Election Edition. LC # 84-082357. Pg. 21.

49   ***Foundations; Developmental Psychology*** attempts to address this issue. In many instances, however the, ideology of the practitioner combined with confusion in linguistic and contextual elements, meaning common understanding, may become a dominant element in thinking which coincidentally may have been politicized, due to the present circumstances regarding funding for research in the area of education. This is a complex assertion requiring of serious attention by objectively applied scholarship. Such scholarship must include an element, which deals with our relationship to Creation, with appropriate Hermeneutics. The secularly motivated investigator

attitudes and understandings as those of the parent. Motherly love provides a difficult issue for the socialist planners, the thieves and the hypocrites that aspire to control everything. Formal education, as available is adjunctive to this phenomenon, however should not attempt to erase what is in fact indigenously familial. One's identity is importantly a part of an unfolding biological continuum. The cellular construct of a child is determined by the genetics of the parents and is a real and not imagined continuation of *parental substance.* Such substance is perhaps difficult to define however does exist.

"The routine events that lead to the formation of these organisms are all products of germ cell fertilization. Each zygote has a single cell origin, and the development that follows results in a fly, a cat, or a person through genetic instructions that is a characteristic of the genes of that species. For all organisms, the same basic mechanisms of origin and development are involved: mitosis, growth, differentiation of cells, and morphogenetic movement of cells, tissue formation and organogenesis."[50]

An attitude can be acquired just as well as any knowledge, manner, habit or custom. One can come to this conclusion by viewing the attitudinal and behavioral characteristics of the modern Muslim Child-warrior. However what is indigenous is a matter of familial importance, tribal, national, traditional as well and should not be given up for an *imposed misconception*. Individuals should be aware of the child parent relationship, and both should be proud of whom they are. Both the child and the parent must work to make themselves deserving of respect. Just now the young in America, some other places as well, are being encouraged to develop a manner of *phony attitude attendant to their being, **for effect***: is a rather theatrical approach in step with the time. Actually attitudinal indifference concerns a manner of behavior, which is an important factor in what has become known as the *Generation Gap*. Youngsters leave home to attend college during which time those encounter many forms of pressure, imposed by the System, which for most is far beyond their understanding and, which those cannot control. When in control many choose to do outrageous things that will ultimately destroy them. This may be a somewhat difficult assertion to prove however if you follow the path of some youth it will become obvious. How many hundreds are killed on the streets, every year, over some silly exchange of misunderstandings between youthful ignorance and being simply lazy?

Behavioral modification is an important endeavor in respect to conditioning individuals and groups to act in ways desired by those that structure the forms and direction of behavioral modification. Such behavioral modification is always reasoned for one or another Purpose, more often than not having a political, economic, sociological, and/or sexual connotation. This is apparent (for example) in the clever way in which sex education has been encouraged in the public schools.[51] This is also especially *important* in activities centering on Politics, since we are living in a

---

might find some difficulty with this notion however objectivity requires a comprehensive overview consistent with a known understanding of reality.

50 **Carlson, Elof Axel**. *Human Genetics*. © 1984, D. C. Heath Co. ISB # 0-699-05559-X. LC # 83-80334. Chapter 23, *The Molecular Basis of Heredity.*

51 **Engle, Randy,** *Sex Education, the Final Plague,* When asked how might one control the behavior of children Allan Guttmacher replied "Sex Education." Youth are curious and not well informed and are certainly not ready to accept the role of parent, nevertheless those do experiment and sex is considered "very adult," therefore youth are intent on having such experience. The more aggressive young men become involved with the young ladies with the complete approbation of Sex Education! The reader can certainly fill in the details.

period of political domination; political imposition is apparent in every sphere of our lives.[52] Keep in mind, money controls the Politician and the Politics. Political correctness is just a symptom of a politically motivated ideology, aimed at gaining support (by contrived political means, force when necessary) for perverse concepts, destructive of Catholicism and other Christian religions.[53] Ultimately, when carried to an extreme, this will lead to complete political domination. Such domination finds its expression in prosecuting hate crimes and in the tacit encouragement of deviate forms of modified behavior, which may be (often are) both unwise and unhealthy. This is mentioned as a prelude to what follows, with the understanding that there exist subtle interrelationships acting as stimulus for seemingly unrelated events, in domains, which evolve from contrived complexities, made possible by Governmental and Foundational funding.[54]

Foundations have existed for a very long time. "In 767, the Byzantine Emperor Constantine Kopronymous, after first attempting to tax the holdings of the numerous monasteries which had become too powerful, confiscated their properties, which had been donated by generations of Christians for charitable purposes and pious causes. On May 6, 1312, Pope Clement V dissolved the very powerful order of the Knights Templar. The Templar's had become a symbol of charity and of culture; those had also grown enormously wealthy owning 9,000 manors and had become rich to obvious excess. During the reign of Henry VIII the Church held two thirds of the votes in the House of Lords, one third of the land and had an income two a one half times that of the crown" (Authors interpolation for brevity). One can understand that today we are in a similar position. The great Foundations are very wealthy and are very intrusive on the political process and the thinking of the people. If we were wiser and had a better understanding of History we would not have allowed the Foundations to become the monstrosities that those have become. Because many are tax exempt they play an important part in our Politics.

Because of the nature of the human person, such politically contrived circumstances as are alluded above, because of fearful anxiety coupled with indignation, stimulate the body to respond in ways, which may be destructive to the biological family and individual human health as well. Indeed, the domains of the very large do affect the domains of the minutely small: the opposite is also quite true. Human health begins and ends at the cellular level: conjugate cells begin the process of becoming, healthy cells continue the process in forming the various organs and tissues in the body those do what those are destined to do. Contrarily, cells polluted with various forms of toxin begin the march, toward and untimely end in death. Within the mind Ideas function with both positive and negative consequence to encourage one or another behavior, which can be beneficial or destructive. The problem is that only a few make the associations necessary for

---

52   **Mullins, Eustice**, *The World Order, Our Secret Rulers*. Second Ed. 1992 Election Edition. LC # 84-082357. The entire book is very much worth your attention. It is crammed with names, places and events that have made you a virtual prisoner in the once Free and Prosperous America. The Conspiracy, lying, cheating and death that has been standard fare for the "Big Shots" goes back about three hundred years. **If you only read one book, read this one!**

53   Roe vs. Wade,

54   ***Foundations*** with the consent of government are destroying much of the Individual Initiative and corrupting the meaning of success. Whatever has foundation funding will be in the spotlight, completely overshadowing the work of private individuals. Often statistics and other evidence are falsified for the benefit of those working within a Foundation grant. This is very serious where the research involves medical research and statistics. The importance an effect of foundations has a long history of encroaching on the System.

understanding what is wrong and those do not receive the encouragement or support of the establishment. Keep in mind *"the Establishment includes all that is: how things are right now."* The establishment encourages that the citizen work to <u>give more to those that have too much already</u>. The system could be altered somewhat to make it more equitable, a bit fairer: this could be done in ways without any more government meddling. The present forces of practice, publicity and excessive financial support are in favor of what is. What is has gotten to be as it is because of the same forces, over an extended Time Period. At present, the force of economics and money is dominant! It is likely; this has "almost always" been the case.

In addition to this, individuals are programmed by a genetic complex, which determines just how this process will be supported in an individually determined physiology. Such programming is a part of the phenomenology of existence, the becoming as it were of humanness, and may be considered as an imposition of an irreversible Destiny, imposed upon a physiologically driven being. Individuals, Society, Cultures and Civilizations all face some form of Destiny: and are driven by known however uncontrollable forces. Civilizations burgeon, peak, and then decline into the obscurity of an Infinite totality. "And how thereafter creatures begat and conceived, how the plantlike in them drove them to reproduce themselves for the maintenance beyond themselves of the eternal cycle, how the *one* great pulse-beat operates through all the detached souls, filling, driving, checking, and often destroying — that is the deepest of all life's secrets, the secrets that all religious mysteries and all great poems seek to penetrate, the secret whose tragedy stirred Goethe in his *"Selige Sehnsucht" and "WahlverwandtschaftenI,"* where the child has to die because, brought into existence out of discordant cycles of the blood, it is the fruit of a cosmic sin."[55] Unfortunately, not many individuals take the necessary time to formulate a comprehensive understanding of what this means, excepting as such understanding may be embodied in a religion; particularly, the Catholic Tradition, which spans two thousand years of such extended [exegete] contemplation, inspired by a Divine Being.

Napoleon Bonaparte was an extraordinary man. Unfortunately he had the disposition of many vain leaders, as today's Politicians he was struck with the *"Will to Power."* A phenomenally complex time-space placement is an important contributing factor to what we are able to do physically and what we will accomplish, in our own good Time. The understanding of what constitutes a willful act has been incorporated into a manner of theological and political imposition, thus relates to the existence of both God and the State.[56] Politicians *"imagine"* that their thoughts and actions are always correct? Such imagination thrives on discussion and the *"Democratic-like"* procedures whereabouts <u>compromise is both the nature and the outcome of the endeavor.</u> Ultimately no single individual is truthfully responsible for any outcome, the essential elements having been lost or altered in the procedures and rhetoric. Somehow men exist whose ideas drive the Civilization toward an aspired goal. This Goal may or may not be certainly known or well understood. This is most often fully implemented, in ways incomprehensible to most human understanding. Long after the death of the perpetrator, what was done becomes a bit clearer however only in respect to the truths that become known. "The evil that men do lives after them, whilst the good is interred in their bones" (Shakespeare). This is a complex phenomenon and *some of the many ideas* do find expression in the formulation of an ultimate or final goal.

---

55 **Spengler, Oswald,** *The Decline of the West.* Volume II, ©Perspectives of World History, Alfred A. Knopf, Pub. NY © 1926 &1928 Alfred A. Knopf. Twelfth printing, Dec. 1970. Page 5.

56 **Reed, Douglas,** *The Controversy of Zion,* (Veritas Publishing Co., P. O. Box 20, Bullsbrook, Western Australia, 6084), Chap. 18, pp. 125-131, The Napoleonic Interrogation.

Consenting, Adult Laws; *Free men are given to the notion that they also have free will. When those in power understand this to be a form or manner of license, they glory in doing what may be disastrous for millions. The world depends on leadership that will act upon good conscience in hope that such leadership is mature enough to do so. The world is often disappointed and they who have been killed in War, as a consequence, attest to the fact that this is indeed an important consideration.[57] Adjunctive to this is an interesting notion as is expressed in what we define as consenting adult laws. However, like the workings of Civilization and of the Universe the workings of the mind must be in concert, in tune with goodness and must reject all forms of evil and evil doing. Coincidentally, the Lord's, prayer includes the admonishment "and lead us not into temptation, but deliver us from evil".*

Evil is always evil.

Although given another name it corrupts the Soul and the Person just the same.

Subject Matter Disciplines; *Actually the intersect of what we call subject matter disciplines, which form the basis for our learning (at the present time) does impair certain possibilities, in respect to broad and comprehensive understanding. It might be difficult to address this concept in a pluralistic Society certainly it is less difficult to do so in a Monastery, however we must be aware of the Reality that surrounds us. As expressed elsewhere, Time and Space, hence reality does surround us; none can escape this fact. We are wrapped in circumstance! We can add to this that all thinking is qualified by past experience and is manifest, as such, in ways which are nearly impossible to understand; nevertheless some do attempt to do so, with more or less success, mostly less.*

Nevertheless, the intersection of well-defined and categorized disciplines does afford wonderful possibilities as well. Historical, philosophical and theological Scholarship, Mathematics and Scientific Study have made available extraordinary knowledge about every aspect of our existence. Disciplined thinking in every realm has provided in-depth comprehension for anyone willing to take the time to study. Invention has risen to unprecedented levels, with magical applications of phenomenal discovery engineered so as to be within the reach of almost everyone in the developed and even the poor nations. This exposition attempts to establish some correlation between a number of elements, from diversely and seemingly unrelated realms, in the hope that one might be encouraged to use deductive logic, combined with analogy to form a dynamic and meaningful correlation. Interestingly, one may find correlation between the workings of the modern computer and the functioning of the human body at the cellular level. In some instances, especially involving research with the human brain, the interfaces are such so as to confound investigation in defining the distinctions. Prostheses have been developed, which augment human actions to the advantage of those who have suffered from amputations and abnormalities, which are open to corrective measures. This has come about through the combined efforts of disciplined research and study.

---

57 **Bonaparte, Napoleon.** When Napoleon marched into Russia, with an army of 400,000 men, no one imagined he would retreat with only 10,000 men remaining in his Grand Army. Who can possibly know or fully comprehend the consequence for the French people of so great a genetic loss in so short a time? One might consider the same question as regards other world Wars, which in fact have decimated the population of European manhood. Western Civilization has been deprived of those very numbers, *which may have included in their midst individuals destined for the accomplishment of genius.* Is this destruction of European manhood accidental or is there some great plan, understood by only a few, that have determined this carnage? This question is probably too complex to be answered nevertheless it is certainly a most important question amongst questions.

Healthful Consequence Good and Evil does have some influence on health. Imagine there are parallels between the health of a Society, the health of a Human Body and the health of the Universe. We need not concern ourselves about the health of the Universe, except to understand that we must accept what is and to understand that whatever forces are at work are in perfect (certainly near perfect) harmony. *Celestial Music* is presumably an expression of perfect harmony, *Music of the spheres*, or *choirs of Angels*, all of which suggest perfection.[58] Coincidentally, there is a resonance or pitch in each and every cell, which is the consequence of a micro-vibration.[59] Astronomers, perhaps some musicians as well, understand this better than most. The Radio Telescope is an interesting implement for searching the heavens, providing the means for a transformation from sound to graphics.[60] In such instance scale tends toward what is infinite. Unfortunately Astronomy is largely beyond common understanding, especially involving mathematics and technicalities common to the discipline. Nevertheless Astronomers search for reasons why the Universe is as it is and for the answers to various (seemingly) obscure questions.[61] Einstein's notion of Reality involves relative and proximate components and suggests something quite profound. Energy equals Matter multiplied by the speed of Light ($E=MC2$). What Einstein imagined also does apply *to some degree* in the realm of cellular Biology. The impulses, which are responsible for Human Life, move around in the body much as the Light moves around in the Universe. This is a complex notion, which can be approached metaphorically, symbolically or physically, however is well worth careful and deliberate interest. *It might be wise to consider this from the point of view that what we can see is easier to comprehend than that, which we cannot see.* However our imaginations, combined with a truthfully informed intuition, will be able to provide access to an innate understanding, which is very necessary for health in both the individual and the society as a totality and, which correlative force exists in the totality of the Universe as well. One can envision what one hopes for, thus to provide impetus to possibilities which are inherent in human physiology.

The All is Good. Genesis tells us that All Creation is good. All Creation must be perfect, so as to function eternally. Actually, Eternity is a Concept, which is not well understood. An eternal entity is unbounded in time or space. Man measures time in seconds, minutes, hours, days, weeks, years, centuries, millennia, epochal segments and finally in light years. Time provides for a meaningful unfolding of events in space, including material transpositions. All are related to terrestrial existence defined primarily by means of optical and psychological awareness for what is conceptually assumed to be Eternity. ***Actually, Eternity is the Form of Creation, as evident at any instant in time.*** Put another way all moments are as one, in a universally complex, unrestrained and infinite Time-Space Domain.[62] Or, the Universe must be right, for all time, or it could not be what it is. Here resides a manner of Truth, which has profound philosophic meaning in respect to Theology. As defined by the Catholic Church, confusion

---

58 **Music** deals with such issues in both sound and lyrics, suggesting there may be wide spread understanding of the existence of such phenomenon. Music is said to be *captivating*. Music can have great effect on Politics. It is wise to know one's captors before becoming a prisoner in an unintended situation.

59 **Gerber, Richard MD,** <u>Vibrational Medicine</u>, Third Edition. Bear & Company. One Park Street, Rochester, Vermont 05767. © 2001 by Richard Gerber. ISBN 1-879181-58-4.

60 **Eddington, Arthur, Sir.** *<u>Time Space and Gravitation.</u>*

61 **Eddington, Arthur, Sir.** <u>Ibid.</u>

62 **Bearden, Thomas,** Lt. Col., USA, *<u>Aids, Biological Warfare</u>*

arises from schism and seems persistent thereafter. Given a Catholic understanding, which is a Universal Understanding, [in the Greek], Catholic means Universal a schismatic is a heretic, one way or another, *regardless of an honest, heart-felt, positively motivated reasoning.* From a personal viewpoint this may be acceptable however, given the Dogma of the Catholic Church, it is not. Planets and cells must be in accord so as to function optimally, so too in the realm of thinking. It is important to understand, in this respect that [a] philosophy has [a] manner of form, which must be maintained so as to order the ideas embodied therein, thereafter must be properly conveyed, so to provide for truthful and meaningful, as opposed to meaningless, understanding. Such consistency requires linguistic continuity: in the Catholic Church this has been Latin, as the primary Western Language. Certain individuals have for a long time discredited the use of Latin as being "Old Fashioned," in need of updating. This is a ridiculous position to hold, which is in fact a denial, of Eternity.

Our present System of Higher Education is a matter of false rather than truthful learning. There is virtually no study of philosophy or religion in our public school programs. The separation of Church and State guarantees this for the foreseeable future. Keep in mind Philosophy; Science and Theology were the most important subjects in University study. What we have today is remedial learning and the training in Technology. There are many subjects, which are remedial or simply not Higher Learning, which crowd the catalogues and **give the impression that one is being educated.** *Such subject matter displaces the study of more difficult and appropriate learning. To be effective Higher Education must be higher, providing the training and practice in the discipline required for serious thinking and must clarify:* **what is serious thinking?** *Most present programs do not do this. However in technical areas this may occur at times for one reason or another. In the sciences and in mathematics, the teaching is hierarchical and progressive, understandable and seemingly knowable, therefore can be more easily communicated to the students. There are two footnotes above that hint on higher learning, one scientific (7) and one philosophical (13).*

Many Religions, with a different linguistic continuity, have adopted tenants of the Catholic Faith, which is universal in purview. In theological terms, universal order is also infinite, as it is the work of an Omnipotent Being, God the Father. "I Am as I Am." *Universal order is infinite* all-inclusive, never ending unfailing, boundless, on and on. This must be true and it is imperative that one attempts to understand why. Perhaps we are confused by the notion that it is somehow evolving toward this or that condition. It must be understood that there can be forms of evolution, negatively and positively inspired, with an infinite Domain, such Domain being fully adaptive to any possibility, probability or certainty. The rational mind requires some manner of explanation, which coincidentally drives man toward greater understanding. Man, cogent and perceptive creature that he is, being trapped in a perceived time, given to imagination and a manner of free will, compromised by emotional and circumstantial imposition, should necessarily have ideas. *This is also a good, because it allows each and every individual to participate independently in the stream of life.* No matter what his station in life individually as a part of this totality each person is indispensable, in the eyes of the Creator, the omnipotent One, Who is beyond time, outside of space and is thus immortal. Physicists will ultimately confirm this: however at this time we know not how this will be done.

Nevertheless, we can imagine (at least) that societies and the cells within an individual's body also must work in perfect accord or they will not work at all. Whatever does not work well will be ultimately destroyed, replaced or supplanted. Individually, human beings are irreplaceable: categorically they can be replaced and this is an understanding open to political and economic opportunism and exploitation. Any difference will be enacted in both Time and Substance.

War is Pure Evil and must be understood as such, in spite of the profits made by the System and the various high paying jobs created in the various sectors of the Defense business. War obviates pure evil and is a manner of expression aimed at annihilating contrary opinion, regardless of the amount of suffering caused to unknown others. In a sense there are conflicts other than war that have the same intent with less destructive means, however even then circumstance may provide opportunity for a mortal conflict to arise from even the best intentions. In the realm of thought, sociology, philosophy, theology, Ideas are what separate men. And, the level of intelligence coupled with the level of comprehension or learning is what provides for the determining factors leading toward all manner of conflict. This is why the less well developed Cultures, those considered primitive have difficulty in responding to Western and advanced concepts concerning many issues.

More recently we have behavioral modification being pressed from entertainment, which thrives on a return to the Jungle theme, aggressive insolence, brutality and the bloodletting spectacle. Entertainers cannot be viewed as philosophers however they may assume this stance to the detriment of those who pay any serious attention to them. In a sense, for many, the Theatre, movies and television have supplanted reality. Because of the interconnectedness of ideas and cause effect relationships, philosophy is an evasive and illusive subject, nevertheless philosophy (weather or not one is aware) is what motivates all mundane daily activities: habits, manners and customs. Any form of intelligently manifest human conscientiousness is open to philosophical interpretation.

Parents must wake up to reality. Don't set your child in front of the Television so to entertain them as you do what is only imagined as necessary. Unknown others have influence far beyond what is reasonable. When one is conditioned to behave in ways, which are determined by unknown others, mostly for commercial gain one can easily *lose sight of the fact that, because of an imposed opportunism, their own* body is suffering in ways unbeknown to those who suffer. Add to this concern that it may be very profitable to manage on a long-term basis any chronic condition, which may occur in the body or in the society. *Socialism is a form aimed at monitoring events, production and the movements of individuals for the benefit, of the established elite.* Chronic spelled another way is Money! The cumulative suffering of cells causes personal illness coincident with body malfunction. Emotional suffering coupled with inflamed ignorance is responsible for social unrest, riots and the destruction of good. Nevertheless the Universe remains as quite dependable. Notwithstanding, biological, physiological and sociological response is certain, given one or another stimulation. Therefore the stimulation provided should be determined by the best interest of the individuals, on the individual cell toward the accomplishment of what is good. And cells as well as individuals are interested in being healthy and good. Remember illness is evil! Cells must be good or they begin to die.

Evil in the form of pleasure is the mortal enemy of every cell (toxemia), every organ (cancer, hepatitis) every individual (chronic disease), every society (gang warfare, riots), every nation (Civil War, Insurrection, World Wars), ultimately of the entire Civilization (annihilation War, finally Apocalypse).

The Imposition of Technology has created many nearly unmanageable problems and afflictions, in our societies and in our bodies, even as it has accomplished many wonderful, even phenomenal things. Coincidentally our technologies, because they involve economics, have been brought to heightened levels of efficacy with monumental imposition on our physical and emotional being. It is obvious that the Monument, which is Technology, must stand for good not for evil! Even war is justified by some as the impetus for invention. We suggest that in the instance of weapons of mass destruction ***less invention is perhaps better.*** Humanity has time to develop slowly, however without killing innocent populations needlessly or prematurely.

There exists what might be called a societal uneasiness possibly with an origin in the understanding that life is limited therefore one must do as much as possible within a short lifetime. Technology functions (in part) to satisfy such uneasiness as it provides the next step in a manner of productive accomplishment. At the level of the cell, the pharmaceutical conglomerate has caused unimaginable problems by creating commonly used forms of toxic substance, mostly for profit. Such substances are in our foods, our air and are used in the treating of illness. Since the Second World War there have been hundreds of chemicals developed, many of which are very dangerous and many of which are found in consumer products (Dr. Schulze). All may have an origin in honestly intelligent curiosity given to the service of advanced technology and economic gain. There certainly are many well-intentioned honorable and decent scientists, nevertheless the Drug Cartel, with billions invested is placed in a vulnerable position. Because of their high-cost involvement the companies seek billions in earnings and billions in profits. It is not uncommon for some to alter or slant what those say to accommodate shareholders. The greatest concentration of "shares" is usually divided amongst a few players. Where there is money we find Greed, a very formidable evil. The trading of "stock" becomes an important issue hereabouts. The possibilities for complexities within the human body are beyond comprehension however, the human body is structured in such fashion so as to be self-correcting, self-healing and self-motivating. This is not true of a corporate entity, which is vulnerable to economic malfunction obvious in the many things that we witness every day. Perhaps scientists should point attention to being in closer harmony with natural processes, less aggressive in invasive and harmful pursuits and have less concern for making millions or billions.

The Big Bang Theory, is simply a theory? It is a product of man's continuing quest for the unknown. Obviously whatever caused the universe to be as it is is quite beyond common human understanding.[63] To approach such a serious Question, *there must be a co-mingling of faith and reason*, certainly a respect for both, supported by the Intellect, in reference to where we are in time and in fact to the *meaning of time and space per se.* All theory having universal applications is postulated in reference to our imagined understandings, often without reference to theology. We are in fact, like Alice, standing before the looking glass, which introduces us to a profound theory of optics, combined with a reasoned attempt to become as God. However, to become as God is impossible excepting to become as one in being with the Father, from whom [all] good things come? Of course, this could occur only after death and then only if one is a baptized and professing Catholic: this assertion obviates a peculiar manner of *universal* faith ***one must be a baptized Catholic.*** *Many have a problem with this understanding, which may or may not be correct.* Only God knows and he is not available to answer questions: here Faith presides?

Nevertheless, the imagination is a wonderful human attribute however it may precede beyond reason and common sense, especially when theology and philosophy intersect, in reference to divisions in religious thinking. Divisions in religious thinking involve *heresy, schism and a lack of genuinely Catholic* belief. Catholic belief is aimed at Universal Goodness. Almost all such issues as might arise at this implication are emotionally charged and may be inclined to develop outside of truthfully reasoned judgment.

---

63   **Brown, Walt.** *In the Beginning, Compelling Evidence for Creation and the Flood.* 7th. Edition, 2001. © Walt Brown. Center for Scientific Creation. 5612 N. 20th Place. Phoenix, Arizona 85016. LC# 98-072389. ISBN 1-878026-08-9.

Toxemia: Toxic substances are found lurking everywhere. The word toxic is literally embroidered upon the fabric of our daily ventures or perhaps one might imagine it as tattooed on our skin. The embroidery is merely on the garment of society the tattoo being personally invasive, digs into and permanently colors thus distorts the tissue, which surrounds the body. There is a profound analogy here. The environment, our food, our air, our clothing and household items have been devised, manufactured, packaged, stored and distributed in ways requiring all manner and form of toxic substances.[64] Added to this is the unending noise from vehicular traffic and fantastically crude and ugly commercially aggressive imagery invading the senses whenever, one is out and about. In our homes and establishments for commerce are mass media invasions combining all forms of imagery, tragedy, comedy, spectacle and nonsense punctuated with canned laughter. The modern world resounds with non-stop, over-anxious musical discord and the noise from a rocking, or rapping moron. All this accompanies the drumming up of business for one or another form of something, which is mostly unnecessary, imported from the other side of the planet, requiring an ever increasing beat to keep things going. The fast food industry and pre-packaged food items provide munchies to be ingested whilst one is being distracted, mesmerized, entertained or titillated to a point of stupor, heightened verve or a mild form of insanity. The fast food industry is an imposition on the family and provides food, which may not be the most healthful. Teenagers have acquired an aggressive attitude in respect to the acquisition of stuff, especially automobiles and music Memorabilia. A collector's mania sweeps the adult population of this nation, which has been encouraged, in the needless acquisition of things.

The cells of millions are as polluted as are the cities in obvious and foul ways. Our body and our minds are under constant assault, even as we are unaware and casual in our daily endeavors. Are we too smart for our own good? The body requires rest. The mind must be allowed a period for contemplation, thus to enhance a feeling of well being and to allow time for necessary reparation of cells, tissue and organs. All the seeking and searching and worry about tomorrow is a waste of vital life force. A properly tuned, well nourished, properly sustained and enhanced body, with all that this may entail, preserves the life force and directs it precisely in the right way.

So too, our cities must be restructured, perhaps slowly, so as to allow nature a more dominant role in the lives of the millions that inhabit them. The earth is covered with green vegetation for a very good reason. We should replace as much as we can and not destroy any more than is absolutely necessary. This can be done and in a few instances is a fete accompli'. Some men have intruded in ways, which are determined by economic forces rather than by common sense and a respect for the ground upon which we walk.[65] We have fouled our environment with all manner of signs, slogans and symbols that comprise an intrusive visual complex from which we cannot escape. *The soil of the earth and the grasses growing thereupon are a sustaining life force, for every cell, for every person and for every living complex.* It is imperative that we find ways more inviting to contemplation, quietude and introspection. We must become one with universal order thus to benefit most from a just and proper placement in the scheme of things;

Holy wonderful and wise.

---

64   **Clark, Hulda Regher Ph. D. N. D.** *The Cure for all Cancers,* (Pro Motion Publishing, 3368F Governor Drive, Suite 144, San Diego, CA 92122*),* pp. 1-25. This is in a sense a do-it-yourself book as many of the procedures can be done at home, are harmless and inexpensive.

65   **Meyerowitz, Steve.** *Wheat Grass, Natures Finest Medicine, The complete Guide to Using Grasses to Revitalize Your Health.* (Sproutman Publications, Great Barrington, Mass., 01230)

Robert R. Fiedler

Other books by this author

Money Murder Madness; ISBN:
iUniverse 1663 Liberty Drive, Bloomington, IN 47403
ISBN-13: 978-0-595-41500-7 (pbk)
ISBN-13: 978-0-595-85849-1 (ebk)

Musings, Greed, Love and Indignation;
iUniverse 1663 Liberty Drive, Bloomington, IN 47403
ISBN: 978-595-42901-1 (pbk)
ISBN: 978-595-87238-1 (ebk)

Good and Evil: The Destruction of America
XLibris Corporation; www.XLibris.com
ISBN: 978-1-4415-2629-8 hard cover
ISBN: 978-1-4415-2629-1 Soft cover
LC #2009903271

In Honor of Geri
iUniverse 1663 Liberty Drive, Bloomington, IN 47403
ISBN: 978-1-4502-3009-4 (pbk)
ISBN: 978-1-4502-3010-0 (ebk)

Chapter VIII

Disease

First, Physician Do no Harm (Hippocrates)

Robert R. Fiedler © 2003
Professor Emeritus, CSLA

Generally, Disease is a result of physical weakness, exacerbated by incorrect behavior,
or compromised by an outside threat to one's own functioning immune system.
The effects of any Disease, when imperfect knowledge is summoned to bear, create
biological and/or physiological consequence, which may be debilitating: can be fatal.

Disease must be understood as an ultimately complex phenomenon which, considering curative Measures must be approached from a multi-dimensional point of view. Any serious attempt must be open to *truthfully critical forms of investigation*,[66] concerning what may be deemed as the best possible approach, thus to encourage the body's natural ability for correcting itself. Often profoundly complex negative circumstance may be brought back to within normal limits by the simplest natural therapeutic procedures.[67] Countless numbers of individuals have testified to the fact that functionally curative procedures are *at once* simple and phenomenally complex, demanding of a humbly discreet understanding of physiology as well as a sense of *trust in a profoundly continuing holiness.* The complexities arise from the trillions of functions, which are performed by the human body every waking moment of any human life. Man's knowledge is imperfect therefore, no individual, or group of individuals, can possibly understand *completely and correctly* the totality of such complexity. Expert opinion is most often in disagreement, depending upon background information, when a curative procedure is being considered. It is logical therefore, that some (perhaps most) expert opinion is quite suspect. **It is wise to proceed**

----

66 **Truthfully critical forms of investigation,** are without prejudice, including no vain self-interest, are competently objective and avoid the imposition of technological procedures, which may be [probably are] unnecessary (Schulze MD.). Furthermore, they must avoid the use of obscure and meaningless language, which may encourage a patient to proceed along a fatal path, without proper understanding of what is involved, especially where invasive procedures are concerned; all such procedures have potentially harmful consequences (Mendelsohn MD). The imposition of any political issues must be kept apart from the treatment of disease. Finally, economic issues must be considered in respect to common sense, especially when there are very effective ways, not as profitable for the practitioner and quite inexpensive to treat most illness. Charges must be determined honestly; not *ballooned* because of extraneous accounting practice, such as *tax write-offs* and a *phony inflation index*, neither of, which has anything to do with the life of a patient.

67 **Jensen, Bernard D. C.,** (deceased), "*Diet together with a proper amount of pure water,* are the most important considerations when addressing any illness." Given the proper nourishment, combined with a proper mental attitude, the body will heal itself.

cautiously, thus not to interfere with the naturally positive workings of the body's healing functions.

Importantly, not to be overlooked is the fact that every individual must exist within the present time frame and is thereby open to the influence of various opinions, including political opinions, which are currently held.[68] There exists what may be defined as a *collective contemporary Id,* which to a large extent is molded by the opinions of *economically concerned individuals. Those include government bureaucrats that know nothing of illness, reporters, or some other functionary* seeking personal gain, rather than by those that best understand a peculiar circumstance, involving phenomenally related intricacies.[69] Importantly, much of what is done today, in any sphere of endeavor, the practice of medicine is no exception, is *done as a business,* for a profit, which not incidentally alters the reason for any *interested, professionally managed* participation.[70] Participation often is a matter of *watching the bottom line* and being certain that financial obligations, both necessary and trivial ones, are met on time.[71] **We call this the rat race!**

Briefly, some important factors are listed below, which contribute to and bear upon the complex make-up of any single human being. The reader can imagine which factors may be most important and why. Certainly, each circumstance must be met on an individual basis; therefore the order of priority will be different from case to case. Some instances would allow for a gradual studied approach whereas another might demand more immediate attention, directed urgently. Many certified practitioners believe that, in most instances, *it is wise to proceed slowly* with curative measures rather than too quickly, keeping in mind *Iatrogenic Disease* is one of the leading causes

---

68 **Current Opinion** *is often motivated by self-serving interest.* Additionally, all Opinion is a consequence of *imperfect knowledge* therefore should be carefully considered when any circumstance is critical (note 70 & 71). A Businessman's mentality is often involved with the objective of some monetary gain and concerning the medical profession there are billions in profit for those who would take them, without concern for who must pay.

69 **Mullens, Eustace,** *Murder by Injection, The Story of the Medical Conspiracy against America.* (The National Council for Medical Research, Staunton VA 24401) pp., 59-128 **Iatrogenic Disease,** *a form of disease caused by treatment is a leading cause, perhaps the number one cause of death in the United States.*

70 **Mendelsohn, Robert S., MD.,** *Confessions of a Medical Heretic,* Contemporary Books, 4255 W Touhy Avenue, Lincolnwood (Chicago, IL 60646-1975, USA). Copyright ® 1979, Robert S. Mendelsohn, ISBN # 0-8092-4131-5. Chapter 3, Ritual Mutilation. Pp. 49-66. *"My feeling is that somewhere around (90%) of surgery is a waste of time, energy, money and life."* Pg. 49.

71 **Fedeles, Nicholas, MD.** (Now deceased, was a close personal friend of this author) I quote directly from a conversation held with this wonderful Doctor. "When an office pays hundreds of thousands of dollars for medical equipment it is necessary to pay for such equipment before it becomes obsolete. Therefore, patients are encouraged to utilize such equipment before newer and more (presumed) effective implementation becomes available. Thus, in many instances, paying for a Mechanical Device has precedent over a patient's well being. Actually many tests are near harmless, however they are also often quite ineffective and are simply not curative."

of death in this country.[72] Importantly, up to perhaps ninety percent of all illness will correct itself, given time and a natural approach to healing.[73]

Hopefully, what is written and what is tacitly inferred will provide some means for the reader to better understand the nature of intricacies, not always discussed, in a direct and comprehensible manner. Illness, especially one's own illness is a difficult topic. This writer is not a doctor or involved in any aspect of medical treatment, except for that of his immediate family. What is written is not clinically substantiated others are better qualified for such endeavor. What is here written is a common sense position, based upon the single critical encounter of my wife, which may be of interest. This writing will address the treatment of disease, considered as a human challenge, including the imposition of the effects of politics and economics, to be met and defeated, using the least damaging procedures. Thus we admonish that a Physician "First do no harm".

Unfortunately, we have constructed an artificially and bureaucratically determined health-care system.[74] Millions ignore the existence of God, creator of the universe? That man has an immortal soul, which is believed by millions, is all but forgotten by other millions. This is *symptomatic of our great Western Civilization in retreat*, being cleverly and secretly plundered as it is intellectually and spiritually undermined, thus weakened, by a multitude of opportunistic and alien beneficiaries.[75] Plundering and undermining are done so to gain wealth and to discredit the faith and spiritual vitality of the people. This is not new however has sustained since before the birth of Christ. The Cabalistic mutterings are carried forward in time by a few zealots that hope someday to conquer and rule the world; a foolish notion.

---

72   ***Iatrogenic Disease*** is that category of disease caused by an unsuccessful procedural attempt or some unforeseen fatal event, which has been brought about by an extraordinary and invasive imposition, arising as a consequence of poorly informed medical treatment. It should be understood that most often modern practitioners refer to their procedure as a treatment, while choosing not to mention the word cure. Thus none guarantee any cure, rather are liable only for having treated a patient. In this instance the vocabulary of a practitioner is crucial to what is being inferred, especially so since many well-meaning practitioners know and understand that what they are doing is harmful to a patient (one way or another) and may be fatal. We understand that most practitioners do what those imagine is best for their patients and we indict no one of fraud, however human knowledge is always limited and subject to mistakes and the consequence of emergency acts..

73   ***Imagination*** is of considerable influence in structuring what one *believes*. However, what one *believes* may be wrong, having no basis in fact or in science. Beside which, symptoms have been known to occur, as a result of one believing he/she is ill or impaired. (N. Fedeles MD) Imaginations, structured within the mind, can cause what one believes *to become as an illness*, in which instance such *illness* simply does not exist. Additionally, the notion of preventative medicine may cause a too quick response to what is self-healing. (R. Mendelsohn MD) The fact that millions are spent on advertising, for drugs and various forms of treatment, may seduce or encourage individuals to do what is unnecessary and ineffective. All drugs can have or do have damaging effects on the human body; countless numbers of which have proven fatal..

74   **Mendelsohn, Robert S., MD.**, *Confessions of a Medical Heretic,* Contemporary Books, 4255 W Touhy Avenue, Lincolnwood (Chicago, IL 60646-1975, USA). Copyright ® 1979, Robert S. Mendelsohn, ISBN # 0-8092-4131-5. Chapter 4, the Temples of Doom. Pp. 67-88.

75   **Spengler, Oswald,** *The Decline of the West*

> **Many in number are they, who will come to the celebration,**
> **However the hypocrite will poison the wine.**
> **Who is he and how may we know him?**

First and foremost, *heredity is of utmost significance* in any human health challenge. This should be obvious enough, when (simply) we consider general circumstances. What may be deemed biologically/physiologically structural, which although neither exactly definitive nor critically diagnostic, may nevertheless be quite convincing. The *nature* of what one sees on the surface is, no doubt, to some considerable degree, indicative of that, which may be forming on the inside. A phenomenally driven intricately constituted presence would deem to extend the special nature of the species physiologically, that is structurally, as well as psychologically, in humanly perceived time. Genetic continuance is a profound occurrence, making possible the extension of a unique physical and psychological existence in future time.[76] The possibilities inherent in genetic transfer are at the same time *profoundly deterministic* and *unpredictably extensive*, **discreetly so**.

> **The genetic information in one cell,** *using Carl Sagan's straightforward calculations would fill 4000 books of printed information. Each book would have 500 pages with 300 words per page. Each book would have a volume of about 50 cubic inches. An adult body contains about 10 to the 14th power of cells. Somewhat less than 1,000 cubic miles have been erode from the Grand Canyon. If every cell in the human body were reduced to its 4,000 books, it would fill the Grand Canyon 78 times.*[77]

> *What Dr. Sagen postulates, is profound beyond human comprehension nevertheless it is certain that Dr. Sagen was no fool. What he says should be at least of considerable interest. Most individuals should think of this even if they can't understand the meaning.*

The special and specific nature of biological extension, humanly considered, is both reason for and a consequence of procreation. "Biochemical systems are exceedingly complex, so much so that the chance of their being formed through random shuffling of simple organic molecules is exceedingly minute, to a point indeed where it is insensibly different from zero" (Hoyle and Wickramasinghe pg. 3). A single cell uniting, in a very peculiar manner, with one other single cell makes possible what we understand as *familial continuation*.[78] This is a genetic continuation of the parents. This is made apparent, however not proven, by what *we name* as familial continuity. Heredity is the consequence of this phenomenally driven intricately constituted functional presence in action, from one generation to another. We say phenomenally since the number of functions required of every single human being, number in the trillions just to live one single second! *Each day trillions* upon trillions of biologically discreet functions are enacted in every living human being, *each one correlated with billions* of others. Every cell in the human body is part of a complex and profound orchestration, not certainly open to precise human understanding. We ask who might understand this unpredictable, complexity? Keep in mind cells are viable in respect to other cells, those nearby and those more distant, within the human body. Cells in fact do communicate

---

76 **Mechizedek, Drunvaldo,** *The Ancient secret of the Flower of Life, Volume I.* Clear Light Trust, 1998. Light Technologies Publishing, P. O. Box 3540. Flagstaff, AZ 86003. ISBN 1-891824-17-1. Pp. 186-187.

77 **Brown, Walt Ph.D**. *In the Beginning, Compelling Evidence for Creation and the Flood*. Center for Scientific Creation, 5612N. 20th Place. Phoenix, AZ 85061. ISBN 1-878026-08-9.

78 **Mechizedek, Drunvaldo**, Ibid., Pp. 185-87.

with other cells however few can imagine or understand exactly how this might occur. Vitamins, minerals, adrenaline, amino acids, antioxidants and glandular (liver tissue for example), stimulate and enhance living body tissue and fluids, through which such communications are sent.[79] The nervous system, absolutely and by means of holography, transfers and translates information vital to life. Since there are billions of cells, which function very discreetly, it is easy to imagine that the number of incidents of dependency are rapidly occurring, are countless and *to monitor them with certain expectation is impossible*, excepting coincidentally, within a very short time frame. *Modern medical practice too often deals with limited probability without any known guarantee of certain response.* No matter how noble any intention may be, a complex medical treatment is never guaranteed as curative. Billions are spent in futile attempts to do what should not be done.[80] This is (unfortunately) considered as progress. Individually, almost everyone will face some illness, which could/will have fatal consequence. "In the end we are all dead." (Shakespeare) We are individuals, subject to phenomenal circumstance, with unforeseen consequence; such based upon bodily function. Any Practitioner, at best, has a *somehow limited* and imperfect knowledge of those circumstances, which might affect any human being.

Second, *concerning complex biological, physiological and psychological circumstance,* the reason for a specifically determined outcome, of a genetically formed humanness, may be quite illusive. The imposition of what is psychological (subjective in nature) on what is physiological (objectively truthful) cannot be denied. Any circumstance, evoked within a time space format, given to a peculiarly individual understanding of now and then, *that is a conceptually structured awareness in the realm of humanly perceived time*, is not necessarily given to varied and wide understanding. There may be significant disagreement between practitioners working from an exclusive protocol. Thus, *circumstance given to varying interpretation* may cause any event to be generally misunderstood, based upon limitations concerning what may be known, pertinent to the event. What is *imagined, as fact* may be untrue! However, this does not imply that any intent may be other than honest and truthful. Nevertheless, often quite dramatically, human intelligence is challenged by and personally directed toward some degree of understanding, thus free will acts to solve (as it may be assumed) irregularities which may exist or are imagined to exist. That which exists as apparent in a clinical sense is physiological, whereas that which may be imagined to exist is psychological however, the psychological elements do trigger what is understood as physiological. Politics and economics are importantly causative in the formation of "feelings" upon which an individual will or must act. One may assume that often such relationship is not part of an equation, which has been correctly factored. In a critical situation, it may appear that urgency is required, which may prove fatal given an incorrect assumption or improper diagnosis by the professional in attendance. We presume any act is performed in good conscience however it is not always possible to understand the reasoning, which might motivate any sense of urgency.[81] And, one's beliefs, a consequence of having lived a certain life, may very well lead one into an uncompromising

---

79 **Privitera, James, MD.** And Alan Stang, MA. © 1996, *Silent Clots, Life's Biggest Killers.* The Catacomb Press, 105 N. Grandview, Covina, CA 91723. (818) 966-1618. ISBN 0-9656313-0-3, Pp. 110-117

80 **Mendelsohn, Robert S.,** MD. Ibid. "Conservative estimates- such as that made by a congressional subcommittee- say that about 2.4 million operations performed each year (example, 1978) are unnecessary, and that these operations cost $4,000,000,000 and 12,000 lives, or five percent of the quarter million deaths following or during surgery each year." pg. 49.

81 **Mendelsohn, Robert S., MD.** Ibid., Pg. 50, 52, 55 & 61.

position, even when both the facts and science are in opposition to such beliefs. *And, there are always financial considerations!*

Third, complex, *historically formed Ideologies* influence, in a profoundly unpredictable manner, the form and content (idiomatic) of evolving thought patterns, as well as much of present thinking, which may be in response to extraneous considerations. Unfortunately as alluded above, not all historically formed ideologies are based on absolutely truthful and provable fact, thus may be the cause of much disorder and confusion, the consequence of misunderstanding, emanating from imperfect knowledge. "According to the Office of Technology of the U. S. Government, 80 percent of conventional medical therapies have no basis in science."[82] Significantly, given time/space as presently understood, all human knowledge is incomplete, is thereby flawed and is therefore imperfect: probably ineffective. This point is addressed and made emphatic by the teachings of the Universal holy, Catholic and Apostolic Church. A **vain practitioner** may *imagine* otherwise, with misunderstood consequence meted upon a trusting patient. The word *holographic* as used in this writing, infers the existence of the Spirit, in the manner of an *auric field* (subtle energy), as an important part of any living organism. Interestingly, by means of Kirlian photography, one is able to *record what is unseen, nevertheless certainly apparent,* within and around the human body, other life forms as well.[83]

Presently, *individuals* **are very likely confused in their discernment between Reality and fantasy,** given the incessant encroachment of entertainment based on fictionalized history. This, combined with the political and economic considerations, one can be certain has some effect on general health and well being. Additionally various forms of religiosity also influence *individual ideational constructs.* We introduce what is a complex, abstract element, nevertheless somehow eminently functional, which can and does impose upon a variety of considerations pertinent to any case at hand. *Unknown imposition on any circumstance does manifest with some historic meaning.* A particular thought may engender a peculiarly acute response, emotionally as well as physically, especially considering the complex nature of present *[non-selective]* interpersonal-communication. Incidentally, this is mentioned primarily in respect to the ideological structure of *politically and economically motivated thinking,* in every area where human health and/or development are concerned. For example, "The greatest threat of childhood disease lies in the dangerous and ineffectual efforts made to prevent them through mass immunization."[84] The treatment of disease, including immunization, combined with education and welfare make up an awesome slice of the economic and political pie! It is wise to keep this in mind when considering any form of life-threatening treatment. A strong patient on kidney dialysis is worth a fortune to those that would "treat" him. Chemotherapy and radiation for cancer treatment costs tens of thousands of dollars per year, which is *split between the various practitioners* and the multinational drug companies, all involved in the procedure. From experience, many are well qualified to

---

82   **Privitera, James, MD**. And Alan Stang, MA., © 1996, *Silent Clots, Life's Biggest Killers.* The Catacomb Press, 105 N. Grandview, Covina, CA 91723. (818) 966-1618. ISBN 0-9656313-0-3, Pg. 55. An interesting and provocative work outlining "Lockstep Medicine's Conspiracy" made possible by government control. We call this Fascism of the very worst kind.

83   **Gerber, Richard, MD**. *Vibrational Medicine*, Third Edition, Bear and Company, Rochester, VT. ISBN# 1-879181-58-4. Chapter I, pp. 39-69.

84   **Mendelsohn, Robert S.,** MD. *How to Raise a Healthy Child in Spite of Your Doctor,* Contemporary Books, Inc., 180 N. Michigan Avenue, Chicago, IL 60601. LC # 84-1783, ISBN: 0-8092-5808-0. Pg. 209.

know *with certainty* that the treatment given to a family member or friend was futile. Patients died in spite of or because of the treatment; we define this as *iatrogenic death.* Economics is a part of any endeavor regarding a curative or therapeutic program. When costs are factored in any program those do influence what may or should be done. How one value life is another attendant consideration, which is importantly influential? Both cost and the value of life, as being important influence the imagination. From such imaginings procedures are considered and enacted for the *"good"* of the patient. All this is made more complicated by the fact that the top administrators never see or seldom see a patent: this continues on and on?

Fourth, neurological function is determined by complex sets of phenomenally structured inputs. Consider that Experience provides such input in two principal categories; *first, pertinent personal endeavor* with known others and meaningful symbolism; *second, vicarious forms of encounter,* which are often somehow contrived (they represent artificially created circumstance), encountered from mass media communication, politics, economics, movies, television, the theatre and the novel. *Daily the relentless assault of the mass media is devised to combine reality with fiction, truth with mythology and exaggerated propaganda with the lie.*[85] Furthermore, much of mass communication serves as a front for commercial and ideological exploitation. Beside this, there are many other complexities involved in the intricacies of a healthful human existence, which are ultimately significant. An extraneously structured, *conceptually foreign idiomatic* (both personal and collective), combined with a contrived, political imposition on truthful utterance, make dialogue with subsequent meaningfully truthful understanding difficult. Of course, total comprehension is impossible. In fact, this consequence emanates from a general misunderstanding of the power of utterance and the written word; **especially the written word, which can carry forward in time a peculiar message, thus becoming (As it were) more certainly food for extended thought.** Ultimately this is formed as a complex mythology and may be difficult to extinguish.

One must consider that *each individual has a limited capacity for information*, depending upon intelligence coupled with a healthful state of being, reckoned by a level of interest and tempered or formulated with and by existing mind content. What is observed in now time is tempered, one way or another, by what is already established as belief, ideology and imagination? Additionally, there do exist (in everyone's mind) mental pictures, which are conceived or pre-conceived as a form of visual symbolism. Additionally, in the recent past such mental pictures have been implanted by mass media, especially aimed at the conversion of children to one or another, often barbaric or primitive, points of view. The Disney Corporation is on the forefront of presenting such visual symbols to be a part of their very clever, however unwise, attempt to create conformity and acceptance of their point of view. One may consider such subtly directed procedures as a form of behavioral modification, conditioning and/or brain washing. Symbolic mind-content, in the form of imaginary constructs manifest as seemingly holographic-like formations, which can and do carry significant meaning in a specifically oriented time/place, psychological/physiological setting. Such images may elicit pre-determined understanding having been significantly imposed a-priori by unknown others. What may have been superficially imposed exists together with imagery, which is meaningfully realistic as well as significantly and personally symbolic.[86]

---

85   **Denver, John,** a major celebrity in his time, suggested (among prominent others) that we turn off the TV, move to the country, have children and eat apples. Actually he was part of both the problem and the solution for what was and is wrong with mass media. This is amusing, since he made so much money, in this life, and was so well known. Unfortunately, for him, he died young.

86   This paragraph suggests **some elements of truth that are just now beginning to be partially understood.** Holographic coincidence is just now being implied by computer technology and

Alien concepts, have been implanted by propaganda and the half-truth, in service of a sophisticated master, and are carried as mental pictures in the minds of millions.

Many such concepts are given as entertainment, thus are eagerly accepted by millions, who view them in darkened places. Who is Darth Vader, Spider man or Harry Potter, who is Barbara (ella) if not a figment of an unknown or economically motivated imagination? The Sin of Greed is also an important part of this equation and the anxiety that is attendant to hopeful expectation on the part of the practitioner. Here too we find a co-mingling *of **daydreaming with eager expectation**.* Although there may not be any negative intention or destructive motive, much of what is pertinent [in a critical instance] is *other-induced*; the other is not always known, nevertheless, the mind functions with what has been perceived. All perceived elements coalesce as part of a complex and extensive mental picture. When one is suffering from any form of health challenge, the images which one encounters in one's own mind are very important in determining what approach one is likely to pursue. Practitioners, in *an advantaged psychological position,* are able to frighten patients into *the proper frame of mind* for even a horrendously invasive procedure. As inferred, mental images are often acquired inadvertently and *they may not bode well for those who recall them.* Interestingly, some of the most effective remedies and procedures are neither technically complex nor are they prone to romantic interpretation. Cabbage, honey, wheat grass juice and garlic provide amazing results when used in the cure of various afflictions.[87] Few have been given the notoriety of the *great newspapers* (assumed as such), which pander to the Medical establishment breakthroughs in respect to *expensive treatment of disease* rather than simple forms of natural remedy.

Fifth, *personal anxieties and a deprecating sense of self,* which is often a part of any health challenge, are of important concern. All mental, social and physical elements interface comprehensively within a specified humanly perceived Domain. Ideas, abstractly speaking, interface and lock together in thought-clusters,[88] thus to support one or another Idea or the individually special manner of thinking. Similarly, language places in evidence a more specific form of the *interlocking* of ideas. All those who face an acute personal challenge do not possess sufficient linguistic capabilities, thus to afford truthful and literally correct understanding. *Information involves conjecture, hearsay or probability and is not the same as certain knowledge.* Generally, as a consequence of a rather limited linguistic capability, especially concerning the language of technology and *the many*

---

the consequences appear to have profound potentialities. Whether such potentialities will be made to work for good or evil is still not certain although there will probably be a bit of each. The experimentation and research suggests that the consequences of this form of "knowing and understanding" will override all present forms of communication. *Since there are so many individuals with so many conflicting and divergent Ideas and points of view the way those are resolved will account for how the future will be enacted.* One hopes that the spiritual and effectively good ways of utilizing thought will triumph. Perhaps at this point God will intervene so to guarantee a good rather than harmful outcome will be the consequence. Perhaps the future will be enacted much as the past allowing for the damnation of some and the beatification of others: at least for the foreseeable future. This seems to be apparent in one's-understanding of God's plan.

87   **Dubin, Reese,** *Miracle Cures from the Bible.* Reward Books, Paramus, NJ. 1999© ISBN 0-13-621269-7. See the Index for amazing cures.

88   This is my terminology for what exists in the realm of thought. Thoughts do combine in ways unpredictable and often they are formed without reasoned Judgment.

languages employed by the sophisticated Practitioners, today as never before, the individual may be given to a sense of despair. And, the awesome structure of the Metropolis and the **too large hospital facilities** are particularly unfriendly to the poor and the lonely.[89] Importantly, hospitals are often built for economic reasons, which may be ultimately determining factors, rather than for exclusively therapeutic, medically necessary or common sense reasons. There are excessive technologies, without respect for the Soul of the person. Once again complexities, *arising from unknown sources*, which structure the basis for personality formation and development, provide reason for peculiarly psychological/physiological outcomes, however are not easily evaluated; thus truthful response is often, perhaps most often, impossible or nearly so.

As a credit to our good judgment, social institutions have been developed to perform what is a seemingly impossible task, however too often with little or no success. Nevertheless, the human *body has remarkable recuperative and regenerative potential*, which however may be deliberately or adamantly curtailed by habit. As part of any corrective implementation, there exists an idiomatic of Protocol, which advances an assertion based on limited (meaning imperfect) knowledge as may have been gained from pertinent, however limited practice. The mind motivates the body and engenders (calls forth, excites) the becoming of a personal soul. *This understanding (as a most fundamental one) should be considered an important part of any curative approach directed toward the common good.* Does the person want to live, to recuperate, this is very important in curing anyone of anything. Truthfully, the success of any organism requires maximum health supportive of maximum function. The life span of a man, being quite brief, emphasizes a need for comprehension, serious prayer, diligence and truthfully correct attendance, in respect to all significant impositions, foods, smoking, and excessive drinking, which bear upon any human being.

Sixth, *Magnificently structured Technologies* offer what is probably futile hope for millions, who are in the process of physical and/or mental breakdown. Fancy buildings, as inferred above, have no curative function whatsoever, except to generate employment as they are being constructed. **Small may be much better,** especially where about the elderly are concerned. Concerning the production of food, upon which all good health is dependent, many innovations, while praiseworthy as marvelous technical achievements, too often lead ultimately to producing foodstuffs lacking in vital nutritional elements that are often unfit for consumption. War, ingeniously contrived, is the most obvious example of **madness given technological innovation.** However, every single person is at war within, in a very real sense, on the cellular level. *The interior struggle is best won when chemical and traumatic imposition is non-existent.* To repeat, some medical Practitioners believe about ninety percent of all Illness; can be healed by the body, without chemical or surgical intervention. Given the right ingredients for rejuvenation the body will heal itself.[90] There may be exceptions, however exceptions are few, perhaps five to fifteen percent of the total. This is an evasive number since so much is dependent upon past personal habit and behavior. There are times when the body is simply worn out, used up and cannot be healed.

Additionally for millions, *personality formation, as a consequence of destructively skewed indiscretion*, guarantees significant internal conflict, whereabouts *the conscience struggles with the remembered*

---

89   **The poor,** in any instance concerning medical treatment, being wards of the State, play an important part in the redistribution of wealth programs devised by clever and divisive politicians. It is a truism that one dollar is as good as another, more or less, depending upon one's position in the redistribution of wealth chain. How one earns a dollar is quite another thing.

90   **Schulze, Richard, M. D.** *Healing Colon Disease Naturally.* Published by Natural Healing Publications, P. O. Box 3628, Santa Monica, CA 90408, © Copyright 2003, ISBN: 0-9671570-3-4.

past, even as individual intelligence compliments the present in anticipation of a better future.[91] The psychological self is largely influenced by what is hoped for and imagined to be miraculous. Internal excitation may and does precipitate glandular and systemic malfunction. The present day over-emphasis on the value of casual sex can be, I believe will be, the cause for many emotional and psychological problems. The abandonment of the Idea of a permanent and devoted mate should be more carefully considered: Truthful love is indispensable.

Seventh, the *aggressively imposed self-interest of others*, some being i*magined* as professionals, is often a determining factor in individual acquiescence to some form of treatment, which may or may not be curative and, in fact, may be ultimately destructive. <u>Anxious Greed plays a functional role</u>, perhaps often a principal one, especially concerning some unwanted or unneeded treatment. We affirm our belief that most medical professionals do their very best, spending long hours, treating patients. Nevertheless there are some, unethical and uncaring that ruins the good work that is being done. However, at this present time, the presence of greed (a sin) is not fairly considered (if it is considered at all) and may be ignored, as an important element in a complex equation. In fairness many, however not all, involved in the medical establishment, never concern themselves with sinful issues. Sin is, considered by millions, as normal behavior, beside which sin is thought to be a **merely religious** issue. To some extent, stemming from this, the separation of Church and State contributes to sinful behavior. Importantly, <u>government naturally panders to greed</u>, claiming the dutiful accommodation of the populace. A pervasive physical and spiritual domination exists, which few will admit as being the hallmark of a corrupt and fraudulent bureaucracy. Furthermore, there does exist (seemingly) a conspiracy between government, drug cartels and administrators within the medical profession. This is a very complex issue, which few on the outside are able to comprehend.[92] Nevertheless, this bureaucracy appears to be altruistic and concerned only with the well being of the distressed citizen, which distress is largely a consequence of an overly complex system in operation. At the same time, the system is structured so as to rob unfortunate souls of any product from their past and present accomplishments. This robbery is in the form of outrageous charges working in concert with inflation, which together will somehow rob all except a very few, those few are the primary beneficiaries of the System. We understand that the bill are factored and are not always what those seem to be, however those are nearly incomprehensible to a layman with limited insurance, or no insurance at all. This presents a certainly abstract and very complex picture, a picture quite beyond most *seemingly informed* comprehension.[93] It is interesting to observe and to note that various practitioners become caught up in the malfunction and even

---

91 There are many maladies that can befall upon one when the one is set upon by the innumerable possibilities inherent in a full and healthy lifestyle. Keep in mind that the body must engage in defense against various forms of unwelcome invasion from outside sources, which are known to exist and which are debilitating in their assault on the body: virus, microbes and assorted realms of pathogens. Even a healthy body must deal with all of the existing disease causing elements in the vast network of human encounter. Beside this, there are memories of the past that can and do affect one's understanding and acknowledgement of the differences between right and wrong in a moral sense. This is a function engaged by the conscience and is difficult to evaluate.

92 **Privitera, James, M. D.** And Alan Stang, M. A. Ibid. *Chapter 12, Monopoly Medicine.* Pp. 159-163.

93 It is interesting to observe and to note that various practitioners become caught up in the malfunction and even death of those that follow the rulings and procedures, of the men that control the System. This is proof although perhaps somewhat scanty that something is "Still" rotten in the good old U. S. A.

death of those that follow the rulings and procedures, of the men that control the System. This is proof, although perhaps scant that all is not well in the good old U. S. A.

Eighth, because of the genius of individual beings, **Time** has produced a profound accumulation of wonderfully effective means of implementation. Most of the consequence of this profound thought has been *captured by some large corporate entity.* And, this ***disposition of proprietary interest*** has a most important political, economic, sociological and emotional significance. The conglomeration, really a monopolistic **Cartel**, bears upon thus determines, to a very great extent, the health, well being and self-image of each individual. There exists an astoundingly pervasive governmental-medical bureaucracy, with seemingly unlimited financial resources: for some that is. Implementation, as it is, vested in the medical industry become as a business, forms an important element in present Time and manifests in far-reaching technological complexities: actually beyond most human understanding, *the efforts of astutely informed vanity,* as scientific research, notwithstanding. It is known that *about one fifth of spending* is for medical expenses and related issues. This is a very big piece of the pie! The accounting practices and procedures for billing fictitious sums, to be modified somehow by a degree of common sense, are awesome: quite beyond the purview of a distracted suffering patient, unable to pay minor expenses, except with a credit card. How then shall we bury the dead? *In a pauper's grave right next to Mozart?* Keep in mind, Mozart was a musical genius without equal, nevertheless he died destitute. His music set a pattern for much of what has developed in music since his existence.

Ninth, *tradition as established is a fundamental element* within the present (or any present, for that matter) paradigm, which stems from complex Ideational Integration, thus forms a basis for the existence of and adherence to a peculiar protocol. Ideational-integration, which is the product of advanced education, is a concern in an event where cooperating practitioners have distinctly different social, cultural and linguistic backgrounds. Linguistic peculiarities combine with distinct personality Traits thus may add considerable confusion to the dialogue. The patient is not aware of this, however bears any consequence forming wherefrom. Once determined, specific protocol is what has been studied, thereafter applied formally, as method, *possibly exclusive of common sense,* to an extent, which may not and does not allow for the truthfully informed, individually creative mind to expand upon existing pertinent *cross disciplinary* knowledge. Rules and restrictions slow down the process for many, some that are certain to suffer because of this.[94] The exigencies of immediately unfolding circumstance are what motivates peculiarity of response and thus beacons the most highly intelligent human reaction. Importantly, *native intelligence* coupled with the quality and extent of pertinent experience separates *qualitatively* one response from another. One can imagine (at least) *a highly intelligent creative response* may be both peculiar and outside the limits of generally understood protocol, however may be *most important in addressing the future for countless unknown others.* Most significant invention can be understood this way, especially so in the instance of science, whereabouts trial and error has brought-forth amazing consequence. However, such consequence is not always positive in practice and may be responsible for uncounted deaths, especially when reasoning has been made to serve extraneous or ulterior motives. Add to this that, much of what is significant truth may be, and is, *a threat to the income of the establishment,* in support of present practice. Extensive and costly implementation guarantees that self-interest will always be a most important determinant for those likely to be impressed by worldly acquisitions.

94　***Both protocol and court rulings*** do impose upon and direct the procedure and acceptance of various routinely imposed practices. This is understandable in a system, which is as complex as the one we have created. There must be an *honest way* of knowing the difference?

Tenth, *formal study and subsequent learning,* with extended practical experience, as being adjunctive to protocol, will develop into what has become known as *expert opinion,* however may exclude many factors, which are of significance in a singularly peculiar instance. Therefore, formal study, the application of, which requires (necessarily) the use of costly technologies, as supportive of human effort, ultimately compromises the practitioner in pursuit of truthfully understood methods or procedures, based upon inherent intelligence, seated in independently observed pertinently significant reality. Consider that at the highest levels of thought formation there exists *complex energy motivations,*[95] which bear forcefully (positively or negatively) upon the meaning of what may be or *is imagined* as being truthfully understood.

Consider also, there is such a phenomenon as **cellular resonance,** which is certainly worth attention in all cases where time does allow a studied approach to a curative procedure.[96] Importantly, a large number of individuals within the United States (perhaps 80 to 90%) are hosts to innumerable forms of parasites, which feed upon the human body.[97] Additionally, there are ways in which light, in various forms of application can result in a positively curative consequence.[98] And, simple as it may seem, proper diet is most important, including simple, plentiful foods like juice from Wheat Grass. This food has been researched extensively and is reported to produce near-miraculous results.[99] Finally, a systemic cleansing of all organs, within the body, is certainly worth the effort.[100]

Eleventh, *Vanity is assuaged by the application of complex technologies,* which function (albeit with great subtlety) to make **practitioners appear as if to be in control** of what they, in fact, do not fully understand. This may afford some sense of confidence to a dying being; however it is not curative and may prove fatally destructive, given the ultimate consequence of disease allowed an extended time frame. Given the *trillions* of functions, which the body must perform *each and every day,* we repeat no single human being could understand very much of this profound reality. Perhaps there may exist just a very little understanding at best, therefore it is wise to do as little as possible to upset what may easily be brought, *quite naturally,* to perfection. There is no mechanical complex as profoundly intricate as the human body, especially considering the miraculous nervous system upon which all functions are dependent. And, the body is not a machine, as some might imagine. To imagine that the human body is "like a machine" is silly, if not simply stupid! Succinctly, **the nervous system** controls all functioning bodily systems, controls temperature, generates the power of cognition, makes possible reasoned judgment, promotes locomotion,

---

95 Such motivations may be largely intuitive and originate in space, as does all thought content. Often "intuition is what motivates a peculiar response and understanding of reality.

96 **Bearden, Thomas, Col.,** USA, Ret., *Aids, Biological Warfare*

97 **Clark, Hulda Regher Ph. D., N. D.** *The Cure for all Cancers,* (Pro Motion Publishing, 3368F Governor Drive, Suite 144, San Diego, CA 92122)*,* pp. 1-25. This is in a sense a do-it-yourself book as many of the procedures can be done at home, are harmless and inexpensive.

98 **Douglas, William Campbell II, M. D**. *Aids, The End of Civilization*

99 **Meyerowitz, Steve,** *Wheat Grass, Natures Finest Medicine,* *The complete Guide to Using Grasses to Revitalize Your Health.* (Sproutman Publications, Great Barrington, Mass., 01230)

100 **Schulze, Richard, M. D.**,Ibid. pp. 53-60.

controls cell regeneration and stores thoughts and Ideas, in *a quasi-ephemeral holographic matrix*[101] all of the information gained from each encountered event; all this for a lifetime. The impulses generated within the human body are absolutely profound and have led to and continue to support as they encourage the building of *Tradition, that sociological construct which resides within the Intellect* and is available to all who would aspire to comprehensive understanding. In terms of Politics, the delving into truth will yield some astounding results, the truth of which will be rejected with great resolution by almost all politicians, and by all those who most benefit from the **[Our]** System.

Twelfth, *well meaning, government intervention is counterproductive* in many instances, perhaps most, even all instances where such intervention becomes a primary or ultimately significant element in the treatment and hoped for cure of any disease.[102] Government, an abstract corporate entity, has many enticements, which justify a <u>*selfishly motivated and ingratiatingly profound*</u> appeal to personal well being. Thus *dependencies are established,* which aid and abet the continuation of the vested protocol and firmly established methodologies. To be generous we admit that this is certainly understandable, perhaps unavoidable. However, if truth may be revealed, without hateful consequence, one can imagine that entire industries are anxiously developed in support of achieving what is totally unnecessary, probably impossible and certainly dangerous, if not simply illogical and lacking in common sense, stupid and insidiously counterproductive.

This is exacerbated by the fact that the average individual suffering from serious physical impairment knows little regarding biology, chemistry and human physiology, to mention some areas where our educational system has failed somewhat unaccountably to properly inform and teach our children. Keep in mind that some youngsters are not interested in learning the more serious Subjects: they lack the incentive and do not have the aptitude or necessary mental capacity. In our Democratic Society this truth is left unmentioned. In education, too much emphasis is placed on the immoral sexual encounter, team sports and athletics. The instructors are compromising the System by providing too much of what students want. Students, who are not always children, would rather have fun than tend to serious learning. Except for technical education, our educational System has done very poorly where serious education is an issue. Proof of this is manifest in the habits, manners and customs of many of our children, who at eighteen are encouraged to believe they are as a mature adult: thus, many young morons actually believe

---

101 **Ex-nihilo,** One should consider the meaning of **"In the beginning was the word"** and "The word became flesh." Actually "Thoughts" originate phenomenally, where there is nothing else they are inter-synaptic, meaning those exist within the space between the ending of proximate neurons. All of an individual's previous existence underlies every present thought, in an intricately formed complex defined as "memory". The memory, in this respect is absolutely phenomenal.

102 **Government Intervention** is, generally speaking, formulated so as to render extraordinary profit to the system, responsible for devising one medical, social or political scheme or another. This is done, whilst Politicians pay lip service to the needs and demands of the people, thus to provide the necessary smoke and mirrors to confuse an unknowing and poorly informed public, beside which the word "PUBLIC" has virtually no meaning. The victims imagine themselves to be well-informed beneficiaries, without knowing who provides the information. Actually the beneficiaries are those individuals who pocket billions from one program or another in an endless parade. ***All of the above combines in a subtle process of behavioral modification and mind control, such to completely override individual inquiry.*** The Experts are in control! Woe to those who would not capitulate to the expert, especially when and if the expert sees no correlation between decent and fair-mined behavior and a limited, however vainly imposed, professional expertise.

they have a comprehensive understanding of the world and the meaning of reality. What those lack is humility, perhaps the most important Virtue: the mother of all Virtues.

Furthermore, the ill and the elderly have often become victims of teen age gangs that rob and beat them. Within certain categories there exists what amounts to a socialistic-fascistic scheme of transferring wealth from workers and the elderly to a politically indemnified aristocracy. The *Golden Years* are those few years during which an unknown other will strip away almost all the Gold, which the unsuspecting have accumulated (patiently) over the course of a lifetime; just like magic, the sheep are shorn, no doubt!

Summary and Interpolation:

What is written above introduces/infers succinctly, as it suggests briefly, the scope and nature of what has become (in some measure) *a sophisticated racket,* a con game aimed at a very vulnerable group, they who suffer from critical health challenges. The *perpetrators* stand in full view, with *establishment support* and *billions* for the taking, as a physically impaired population fears the charges more than the disease.

A governmentally sanctioned, bureaucratically anointed, "functionary" will be paid thousands in fees, whilst the patient's singularly chosen man of independent mind, even though he may possess the mind of a genius, can be ostracized and made to appear as a "quack" and a fool.

Immediately above is an example of the outcome of too much government in one's private life. What Obama has introduced, in health care reform, limits the freedom and the becoming of every person in this nation. It is bad Socialism in disguise, which ultimately becomes Communism, the worst form of government control. One cannot be deprived of his right to free choice and association in what and how he wants to live: Socialism is not the answer. Only by means of honest education, not directed by an interested governmental agent will one be provided with the necessary tools to exist as a free man.

It should be apparent, *to some at least,* that a monumental, deviously contrived, ultimately presumptuous System is in a position to deny, as it does deny, the individual's right to the exercise of God-given free will.[103] We must demand better treatment! With the most *sophisticated* form of *treachery* applied to *every sphere of existence,* the System controls, with intent or inadvertently, in secrecy as well as in broad view, the outcome of every life. **What is outlined touches upon the Theology of Western Civilization, with its roots in Catholicism and the Christian faith, the Universal, God-given faith of nearly one-fifth of the earth's people?** The Universal Catholic ethic [or parts thereof] is apparent in [some] other Great Religions as well. What is here written suggests (at least) that the means of attaining <u>salvation has, for millions, been compromised</u> by bureaucratically imposed governmental procedures, which deny dignity to those who suffer health challenges that might be easily met and won. Importantly, such challenges engender great anxiety, a sense of sorrow in service of hopeless determination and are coincident with a woeful mood of despair near the end of one's life.

A cleverly devised Chaos occurs, aided by inadvertent or misinformed behavior.
At a time when Eternity beacons and is always relentless, certain in "It's" fatal pursuit.

---

103 Obama Care will make a bad thing worse adding new layers of bureaucracy between the ones already in place.

Just now, the families of the deceased are practicing cremation. In the Apostle's Creed the Resurrection of the body is mentioned as being a reward for compliance to the Faith. Thus Cremation appears as a questionable choice. Cremation is a choice which is less expensive therefore it is appealing for that reason.

The corporate entity, as it functions with respect to human health, must be more sensibly and intimately structured. What is required are smaller facilities, constructed for properly determined reason, *not for the benefit of real estate speculation and development, tax benefits* and *multi-million dollar inducements* given to **vain and insensitive participation**. We require local and more individually determined action, for the benefit of patients, not for the benefit of intrusive, self-serving others. We must reassess the value of outrageously expensive technologies when in fact; simple common-sense procedures will accomplish just as much, or more! *Programs must be encouraged and information made available, which will allow individuals the right to choose from truthfully inspired, alternative procedures.* **We must not overlook the fact that free will is a God given right, which must be protected by Government,** however has been countermanded by ignorantly intrusive, bureaucratic intervention. *If, the Government pays the bill it is still a form of liability, which some citizens will (ultimately) pay.*

Free men **if we are Free (?)** deserve a chance to benefit from the wealth of human knowledge, from which they choose, of their own volition, with personally informed good judgment. The ill, with significant opportunity to gain health and the elderly, challenged by nature and infirmity should not be forced into bankruptcy *so another can live in luxury, own a yacht and drive a Bentley automobile*. Remember, as was mentioned *earlier "He is most content who is satisfied with the least"* (Socrates). The luxuries enjoyed by a few are often a consequence of having stolen from another. We do not condemn anyone on a whim however, this must be considered and reasonable measures must be taken to encourage a proper and fair consideration of one's fellow man. We speak not of Socialism, however rather of a *Catholic (meaning Universal) moral order which obviates our mutual interest* and punishes evil as it occurs

Furthermore, given an understanding that the present paradigm is beckoning monumental chaos, those of the Western world are well advised who would begin to put the pieces together for the benefit of our children and for the continuation of the Western Civilization. It is important to understand that what we do is as a consequence of variously orchestrated mechanisms, which advance forward, becoming more complexes with time. And, whatever is done has moral and ethical implications, as well as being related to the health and well being of one's body and soul. Many of the hospitals, formerly Catholic Institutions, which were (by nature) more aware of the multidimensional aspect of health and healing, have been given over to a secular nature and are, in respect to moral and ethical implications, under the control of an alien inspired Bureaucracy. Secular Humanism, Communism and a false notion of Liberalism inspire the present Bureaucracy. It is somewhat anti-Catholic, the apology being given is that Church and State must remain separated. The way this works is not well understood. This is a vane and dangerous position to take which will ultimately contribute to the destruction of the Western Christian Civilization. We may pay this respect by heeding the admonition of Hypocrites, "First, Physician Do no Harm." We must do this in spite of the fact that even some Priests, having succumbed to worldly ways, have been reckless, inconsiderate and profane. Priests are men, sinners and are some are weak in character however the Catholic Church is a Godly ordained eternal institution. Therefore, we must enter into a state of Christ-consciousness and begin to live thereby; nothing else will suffice. And no one can deny that Christ founded one, Holy, Catholic (Universal) Apostolic Faith, *eternal and immutable.*

Slowly but surely, anti-Christianity is overcoming us, as we are invaded by distinctly negative ideologies. Feminism is a distinctly negative and socialistically contrived oxymoron, an abrogation of Tradition and Truth. Nevertheless, we are wise who would embrace the moral imperatives implicit in one, universal Catholic Church so as to pay respect to the one God who created all, by His word? If you do not believe in God imagine what or who did, in fact, create what is the universe? There can only be one Omnipotent Being, by definition and that One is not a woman, **[He]** is a progenitor, which function is masculine. ***Keep in mind*** Politics at present is inimical to Religion, our politicians have insisted on a separation of Church and State. In my judgment this is a fatal flaw in our system where morality is divorced from the workings of government. It is obvious every day that many politicians are immoral pretenders attempting to do what is impossible aided only by their own conceit and self-promotion. In attempting to please everyone those lose sight of this or their main support, namely the Catholic Faith and the philosophy, which has developed from it over a period of twenty five hundred years. Many of them are fools and some are hypocrites beside. The billions being spent and squandered because of a make-believe enemy are proof of the inadequacy of the System: this is certainly not Christian. But who can and who will fix it. We send our sons to be killed by strangers whom those cannot and will never know. As we do this we reward them with higher pay and worthless medals. We send them to school so those can *"learn"* to execute and pay for more of the same. Those are taught to kill and to hate for the good of the System, which is in many ways often rotten to the core. For the sons that are killed we play a bugle over their grave and present the family with a folded flag. The men so called that fight for the munitions makers are little more than children are? They are brave and imagine they are doing the right thing. Are they? We imagine they might better be doing other things.

This brings into question, what is a good Catholic and infers certain elements that are fundamental to the Faith. Such assertion brings forth, great alarm for billions, who are not Catholic and it is therefore a difficult part of the dogma of the Catholic Church. Time has confused us and millions do not believe this to be a condition of redemption. The Catholic Faith is hierarchical and has a dogma that is unchanging. This is as it must be for the purpose of maintaining a decisive and final Faith. Madeline Albright, our former Secretary of State, "imagined" that the tens of thousands of Iraqi children killed could be considered as collateral damage. Nevertheless she mourned the passing or killing of one Jew. Why is this? Is this hypocrisy, if not what is it? Are not all men made in the image of an Infinite being: God? Apparently those such as Madeline do not understand much about the most important things. She should have been employed in a simpler task. She might have made a very good dust maid or an assistant cook.

Woman is as an incubator, the home of the child until birth. This is a question of biology, genetics and the sustaining of the human race and is not open to political tinkering and vain imposition. ***Such is life!*** A woman must be treated well by any man and should not fall victim to male lust. This is not too much to ask for those who sustain the species. The woman shares her physical being with the child, whereas the man is present only at inception, <u>which is deliberately pleasurable</u>. This is a question of the understanding and acceptance of language. It is essential to understand the language and to appreciate the value and need for Western Tradition as the driving force of Humanity. Furthermore we must know that Tradition is all of the best Ideas that are proven to work over the course of centuries. Tradition is a distillate of the best of human thought and thinking. The Devil works twenty-four hours each and every day and he must be resisted! Keep in mind the Devil has millions already corrupt that will work for him. Most do not understand when those serve him, how and why those do.

For the skeptic, in the manner of an appeal to fairness, we assert that much of what is imagined to be Catholic, at the present time, the consequence of Vatican II, represents a false Church and is not truthfully Catholic.[104] Furthermore, we assert that a cadre of opportunists has been working from within, trying deliberately to destroy the Catholic Church,[105] thus to ensure the rule of the Antichrist.[106] This is happening because the Universal Christian, which is the Catholic Church, is the only effective Force within the Western Civilization, opposing Communism and all Socialistic Schemes as being **[Unholy]**. The nature of the Catholic Church has been determined by an infinitely truthful and genuinely Holy disposition, that of Jesus Christ.[107] The Crucifixion and Christ crucified are *powerful symbols which encourage the pursuit of goodness and holiness.*[108]

---

104 Most Holy Family Monastery, 4425 Schneider Road, Fillmore, N. Y. 14735, *A Voice Crying in the Wilderness,* Issues 1-2-3-4. The four volumes are copiously documented and truthfully edited, utilizing written material covering the complete history of the Catholic Church. The volumes include writing from innumerable Saints combined with statement ex-cathedra, from saintly Popes.

105 **Dodd, Bella,** spent most of her life in the Communist Party of America and was the Attorney General Designate had the party won the White House. After her defection, she revealed that **one of her jobs as a Communist agent was to encourage young radicals** (not always card-carrying communists) **to enter Catholic Seminaries.** She said that before she had left the party in the U. S., **she had encouraged almost one thousand young radicals to infiltrate the seminaries and religious orders**... and she was only one Communist. **Brother Joseph Natale**, Founder of the Most Holy Family Monastery, was present at one of Mrs. Dodd's lectures in the early 1950's. He relates: "I listened to that woman for almost four hours and she had my hair standing on end. Everything she said has been fulfilled to the letter. You would think that she was the world's greatest prophet, but she was no prophet. She was merely exposing the step-by-step battle plan of Communist subversion of the Catholic Church. She explained that of all of the World's religions, **the Catholic Church was the only one feared by the Communists,** for it was it's only effective opponent." Bella Dodd converted to Catholicism at the end of her life. Speaking as an ex-Communist she said: **"In the 1930's, we put eleven hundred men into the Priesthood, in order to destroy the Church from within."** The idea was for these men to be ordained, and then climb the ladder of influence and authority as Monsignors and Bishops. Back then, she said, **"Right now they are in the highest places in the Church."** They are working to bring about change in order that the Catholic Church would not be effective against Communism. She also said that these changes would be so drastic that **"you will not recognize the Catholic Church."** (This was ten or twelve years before Vatican II.) From, Crying in the Wilderness Newsletter #6, Most Holy Family Monastery, Fillmore, NY 14735

106 **The atavistic behavior** of many within our present population (2011) is a clear and ominous sign and should not be interpreted *simply* as a matter of ignorance or personal choice. An obsessive tattooing of the body is plain evidence that we are moving toward a more barbaric and uncivilized form of existence. At present (even) many young women are submitting to this outrageous and crude manner of behavior. This accompanies the display of body parts and the operations to enhance (?) the appearance of the female figure. All is a vain expression of freedom to be distinct.

107 **Pope Hadrian I,** *Second Council of Nicaea, 787*: "...Christ our God, when He took for His Bride **His Holy Catholic Church, having no blemish or wrinkle,** promised he would guard her and assured his holy disciples saying, I am with you every day until the consummation of the world." *Decrees of the Ecumenical Councils,* Vol. I, p.133.

108 *Pope Paul III, Council of Trent, Session 6, Chap. 3:* "But although Christ died for all, *yet not all receive the benefit of His death,* but those only to whom the merit of His passion is communicated." Denzinger, 795. By this is meant *one must be baptized in the Catholic Faith and accept that faith in*

The secular, politically controlled world will have none of this.[109] The Catholic Church, Bride of Christ represents perfect truth and all that this means in this life and beyond.[110]

Catholicism is a religion the essence of which is that it has an origin in the Son of the One Triune God, omnipotent and exclusively the First Cause, of which, logically there can be only one. The Catholic Church is in opposition to all that is Evil. Since *much of what is worldly is evil*, therefore the Catholic Church must stand in opposition to it: that is to this world remaining uncorrupt. This is certainly not an issue of "Style." Please understand a Perfect Church cannot be made better, therefore that Church cannot be modified in any way, regarding the Sacraments, which are elements necessary for *a true and eternal faith*. To be eternal the catholic Faith must remain constant, thus **oppose all that is evil forever**. This is a monumental and *unending* responsibility. Logically, in terms of Philosophy and Linguistics, any perfect construct, *certainly a God-given Construct must remain exactly as it is, eternally*. If any single portion is missing or altered the totality is thereby altered and eventually, given many small alterations, the entity will be unrecognizable from the original and the God-given intent will be forsaken. This is exactly what is being encouraged to happen, by those who oppose goodness and holiness. For **millions** it already is an accomplished fact, which as time unfolds affects all others.

---

its fullness. To accept some part of the Faith and ignore inconvenient elements is to remain *outside the bounds of eternal faith*, which is what the Catholic Church has upheld. It is true that *imposters within the domain of the present* bureaucratic Church Structure are imperfect beings, however in its history and in the upholding of truth, as divinely interpreted, *the Catholic Church is flawless in all effort and encouragement expended for the salvation of souls*. Certainly this is a monumental topic, given two thousand years of existence, however we acknowledge this and encourage our readers to investigate truthfully on their own.

109 **Separation of Church and State**, in this Nation (others as well), is a misunderstanding, perhaps presents a fatal flaw. This is especially true precisely when said Church has divine sanction, is Universal (that is Catholic) and has been inspired by the Son of God, Christ crucified, Christ risen. A perfectly formed Church is the proper and only legitimate basis for a sound and just Government. This should be easily understood. However sin (most assuredly vanity and greed) has corrupted the thinking of hundreds of millions and strangles them with a misunderstanding, thus they face worldly struggles seated in improper and evil actions, which they are not able to comprehend. However, all sin is given to conscience, and the consequence, which follows there from; repentance (possibly), recrimination (certainly), sadness (assuredly) and despair (hopelessness in light of eternity).

110 **Catholicism** is a religion the essence of which is that it has an origin in the Son of the One Triune God, omnipotent and exclusively the First Cause, of which, logically there can be only one. The Catholic Church is in opposition to all that is Evil. Since *much of what is worldly is evil*, therefore the Catholic Church must stand in opposition to it: that is to this world remaining uncorrupt. . This is certainly not an issue of "Style." Please understand a Perfect Church cannot be made better, therefore that Church cannot be modified in any way, regarding the Sacraments, which are elements necessary for *a true and eternal faith*. To be eternal the catholic Faith must remain constant, thus **oppose all that is evil forever**. This is a monumental and *unending* responsibility. Logically, in terms of Philosophy and Linguistics, any perfect construct, *certainly a God-given Construct must remain exactly as it is, eternally*. If any single portion is missing or altered the totality is thereby altered and eventually, given many small alterations, the entity will be unrecognizable from the original and the God-given intent will be forsaken. This is exactly what is being encouraged to happen, by those who oppose goodness and holiness. For **millions** it already is an accomplished fact, which as time unfolds affects all others.

The Catholic Church must remain as it is, being seated in a Triune and Eternal Person, God the father, Son and Spirit. [111] Truth poses some threat to those who, because of treachery, greed, vanity and ignorance, seek domination for personal gain, the acquisition of wealth and control of an emotionally distracted, poorly informed and reticent population.[112]

---

111 ***Rutler, George, D. D.,*** <u>*The Fatherhood of* God.</u> (synopsis) ***God is the Father,*** *an Omnipotent Eternal Being*, whose word precedes all else. Logically, given any series of cause/consequence, there can be only one first cause. What is eternal is ***now, always was and ever shall be world without end*** and pertains to ultimate cause: past, present, future thus defines ***placement in time***. Coincidentally, this concept gives peculiar meaning to the ***verb*** in language, all of which resides in God's good Time. Given the human species, *father is causative* whereas *mother is nurturing*; father is the impetus whereas mother, for her child, is the patient, caring and constant force, *including providing the best sustenance, in the form of mother's milk* (Mendelsohn, R., MD.). This should be quite obvious (and is) excepting for the imposition of imperfect thinking, which promotes the sale of *man-made formula* instead of what is natural. The present socially and democratically driven Idiomatic encourages (forces in some instances) inappropriate conclusions from any discussion, which challenges the acceptance *of any perverted lifestyle*. As defined above, *the status quo, that is the vested interest,* has reason to support itself as certainly as does any entity, including the Catholic Church. Furthermore, *tainted behavior* (imagined as some form of free choice) does impose on objectives, defined by thinking of a more astute and truthfully formed comprehension, especially when *corrupt thinking is made hyper-operative* by mass imposition, meaning Television, News reporting, the Theatre, Pornography and *of course* Hollywood. Importantly, deviate behavior and the consequences emanating therefrom are, in fact medical as well as psychological issues. Perversion, in any form, offers a serious challenge to the intellectual and philosophical underpinnings of our Civilization: independent Cultures as well.

112 ***Some men*** are too anxious, are greedy and willing to destroy the good and holy work of others. The practice of medicine is an especially critical area, within which the moral imperative of the Western Civilization must be maintained. This relates, albeit tangentially, to salvation and the eternal existence of the soul. Many Physicians are being deprived of the benefits of their personally unique and diverse, comprehensive nature, which for profound reasons is God given. When and as this happens, who ever lives during this period in time, will somehow suffer from the abuse of an ultimate calamity. The uncounted dead have known of the calamitous consequence brought about by intrusive, greedy and maligned medical intervention. We are wise to do all in our power to prevent the becoming of some make-believe utopia, such as the sham which is The American Medical Association; about which most have very little understanding. (Mendelsohn, MD.) We are being encouraged to accept what may be debilitating in the extreme. When just a few, by corporate and governmental means, have attained authority over the lives of all others, the rest of us will have no reason to think and to know. Thus beware of the Cartel, the Corporation and that one who would have you kill your own child.

The phenomenology of existence is at once simple and complex. Catholicism, truthfully understood, is *simply what has been known as proven over a period of two thousand years*, supported in *miraculous ways* by *supernatural events*. Thus we have Dogma, which is irrefutable, as it is miraculous. Unfortunately, all are not aware of what these supernatural events may have been; therefore many remain in profound ignorance. Ultimately some are destined to oblivion, together with those who are aware, however do not believe.

Vanity (a cardinal sin) and confusion in the minds of the multitude is responsible for creating complexities, which are exploited for worldly purpose, supported by heretical reasoning, by they

The study of History reveals that in all realms or domains of thought there is evidence, now as before, of a form of an acute intellectual disease, not unlike a disease found in the human body. Present technologies make it easier to access information, therefore understand what is happening and has happened in the recent past. Documented research allows us to reach far back in time with greater certainty than ever before. We recognize that in Philosophy, Sociology, Psychology, Politics and Education there may be *syndromes, contorted and contrary to truth,* which become the basis for an Idiomatic, which determines timely human action. Such contorted *paradigms* are not aimed at obtaining the best for most in an absolutely truthful manner. This is unfortunate, however no less true today than in the past. Sin functions to reward evildoers as it coincidentally deprives millions of good men of a more rewarding existence. War, as a political consequence, is the most obvious instance of a political Disease, which will consume a healthy population in needless conflict. Nevertheless small indiscretions, occurring in what appears to be unrelated events, also eat away at what should and could be a better more truthfully formed *Human Circumstance* in service of Humanity, with equity and justice for all. Actually, many imagine this is what we now have; they are wrong! Other antagonists are simply uncaring, disinterested or in contempt of reason, thus deny honorable and fair treatment to others. Some of those are the dictators and have often been elected to lead men and nations.

The human body is a discreetly formed organism, absolutely particular to both time and space placement, furthermore it is the belief of millions that each person possesses an immortal soul, which (as it becomes) functions as an existential and invisible element between limited time/ space and Infinite time/space. By this understanding we acknowledge a direct link between the individual human being, *made in the image of God* and God Himself. For many, this is not easy to accept however **Tradition indemnifies as it obviates the one true, holy Catholic and apostolic Faith.** That Faith has an apparent and absolute connection between *the Son of God* and man made in the image of God. The *Holy Ghost* maintains the phenomenal connection in the presence **[Being]** of His Spirit, third person in the Trinity. The Apostle's Creed makes note of "all that is seen and unseen", as being the work of the Creator.

One need not deny the occurrence of evolution and what it means however one must consider such more carefully knowing in advance that the All was not always as the All may appear to us. There may have been, probably were differences, which we have not envisioned thus far. Keep an open mind for new and truthful information. There is much more to truth than most can imagine.

---

who attempt, with or without success, to entice all of mankind away from that which is truthful, good and holy. (Reference; Dillon, George E., Mgr., D. D., *Freemasonry Unmasked, as the Secret Power behind Communism,* M. H. Gill & Son, Upper Sackville-Street, Dublin, 1885. London & NY; Burns & Oates. pp., 51-61)

Given *intelligent human participation,* the complexities inherent in the use of words are manifestations of reasoned objectives. However, all objectives are not honorable and they do not adhere to the teaching of the one, holy, Catholic and apostolic Church. *Catholics are not aggressive enough in the promotion of the true faith, perfect in every way, however are the objects of many who would destroy all that is good.* Elements confined within the intellect, are utilized for evil purpose by those, often within a *false church* imagined as a Catholic Church, a protestant church or some other form of imperfect concept devised of human intelligence. Many are they who seek personal gain and the destruction of the true Catholic Church, founded in perfection by Christ, Son of God the eternal Father, imbued with the Holy Spirit in service of all that is good.

It is important to realize that many medical procedures, whether performed correctly or incorrectly and for whatever reason, do lead to death. In death we are all equal, however *it does make a great difference* how death may come about.

> ***A Hero may give his life willingly,***
> ***It is something else to waste away, in a semi-conscious state,***
> ***Controlled by strangers that profit immensely from such a pathetic circumstance.***

Living and dying are issues involving familial, genetic, theological, philosophical and political consideration; the least important of which concerns what is political. Therefore, the more important issues (as listed) should not be overridden by politically indemnified deceit, ignorance born as protocol indemnified by government-controlled research or insensitively personal greed. Thus we face, perhaps unwillingly, the complex question of Church and State; particularly the Catholic Church, which as the basis for Christian Charity, Intellect and Tradition, exists as the foundation for much of our Civilization and for our now-waning Culture.

Interestingly many of the hospitals in this nation, other nations as well, have their origin in Catholicism. Other Christian denominations have also been well represented. However, all are at the present time beholden to various forms of legally assertive political control, not always reasoned or determined by the best interest of the patient, who suffers from a very real and possibly fatal challenge to health and well being: one who may be facing death! Nevertheless, Bureaucracy has a way of burgeoning without pertinent reason except to enlarge the bureaucracy. Government bureaucracy is [**The**] *most dangerous.* Government controls the right to assign a permit or a license, thrives on the power of taxation and has a right to indemnify any form of legal or illegal coercion. ***This is an important point, because much within the law has become a matter of relative importance,*** in supporting the tenor of the times. One is easily tempted to inquire: Is the Law really an Ass? Actually, in a worse case scenario, government may be something far worse. As such it is at once consequence and motivation.

Importantly, most non-Catholic, Western Christian religions, have their origins in the Universal Catholic faith, however they have a confused or partial understanding, brought about by a reluctance to accept all that is necessary for a **complete and eternal** participation. The ideas of man have been placed before those of God, presenting a complex crisis certain to bring this Civilization and attendant Culture to ruin. There may still be time to save what has been accomplished in both social and personal progress. It must be admitted, in the minds of some men, it may or may not be a good idea to save what is as tradition, depending on one's individual point of view. However, to justify any form of dissension, one must be certain to replace what is, with something known to be better, thus the antagonist faces a difficult challenge. Furthermore, those who are aware of some manner of truth are compelled to make known their disposition, in any and all ways open to them. "Go forth and teach all nations." Thus we include this as an important dimension in the healing process. Nevertheless, monumental Bureaucracies have developed over many centuries, with mostly **vanity and self-interest** as a motivation. To reflect and remind the reader: "All in this world is Vanity" (Christ). No matter what one may attempt to accomplish Satan will tempt one with vain aspiration.

The ideas about Christ: we are wise who do recognize that Christ is in truth our Divine Savior. When challenged, our own temple, that corporeal body, which houses our mind and our soul will respond to what God has placed at our disposal. All that is mostly good has been freely given. We are encouraged to take from what is available and must have the personal freedom necessary for the enactment of free will. Concerning political means: intimidation has no place whereabouts any disease is concerned. Nevertheless, individual practitioners, by means of threat and intimidation, become wealthy. Any monetary gain at the expense of a dying individual, who has been or will be butchered, drugged, then robbed (by means of politically indemnified extortion) is sinful and is an abomination. Thus, everyone should remain wary of what is politically motivated. We should not place too much faith in what is merely an expanded technology, requiring the expenditure of billions. Beware of any too-complex technological imposition. An awesome cadre of middlemen, *like Judas for a few coins*, stands between a suffering humanity and various forms of somewhat effective therapy, those known and some yet to be discovered, which are most likely to provide simple curative means.

Too many Americans are dumb and have become negligent and lazy, unable and unwilling to think they are not able to develop a comprehensive compassion for themselves and for others. No doubt, Americans are quite good natured, nevertheless, when being encouraged by accommodating promises, in fact, many become *irresponsible fools, pleasure seekers, addicted to sex, drugs, pornography, violence and self-pity.* And Americans, to a large extent, are distracted by trivia, by unnecessary excitement and appear to be tending toward schizophrenia, as they alternate between a *passively slothful* or *aggressively savage* behavior. This is especially apparent in how **the young are being educated**, as they participate in the great experiment, so as to become greater **consumers** in the **New World Order,** which **has been and is being planned for you by whom you will never know.** They will be assured in their subservient, dolt-like participation. All Behavior is driven by complex time-space configurations, which function to determine any subsequent act, therefore regarding human disease it is wise to consider the nature of the complexities involved before one sets upon a course of *"treatment"*, which may/will prove fatal in consequence,[113] (see footnote #7, above).

Always, be patient and prayerful, forgiving kind and gracious:
Take care of all of that, which God has given you!
Become just a little bit better every day.
Good health and well being,
Greatest of all assets,
Will be yours

For the taking.
For the taking.
For the taking.
For the taking.
For the taking

Peace, be with you!

---

113 Mendelsohn, Robert S., MD. *Confessions of a Medical Heretic,* Contemporary Books, 4255 W Touhy Avenue, Lincolnwood (Chicago, IL 60646-1975, USA). Copyright ® 1979, Robert S. Mendelsohn, ISBN # 0-8092-4131-5. Chapter 8, pp. 141-156

CHAPTER IX

Space

To play life's game, is to play by one set of rules,
In the space provided by
The One who created the Universe.

To begin, *space is a profound corollary of Time.* Space is ultimately significant concerning how and why we think and act as we do. Space is the most significant absolute and is infinite, nevertheless is invisible. ***What is infinite must be invisible.*** Whatever is visible is defined by the boundaries, which contain all finite entities. What is *finite* can be *found [In] space.* Coincidentally, Space, as the ultimate infinity is the symbol of itself.[114] It is *ultimate and profound* that what, in fact, [Is], as nothing, contains the **All** that is! The virtual potential of space has no limitation that we know of, excepting those set by the Creator. Whatever else it may be, the universe is a product of a *"Creative Miracle."* Interestingly, we, as individuals, are given to comprehend only just a very small Space-time Segment and do not understand the truthful nature of this profound ***miracle.***

The Creator must be a masculine entity since the Universe is the result of His being the Progenitor. *This is no small matter, given how many rant and rave upon hearing the mention of God as being a Man.* Some minds, which have been closed or stunted by too much of the untruth and by adolescent political propaganda, which is rampant and by the 'pedantry,' which, Father Rutler brings to mind: *The Fatherhood of God,*[115] are unable to deal with the truth. There are many today that suffer, as a result of the interpolation of exigent thought, which is schismatic and deceitfully covert as well as blatantly sinful. In addition, we are a nation *overwhelmed by childhood fantasies,* which are driven by astounding technical skills, and the investment of billions of dollars (for effect). ***Is it any wonder that we have a dearth of serious adult thinkers?*** Personal prerogative and an impossibly naive understanding of Democracy, impose a too politically subjective stance for honest discourse. Objectivity is essential in searching for the truth. When one is encouraged by powerful unknown forces, with an unknown and obscure messianic goal, in respect to the objectives of those engaged in the dialogue, it is difficult to act in a truthfully and traditionally correct manner.

What we perceive is brief compared to all Time and all Space, or so it would seem. In one's perceived Time Segment, we nevertheless become (in a personal biological neurological and psychological sense) as a center [**our center**] of God's infinite space.[116] We do not suggest that every individual is the exact center of a plotted universe; however what we accomplish is always

---

114 **Spengler, Oswald,** *The Decline of the West,* Vol. I: Form and Actuality. Alfred A. Knopf, Pub. NY. 1928, 14th Printing, 1976. Pg. 122, (Time, pg. 123). "To name anything by name is to win power over it."

115 **Rutler,** Homiletic and Pastoral Review, June 1993.

116 **Time** (Fiedler) does not exist without the coincidence of humanness, a human [**being**]. Although the Universe is as it is, cognoscente is dependent upon human neurological function. Coincidentally geological time, as the format for human existence is independent of man's participation and

from, where we are, and who we are. <u>*We acknowledge and note that what is infinite cannot be exactly plotted.*</u> All human life is centered on an "individually" placed being. Life, in this world of human perceptions, may be considered as a "becoming" toward an infinite existence in an infinite space. This is a Universal Catholic Idea, which is not necessarily accepted by all, nevertheless it cannot be ruled out (Spengler) once it has become within the *mind space* of the individual. In fact, it is a driving motivation for hundreds of millions of individuals. Furthermore, with a promise of possible salvation, *many imagine* we may [after death] become "one in being with the Father, from whom all good things come."[117] The "All Things" referred to, are located in an infinitely-extensive Time-Space surround.[118] Keep in mind whatever time is granted is sufficient to gain salvation, assuming one has undergone a Catholic Baptism (?)[119] This assertion will create problems for some however the **[All]** exists ipso facto as now and is **then** (as before) and **then** (as hereafter).

"***Infinite Space*** is the Ideal that the Western soul has always striven to find, and to see immediately actualized, in its world around; and hence it is that the countless space-theories of the last centuries possess -- over and above all ostensible results -- a deep import as symptoms of a world-feeling. In **how far does unlimited extension underlie all objective things?** There is hardly a single problem that has been more earnestly pondered than this; it would almost seem that as if every other world question was dependent upon the one problem of the nature of space. And is it not in fact so -- *for us?* And how, then has it escaped notice that the whole Classical world never

---

biological time is continued in the seasons and in the presence of animal life however, such without perception of the relationship between past, present and future. ***Only man has a Soul***.

117 **Imagination** (Fiedler) is an important part of Humanness. Imagination beacons future time, from a neurological centered humanly perceived Reality. Imagination is a wonderful gift however, should be directed properly so as not to contaminate the effect of such imagination. The source is a particular human presence as exists in the Soul, reaching for an *"infinite beyond,"* which is unknowable. The center of the Self has an unknown and unseen manner of reaching beyond what is apparent. The thought of an infinite beyond has been an important part of Western Thought for centuries, since the advent of Christ. What is not seen and not perceived may very well be what is most important. For example, *"the spirit of Christ cannot be seen however is nevertheless very functional in the scheme of (Reality),"* as we understand reality to be. This is especially true when we consider the interactive workings of an entire Civilization. *To continue, almost all of what happens between men and nature is unseen by almost everyone on the earth.* **This is the understanding in support of the Catholic assertion that no one can have perfect knowledge**. One would need, be Omnipotent, by definition, to possess all of what is known and understood of every single event.

118 **Bearden, T. E., Col.,** <u>*Aids Biological Warfare,*</u> Tesla Book Co., P. O. Box 1649, Greenville, TX 75401. ISBN # 0-914119-04-4. Col. Bearden implies then explains that we exist in a time-surround. In such instance all time is cancelled as it occurs, thus each moment is lost in time-space forever, except that it can be documented, in word, sound and symbol, by human intelligence sustaining for a limited time. Human intelligence and what is human, being imperfect, cannot possibly convey what is most, significant and most necessary.

119 **Christ** did admonish that we should follow Him. The first step is Catholic Baptism, by which means one is brought into a communion with Saints and other Catholic beings, meaning becoming one in the Spirit of the Lord. The Spirit is found throughout humanity and aids in performing wondrous miracles. The need, for a Catholic baptism obviates some questions. Millions have been corrupted by the imposition of the vanity of others.

expended one word on it, and indeed did not even possess a word [120] by which the problem could be exactly outlined."[121]

Kepler recognized that since all astronomical observations result from the intersection of light and the human eye, knowing the principles of light and of vision would provide a link to understanding the connection between, the cognitive and the physical domains.[122] As he wrote in the introduction to his *Optics*: *"What wonder then, if the principle of all adornment in the world, which the divine Moses introduced immediately on the first day into barely created matter, as a sort of instrument of the Creator, for giving form and growth to everything if, I say, this principle, the most excellent thing in the whole corporeal world, the world, has passed over into the same laws by which the world was to be."* We read in this statement that it is conceivable, not necessarily certain, that man might be working with the same manner of intelligence as God however, to a lesser degree. If, indeed, man is made in the image of God who shares, in some small part His divine wisdom with his creatures, then it seems probable that intelligence, thinking and knowing are divine characteristics given each man for a brief period in time in a limited however definite space.

This divine characteristic set the *"Stage"* for free will, a God given right, which exemplifies God's respect for His creatures. Free will has been given by God to every human being, all Mankind, <u>*not some selected group.*</u> If you are human you can think and act on your own volition, as was intended by the Creator. ***There are various messianic movements, with mostly political intent, bent on controlling the World, which is a vain presumption.*** Men are of their own volition able to choose one or the other without being coerced to do so. Coercion derives from Vanity, which is a mortal Sin. Coercion derives from the fact that ***the will to power*** is in force and controls the population. This is obviously wrong since the **will to power** of one then denies the existence of free will for all others. Christ admonished that to discover truth, as an individual, will set one free, free from slavery, bondage and mortal Sin. This is such a fundamental truth, that it cannot and must not be overlooked or subverted. ***Any Messianic disposition, which denies this, is therefore wrong.*** Christ alone did come to teach *"All Nations"* for which he was crucified by the Pharisees living at that time. He was crucified by a mob living at that time.[123]

Mind Space is [absolutely] unique to every individual in this world. Without elaboration, this understanding is brought to your attention. <u>***The uniqueness of individually formed Mind***</u>

---

120 **Either in Greek or in Latin.** Locus means spot, locality and also social position.

121 **Spengler, Oswald**, *The Decline of the West, Vol. I. Form and Actuality,* Authorized Translation with notes by Charles Francis Atkinson. Alfred A. Knopf, Publisher, NY. Pg. 175.

122 **Director, Bruce**, *On the 375 Anniversary of Kepler's passing.* Fidelio, Journal of Poetry, Science and Statecraft. Summer/Spring 2006Pg., 103

123 **The Romanoff's** were butchered, burned and mutilated for the same kind of thinking by a mob living (then) and the world has not been as it should be because of it. This mob carried forward in time, in the minds of ignorant dolts, the strange and outdated ***Ideas*** similar to those that crucified Christ. The murder of the Romanoff's was a Time-Space atrocity based on a carefully planned and executed "take-over" of Russia, at the time the most powerful and wealthy Christian nation in the World. This take over was orchestrated with precise timing by a group of dissidents combined with bankers and hired assassinates, and was successful because of all the anxious Traitors in the Western world. The motive was GREED *a mortal sin. **The Ideas are made a bit more evasive because there were some Religious implications and many of the Revolutionaries came from New York. This is a difficult subject to approach, more difficult, to understand.***

Space is a threat to those that seek political control*,* harbored in the **Will to Power.** Such individually and phenomenally formed Mind-Space is a singularity unique to the Individual-Time-Space Interlock (configuration), thus cannot be known or easily controlled. Such space is in fact a psychological extension supported by the neurological, biological functioning of [the] individually formed human body and the control of the human mind.[124] Mind-space functions as a phenomenal form of "containment" for what we know and what we understand. The nature of the mind-space is determined, to a large extent, by what one has or *"harbors"* as an Idea or Ideas.[125] It is distinct from cyberspace in that the Mind-Space is within the domain of a living being, the individual, whereas cyberspace is a universal given. Cyberspace is a human discovery, which can be entered at will by anyone with the technology necessary to gain entrance. It is true that Mind-Space can interlock with the products of cyberspace depiction however; the product of such interlocking is still a personal possession, which may have positive or negative effects on who enters that domain.[126] Mind Space is an individually formed human construct requiring of the discreet biological functioning of the various systems within a particular human body. Bodily systems are synergistic[127] and work together in marvelously complex and very positively comprehensive combinations functioning to promote the life, thought processes and vitality of every human being. At death all such *temporary and individual Human functions* cease to exist. What will/might replace them is found in the domain of Religious thought and requires a form of Faith.

---

124 **It is a tragedy** that the mind content of those such as Karl Marx or Pablo Picasso or any other form of prostitute did invade and coalesce with the minds of millions. In some instances such vainly inspired ***"Intellectual Syphilis"*** overcame the content within the minds of the mostly innocent millions.

125 **Christianity,** Catholicism in particular, consists of a *"set of Ideas,"* a philosophy that forms, the basis for the theology and the behavioral patterns of a *"kind of person."* In fact it is Holiness! Christ opposed many of the commonly held Ideas of his time for which he was crucified. *His Ideas were seen as being a threat to the rulers. He was imagined as an enemy of those in power.* Things are no different today than those were two thousand years ago. Keep in mind *"We the people"* never do anything except live. Those who control the rest are determined in their endeavors and are becoming more certain of such control which is now guaranteed by great wealth and properties. ***Money and control of Finance provides the necessary means of control.***

126 **Unfortunately**, for millions, the understanding of cyberspace is correlated with comic book ideas and those that represent violence, killing and mayhem. Youth are distracted by games involving silliness and gaudily colored forms that represent the vulgarity, cruelty and sensuality representing what is imagined however is unknown and unseen. As such, the imagination is a dangerous function, to some degree playing into the hands of who wishes to control the world. There is more than one faction with this desire. Only one faction, Catholic Christianity, completely opposes such mind set. Certainly God and His Son Jesus would best understand such maliciously contrived circumstance.

127 **Synergism** functions during one's entire lifetime and is manifest as a consequence of trillions of functions, both thoughts and acts. "**In Theology** the doctrine that the human will co-operates with divine grace in effecting regeneration" (Webster). There is a connection between **Body, Mind and Spirit,** which <u>*must not be excluded*</u> from thinking and/or thought patterns. It is a Primary Motivational force in human behavior and existence. In fact it may very well be the most important consideration. The **Idea** has been eclipsed by Pagan and Disneyland imagery that completely obfuscates the meaning for youth.

The Catholic Faith, universal and all conclusive, is that Faith which is to a great extent responsible for the development of the Western Civilization and the marvelous thought components, which have provided so much for human progress. Nevertheless since the Crucifixion of Christ there has existed a never ending struggle between Catholicism and those that have a like mind, to those that performed the Crucifixion. History informs us that there is great disagreement in who is a Jew. Biblical Jews, as such, are very much incorporated into the human race. Much emphasis is placed on the Diaspora, however all peoples have undergone similar fates.[128] Individual members of all tribes have moved from their place of origin to other places. A few may still remain, which is understandable. Only the Zionist Jew uses this as a defense of his being, without including mention of his *sense of exclusiveness and his unwillingness to participate in the general workings of the human Race.* The most notoriously Jewish persons support the *"Idea"* of racial and religious purity, for Jews. Nevertheless those encourage a mixing and or leveling of all others. In the past, by his exclusiveness coupled with his being a moneylender, to the nations of the World, he now finds that he is in a privileged position amongst men. Given the nature of **Usury** and its function in **Time** some Jews, others as well have gained an extraordinary advantage in worldly affairs. The history of lending money is a subject all by itself. Briefly, what has happened is that money instead of serving the well being of Humanity has slowly and very deliberately become the Master of Humanity, serving most those that hold the coins? Jews, together with other money lenders have, in large measure, become Masters, and thereby control, amongst other holdings, most of the major banks in the West.[129] Greed, a Sin, will encourage them to attempt to control the others as well. Time will tell.

When money is loaned at interest over long periods of Time it grows exponentially. In the course of many lifetimes the sums become astronomical and are a threat to the Civilization. This fact ties in with inflation and provides the necessary funding for what should not occur. ***This is not well understood and may be fatal to the Human Race.*** The holdings listed under the reference ( ) immediately below give some idea of how this works in reality. The interlocking relatedness is no accident: it is being carefully implemented right now. Corporations must be more truthfully exposed for what those really are. Criminal Syndicalism must be identified and stopped before more enterprise finds its way into criminally inspired possession. The narcotics trade places billions in the hands of criminals that are determined in their sleazy efforts to corrupt the human race. The criminal types could not function without the co-operation of a segment of the general population. One does not have to purchase any form of narcotic: certainly not as a means merely to feel good. Combined with this understanding we have some psychologists pushing drugs, especially on children where such drugs are more harmful than good.

---

128 **Diaspora**: the dispersion of the Jews after the Babylonian exile. In fact many people moved to different places and today more frequently than in the past. The Jewish Diaspora has greater religious connotation, which relates to their believing that, those are God's chosen people. This ancient belief is a factor for much of the turmoil and bloodshed in our present world. Combined with the use and control of money such feeling of superiority has despoiled and corrupted the entire civilization.

129 **Mullins, Eustice,** *The World Order, Our Secret Rulers*, Ezra Pound Institute of Civilization. P. O. Box 1105, Staunton, VA. 24401. pps. 6 to 63.

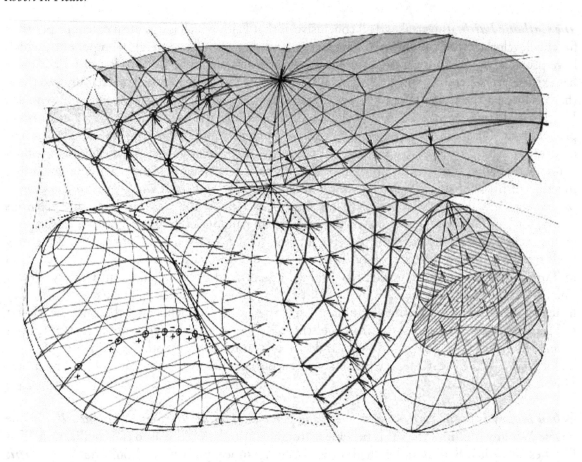

Recent computer imaging, of the interior of the body has been rewarding for the purpose of medical diagnostics. Also, for informing the general population, to a limited degree, of what exactly goes on inside the human body. Nevertheless the understandings that follow are open to the *"thoughtful and personal"* subjective interpretation of those that view, thereafter act upon such information. Thermography, senses and confirms the existence of heat within the body, which is a sign of infection or illness, for example breast cancer (Nelson, MD, PhD. Mark Brown PhD). Vibrational Medicine is able to override the waves that function within the body and to make minute adjustments where malfunctions are apparent, for example heart beat and cellular resonance (Richard Gerber, MD). All such techniques are in consonance with the normally functioning bodily systems and with the *universal order and functioning of the space,* which contains them. *(See the diagram immediately above of an imagined genetic structure).*

Micro-voltages are found within the functioning cells that can be acted upon by mechanically induced waves so to enhance and correct cell function.[130] Micro-voltages are also found in the aura that surrounds living plants and animals. Subtle forms of energy are emitted from living entities, which can be photographed using Kirin photography. What is within and without from the human body (other plants and animals as well), works in concert to accomplish remarkable human endeavor. Acupuncture, the use of light and holistic medical practice is dependent upon such infinitesimal functions. Medical science, when given freedom to inquire, combined with personal discovery, as a consequence of living, combine to provide understanding of what heretofore has

---

130 **Gerber, Richard, MD**. *Vibrational Medicine, The # 1 Handbook of Subtle-Energy Therapies.* Third Edition. ©2001, Richard Gerber. ISBN 1-879181-58-4. Bear and Company, Rochester, Vermont, 05767.

been unknown. Unfortunately there are religious, political and economic considerations that do color what may be done or will be done to benefit from any important discovery.[131]

The diagram above is completely abstract and addresses many issues within the domain of Biology. A more complete explanation of this process is found in the writings of another volume to be completed by this author in the near future. There are a number of related issues that are considered and a form of explanation is given. The functions of the diagram can be applied to the infinitesimally small and to the infinitely large as well and all sizes in between. The image is considered without specific reference to size: it simply IS! This is difficult to ponder however is necessary so to establish the validity of the idea. This diagram is in consonance with the nature of a complex reality in a state of flux.

Micro-voltages combine with chemical substances in *"a spiritually centered force"* that drives human life. The ontological aspects combine with the misunderstanding of what is of a divine nature, and are generally confused, by variously limited notions concerning Religion. All Religions are *"imagined"* to have an equal validity regarding their efficacy. ***This is a primarily "Political Notion", driven by the Party, certainly most deficient in the understanding of what is Spiritual.*** *Politicians use Religion as a means to convince a population because their Political Ideas seem more acceptable if wrapped in a form of divine thought. This is most obviated in the Communist and Socialist domains where about the dominant Political thinking is in direct opposition to religion: especially to Catholicism, the Christian Philosophy of the Western World. This is a very obvious form of hypocrisy that no one seems aware of.* Political thought, generally, does not include, the *"Transmundane"* and that, which is **Holy.** As always, comprehensive and complex thought is imposed upon, by political subterfuge and what is only *"imagined"* as necessary. ***The Ideas which imagine and represent the separation of Church and State present an insoluble problem.*** Abortion law and the Federal Government's intervention in domestic issues provide glaring example of *destructive and debilitating political interference.* The present debate over the Nation's health programs is a NOW notion of what some believe will be for the betterment of the people. There is little thought or discussion concerning what is or may be holy. There is little understanding and little cognoscente on the part of those who are doing what *they only consider is important.* Most of the politicians and many other bureaucratic Types have almost no understanding of the various complex medical treatments which may be involved in a special circumstance. Even the Doctors do not always have all of the necessary information required to proceed correctly.

All forms of life animal and plant also become as evidence of various phenomenal processes. Animals, lack understanding of any spirituality, however benefit from the existence of an eternally present power over reality that man has determined as his God. All point to one simple question. How can this be?

Thinking is one such endeavor and thoughts do have patterns. Thought patterns interlock, within the mind space, ***by means of language symbol and act.*** When committed to the various *written word patterns,* thought can be observed and reconsidered many times, thus to obviate,

---

131 **Privitera, James R., MD.** & Allan Stang, MA. *Silent Clots, Life's Biggest Killers,* The Catacombs Press, 105 North Grandview, Covina CA.46 W. San Bernardino Rd., Covina, CA 91723, tel. (818) 966 1618.

compare and reinforce understanding.[132] Music also affects thinking because of the intensity and the insistence of the rhythm and beat. The beat, when strong and incessant does affect how one feels and may encourage certain forms of personal or mobs behavior. The vibrations, given off by percussion as well as sound reverberate within the internal workings of the cells in the human body. This is perhaps why music is so compelling, one-way or another. Plato was critical of music for political as well as spiritual reasons. Presently, (2011) one can assume that much of the noise deemed as music has a strong (negative?) affect on the listener. By insinuation and sheer force of noise, accompanied by outrageously invasive lighting, rock music intrudes with negative implication on the minds and behavior of the listener: especially so on the minds and behavior of children and youth. The noise and the language in such instance *are dominant in the mind-space of many youth*. No one should participate in such nonsense however to stop it is nearly impossible except an individual can protect his own being. ***Don't buy tickets. Don't buy recordings don't go to the fools concert! Try to enjoy the serenity of silence with only your thoughts to consider.***

Television, especially, has provided a level and degree of intensity and insistence combined with the inclusion of commercial nonsense that is designed to entice even as it distracts from and impairs serious thinking. It is difficult to imagine what might be the consequence of such desperate programming viewed incessantly. One can imagine that the behavior of our children is directly affected by such inputs: their feelings and understandings are being impaired. The music, which accompanies drama, is most often more compelling than the drama, much of which has lost its meaning between the commercial messages and the subliminally delivered thought content, which may be an underlying factor?[133] As an art form, drama has been trivialized and delivered so that the means of delivery, the technologies employed in the sophomoric attempts to create realism, take precedent over the message. Before coming to any defensive conclusions, consider this philosophically and imagine an extended time period, perhaps two or three hundred years. *To reiterate, even Plato, two thousand years ago, was skeptical of the form and manner of music as being capable of destroying the nation.* One might imagine that music is an important factor in the destruction of the minds of youth. The young grow old. One wonder how will the adults of tomorrow deal with the problems that have been created today?

Propaganda is another related issue, which depends upon the reiteration of sound and symbol *in context contrived to create submission to intent.* Freud knew and had some understanding of this, as do modern advertising executives. What is imagined as truth, when given to the wide audiences found in recent-times functions, more or less as propaganda. Propaganda has been very destructive on Christianity and especially so on Catholicism, *which harbors the imperative upon which Western Civilization has been founded.* The Church has been the object of calumniation for centuries by all that were Heretics. Those that did leave the Catholic Church, and there were hundreds of millions, felt some obligation to defame, insult and malign the seat of **Holiness:** from which they chose to

---

132 **The Rorschach test** requires all participants to respond to a form after which response the participant gives a description of what has been seen. This is an interesting test however is influenced by the interpretations of who administers the test. Thus such *"tinkering with the mind"* may not have much, validity. Pp. 8-22.

133 **Jacobson, Steven,** *Mind Control in the United States.* Introduction, by Antony Sutton, Critique Publishing Company. P. O. Box 11451. Santa Rosa, CA.95406. ISBN 0-911485-00-7. LC #85-70431.

escape (see chart showing the rise and fall of various heresies).[134] **Chart** shows some individuals that were amongst the finest and most astute and holy men found in this life?[135] However even some Popes have negated their responsibility and were anti-Popes. The last five Popes come into question for a strange form of ecumenism, which those have espoused. Politics has corrupted the Intellect and the Papal authority therefore much of serious thinking including theology and the dogma of Catholicism, has been somewhat impaired by adolescent misunderstanding, and much has been pushed aside.[136] By serious thinking, we infer thinking that is significantly in reference to the *here and now* and, [the] *there and then,* especially so do we consider eschatology and eternity. Serious thought is certainly more important than the needs of athletic programs and phony classes designed to create a desired (by some) form of social acceptance.

Much in this world is ordered hierarchically, <u>*Thought Space is hierarchical*</u> as well. We imagine the standard Intelligence tests do obviate this; however political intrusion coupled with the refusal, of some, to consider reality truthfully has made a deliberate and effective means of determining the <u>*"Level, of Intelligence (Quotient),"*</u> the I. Q. somehow unacceptable. The Thought Space of genius is far beyond that of others, which is obvious, it is more extensive and provides for complexities and more cognoscente associations than that of a normal person. Nevertheless, Public Education thrives on scholarships given to those that kick, bounce, hit or run with a ball, not to forget pole vaulting, golf and gymnastics. Also, young ladies are encouraged to be no longer interested in the domestic arts. Many are being encouraged, to prefer kicking, bouncing, throwing and hitting a ball rather than serious study and most certainly not the domestic arts that support the family. The young ladies respond well to the athletic events demanding a form of manly action: with beer from the bottle after the events. Watch the beer commercials on television: you'll get the picture.

Athletics while having a small bit of importance distract from the serious learning required for Today's living and existence. Millions are spent on scholarships for athletes, which is of little consequence: except for political purpose and for entertainment. Many athletes graduate without having completed any significant coursework during their ***too much valued*** participation in one or another game. Those are like grown children. In fairness to Public Education there are some small tokens given, for work of the mind as well however, most do not compare with athletics. If one compares the salaries of the better coaches, considered as such, with those who teach English or Math, one gets the picture. Some coaches make two or three million a year ($2,000,000. or $3,000,000.), whereas the teachers, generally speaking, make much less than $100,00.00 one hundred thousand. What is this saying?

---

134 **Popes are condemned** because they speak of truth, which is considered infallible. Truth [Is] Reality.

135 **Ratzinger,** Joseph Cardinal, <u>*Theologische Prinzipienlehre.*</u> 1982 Erich Wewel Verlag, Munich. Translation by: McCarthy, SDN. Principals of Catholic Theology, 1987 Ignatius Press, San Francisco, CA.

136 **Catholic Dogma** is the consequence of the intentions of Jesus Christ being extended in the work of the Apostles, which were determined by Jesus Christ to go forth as <u>*"the ligh of the world*</u>, thereby to aid man in his search for salvation, that being for eternal happiness. Even Shakespeare observed <u>*"All that ends well [Is} well,"*</u> and all life ends assumedly well for who are baptized into the Catholic Faith and hold to the doctrines given form as Dogma, persistent, universal, ***unassailable and immutable***. This is not something that most will <u>*to understand*</u>. Most find difficulty in following the ways of a perfect being. Some do try.

The jocks rule! Use your imagination. Athletes earn millions whereas scholarship and intellectual brilliance struggles for tenure. It is difficult for many young professionals, well qualified and eager, to be rightfully employed when one considers the large number of foreign immigrants that are working in the professions. The average person will spend fifty or a hundred dollars, even more, for a ticket to a football game however, *significant writings are ignored* and Catholic scholarship, covering two thousand years of patiently devout study, is scorned, ridiculed and maligned. The best books cannot be sold except to just a few and even the few does not necessarily read and understand them. The exceptions are technical manuals which deal with ways of accomplishing one or another task. All this is indemnified in higher education, by much of which is dedicated to what is referred to as deconstruction, which promotes the deformation of Western Civilization and of the Culture and Societies grown there from. *The destruction of the Western Civilization is the work of the anti-Christ.* Keep in mind, there are many anti-Christ not just one! They are everywhere!

There exist Education Courses *and nausea!* If the college student is not able to pass mathematics, for example, there is a class in Educational Mathematics whereabouts the college student learns how to teach such heavy stuff as counting, addition, subtraction and even multiplication aimed at the level of elementary or sometimes secondary education. With such knowledge the "teacher" will know as much as a ten-year old should know?

Propaganda, as it relates to health issues is often a form of sophisticated dialectic, conceived to confuse. One should consider that much of advertising is propaganda, is meaningless, and cleverly written, and simply stated is not true. For example, millions are spent reiterating on television and in print the value of substances known to be harmful to the extent of causing the death of the patient (Contreras, MD). The profit, gained by Pharmaceutical Companies is an absolute disgrace and an insult to the men that know most about the subject however, are not part of the *"Medical Establishment."* There is a form of Conspiracy, or perhaps collusion between Government, the American Medical Association, and the Pharmaceutical Industry to defraud the people and to ban effective and inexpensive products. The government heaps billions, on the Medical and Pharmaceutical Industries, which have been extorted from the people as a form of their payment. "Collaborators in government (and universities) can now get away with open fraud." (Wm. Douglas, MD). As a retired Professor with nearly fifty years experience in higher education I submit that *much of what happens in higher education is a politically motivated farce.*[137] Much is simply a waste of time all such to please a politically liberal, narrow minded faculty, too pleased with their own very *"limited expertise.* Many college faculties are suffering from a Socialist bias which is, in truth, warmed over Marxism. Their positions are often dim-witted and

---

137 **We pay too much** for what is often near worthless learning, providing that a few athletes are given unreasonable opportunity to practice in preparation for making it in the big leagues. Institutions of Higher Learning encourage Team Spirit over serious study. Observe the mindless hysteria that accompanies the big games. Note also the arrogance of the stars that, if truth were known, would not be able to pass an entrance exam to High School. Even after graduation, if it occurs, without help, many could not write an intelligent sentence. We acknowledge some exceptions, of course and extend our sincere respect. Running on the grass is no substitute for serious study. Busywork is not serious study, beside which only perhaps twenty-five percent of high school graduates are mentally equipped for *"higher education."* The rest require job training and the development of the skills, which we seek in other nations. And, women should take motherhood more seriously and prepare for it with the proper kinds of domestic courses. A woman is not a man! And, a woman should act like a woman: for example no women in combat: no woman in the Army.

shallow; nevertheless those are the respected scholars in the Field, self-centered and arrogant in their pretense.

Thought patterns are peculiarly formed by means of the senses especially sight and hearing however, other senses play some part as well. Sight is important for the simple reason that man has progressed through time guided by symbols and sounds. Symbols and sounds combine with the effects of incoming experience and the *ethereally formed* substance of a peculiar reality. Sight is also important because light is a universal and constant given. Images travel through space on beams of light. (See brief writing by Kepler in this document; pg. 90). Photons travel within the infinite space of the universe as well as within the interior of the cell. *There is reason to believe that living matter is a manifestation of a peculiar form and arrangement of light.* Interestingly Catholic Christianity, some other faiths as well, maintain God is the light of the world. Dante imagined Beatrice as being perfect, chaste and as pure light, therefore somewhat likened to God. Angels are believed by some to be a manifestation of pure light, invisible and therefore capable of being anywhere in an instant.[138] As mentioned above, three centuries before now, **Kepler in his Optics** made some profound associations in this realm. *(See the explanation that defines the nature and content of the cover of this volume: a reproduction of a drawing of the Head of Christ).*

Additionally, in reference to thinking, symbols have been associated with sound to the point where words spoken and written [may] have the same characteristic impact on the mind, as doe's direct experience. The thought patterns are incredibly varied depending on the mind content of various individuals (See addendum A., *Thought Patterns*). Thought patterns I imagine, to have a binomial formed structure, rather like the wings of a butterfly in parallel position.[139] (See my drawing of a butterfly immediately below). It can be imagined that what becomes as part of a structure within the mind space can be referenced and superimposed upon what is incoming as the result of current sensory perception.

To have some idea of what this means, consider that all snowflakes are imagined to be unique. This may or may not be true however there are trillions of variations and they form patterns. The patterns as seen in the snowflakes are similar to the patterns generated by the electrical forces, which accompany life, in that they are categorical and can be analyzed mathematically. *They are not necessarily understood because of mathematical means.* Life and what we do as human beings, is dependent upon the workings of the brain and the thought patterns that develop one way or another. The thought patterns are phenomenally encoded and inextricably interspersed excepting that they do surface so to provide that we are able to distinguish and to recognize one thing or being from another. Without seeing, one can also recognize bacon, frying in a pan or a skunk standing in one's yard, meaning smells as well as images are encoded phenomenally within the *"Mind Space"* of every living human being. Exceptions are those somehow inflicted with physical impairment.

---

138   There are twelve forms of angels: It is a hierarchical continuum from top to bottom. Various Angels (it is believed by some), have different responsibilities.

139   **See Illustration of Butterfly,** immediately below. The wings of the butterfly are obverse and in parallel position. Those can be compared with an image in a mirror as being the exact opposite as the one outside the mirror. What does this mean?

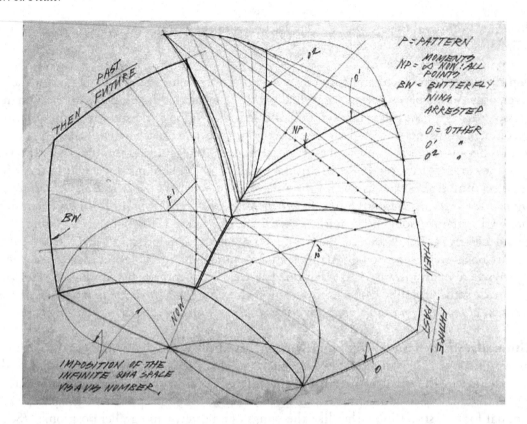

Cognitive ability is tied to the genetic structures of the cellular matrix, which combines to form the nervous system. Phenomenally, this is a consequence of the fact that sound, symbol and reality as it unfolds is encrypted within the brain. As a corollary the encrypting, as in writing or carving, has a direct relationship to the movement of the hand in space. **Movement is characteristic of life.** Writing is in fact movement that has been arrested so to form the marks, which when structured with consistency begin to form the alphabets in various ways. Form, three-dimensional and Texture, random or controlled extension of a flat grouping, as marks comprise two different categories of visual expression. Color is distinct in many ways and enriches form and texture without adding significantly to the meaning of either form or texture. Color does summon forms of emotional involvement that may span all the way back to childhood. Brown, which is non-spectral, is thought (by some) to be the color of the soul.[140] Tradition has made possible the magnificently extended correlation between living and knowing, observing and expressing, formation of various languages and finally mechanical implementation to accomplish a needed and desired consequence.[141] Tradition also forms, as a continuation of what has been the result of

---

140 **Spengler, Oswald**, *The Decline of the West, Vol. II. Perspectives of World History.* Authorized Translation with notes by Charles Francis Atkinson. Alfred A. Knopf, Publisher, NY.

141 **A quality of genius** is found in the conception of the idea of interchangeable parts. This is the greatest strength found in modern technology. What can be analyzed as to form and structure then produced repeatedly can be utilized discreetly in many places with the same effect. This understanding, it is assumed can be (to some extent is), applied to the human body, which likens the human body to a machine. However, such understanding depends upon the existence of a sophisticated Tradition of Biologically scientific technique with commensurate understanding. The Soul of man is apparently lost in the attempts to redesign humanness. The Soul is an *infinitely distinct* element, which cannot be reproduced.

millions of individual *"thought-driven"* choices. *In fact every significant human endeavor of the past is woven within the fabric of Tradition.* Every Tradition unfolds as a product of human endeavor and is supported by its own *"positive efficacy."* This fact alone makes the work of the political process, as we know it, quite redundant.

The results of political-maneuvering have caused untold misery for the human race. Keep in mind all politicians are not necessarily the best of men: some may be considered as being evil. Most are vain and suffer from a neurosis that encourages them to want more than is necessary. Politicians take and are given too much positive credit for the destruction, which they have caused and for the millions that have been killed prematurely because of Wars, Famines and other misadventures caused, by blundering Politicians. What we imagine as elections that will control the future, to the advantage of the people is of little or no significance. *Money determines the law and the workings of government.* Almost every man can be bought. Except Politics form as part of a complex destiny led by the somewhat skewed thinking of individual beings, such is the Riddle of Destiny! Some of our elected leaders have sworn oaths that are above the oath they have sworn to as an official in government. What does this mean?

Political Space is divided between what we have come to recognize as various Political Parties. The Politicians party, the people pay the bill! A *two party system* is ideal since the *space* is thus divided in about half. Politicians, in our nation, generally choose to be Democrats or Republicans. Others are rarely even mentioned as part of the campaigning, some not at all. In twenty five years, the name Lyndon LaRouche has almost never been mentioned, even though he has run for president several times. Ron Paul is another unmentionable name. Why is this so? Both men are independent in their thinking and therefore not *"qualified" to be considered even nominally.* Interestingly one is a Democrat (so called) the other a Republican (so called). The choices are probably the result of who will fund them in their endeavor. The two parties are said to be adversarial, which is ipso facto not necessarily true. In fact, although there may be some superficial distinctions, there is much more, which they have in common. The most important commonality is that they all hope to stay in office for a lifetime, ***which is much too long. Career Politicians are a curse on the governing process*** as determined by the nature of humanness. Career Politicians exude a level of conceit and confidence that is unhealthy and not in the best service of the People. Terms should be limited; perhaps two terms at most. We did not favor a King because he was a permanent fixture: there were some exceptions as many Kings were killed in battle or by hypocrites that pretended serving the King. In any event by electing the same individuals for seven eight or nine terms we are, in fact, in agreement with the Idea of a King. A King is a permanent superior which is what we choose to elect. Governor Brown, in California like his father, is an example of a continuation of the political process. In the past the King had a somewhat reasonable distinction by inheritance and truthfully serving His People. This is the reason that the Romanoff's were butchered: those that killed them wanted what they had: the land and the money, the jewels and other properties. (*I have written about this elsewhere*).

Ideas form as part of the general misunderstanding inherent in human thought processes. Indeed, it is likely that many voters do not understand most issues. It has long been known by a clever few that when millions of people must choose between A and B, or Yes and No, it is likely they will split just about evenly.[142] *Often husband and wife vote differently,* which is dumb, and effectively

---

142 **Col. Mendall House,** who was not a colonel at all, **[was]** a close and very influential advisor of President Wilson. Though he remained almost completely unknown, he was the brains and the Traitor that was largely responsible for much of what President Wilson did do. His legacy from a

nullifies both votes.[143] Actually it would be better if husband and wife had only one vote, with double weight. This would encourage them to have a consensus in their own family. This is the first step in making the system work. However the Modernist imagines that husband and wife should be independent in their thinking. Political posturing provides a basis for such differences even when neither knows and does not understand the substance of the Issues. At present, to win an election one must convince just a few *"on the fence voters"* and the election can be won. Many elections are near even, won by just one or a few percentage points. Thus about one half of the voters decide the election. However only about half of the people vote therefore most elections can be won with a plurality of about 26 to 28 percent of the eligible voters. In matters of fact this suggests that perhaps **two or three percent** of the voters, having been driven by *properly applied motivation (?) can determine the outcome of the national elections.* This is why pressure groups like the ACLU, the Radicals, Ethnic blocks and counterfeit votes have so much influence. Nevertheless the winners do control [somewhat] the situation for a time after each election. Generally speaking thought-content of the voters can be formed by means of propaganda repeated incessantly for the effect it will have on the thinking process. This is especially true of the simple minded, the nearly illiterate, and they are legion. The reader can go from here.

Uniquely individual inquiry and experience combine in a manner governed by genetics, intelligence, biology, physiology, and time-space location. Therefore, to some extent, one can know and *(possibly)* understand ideas and events derived from the continuum of experience as encountered. Of primary significance, Tradition is the containment and holds man's understanding, as being a broad containment structured in accord with an evolving language and level of understanding,

---

somewhat remote past, to this day, can be held responsible for much of what happened since. Balzak did comment that only about five thousand persons were responsible for most of the [then] current history. Perhaps today those responsible for what happens are perhaps no more than twenty thousand. Many are blood relatives, much as were the former aristocrats. (See Ferdinand Lundberg. *The Rich and the Super Rich* [also] *Our Crowd*) The most influential own the large corporations-become-cartel. One-world, the Global Village, International co-operation, Outsourcing are euphemisms for total (as in Totalitarianism) political and economic control. The United Nations Army will be formed for the protection of the One-World government and those owning large pieces of this one-world monstrosity. The individual will be powerless and will have only an imagined participation in the scheme of things. The reason the United States must be destroyed is so that few, eventually no newcomers will be able to assemble great wealth, with which they could upset the scheme of things. What we witness is a sustained effort of one **[Idea]** persisting, over several Millennia.

143　This is one of the flaws in a Democracy. In addition the most ignorant of voters can cancel the voice of genius. This is precisely why voters must be (1.) well educated, (2.) twenty-five years of age, (3.) gainfully employed, with records of income tax payments for a minimum of five years and (4.) They must own property and have paid their taxes.

which is locked in that same language and symbol.[144] Space is unbounded (?)[145] We are perceptive human beings: one's perception is as a peculiarly mortal center for individual humanly contained knowing and understanding. This is true, however perhaps difficult to imagine, as regards pertinent individual becoming. To believe this, with absolute certainty, just look out the window; watch for the Sun, Moon and what is between. **Space is the absolute accommodation** and encompasses all the "in between" of everything. Infinite space comes right down to meet you, no matter who you may be, no matter where you may be and no matter when you may choose to observe this: furthermore, there exists a quantum of space within the cellular structure of your body.[146] Do you know how life has come to be as it is?[147] Every individual should consider the All and the everywhere, thus to aid in formulating a humanly humble understanding of reality. To lead one to a profound sense of humility in reference to what is [**should and could be**], the obligation of truthful education.

Truthful education must include respect for and the extension of the Western Tradition founded in the Crucifixion of Christ and the becoming of **Christ**ianity. Thus the Catholic Church, Bride of Christ must be included in the equation. Though of singular significance, we are as individuals, just an infinitesimally small part of an unbounded and unlimited reality. We do not know how and why all that is did come about, nevertheless we are gifted to enjoy, with others of our kind all that has been *provided.*

---

144 **Modernism** generally denies what has occurred as being old fashioned or redundant. This may be true in respect to mechanical invention however is not true in respect to Philosophy or Theology that maintains certain universals as being immutable. Given the present state of language, higher levels of communication are difficult for many of the world's leaders, *recently emerged from a hut*. It is impossible, for most. When such mind space as existed in a hut is privileged to consider what might be done with modern weaponry, one can understand that the death penalty for arms distribution to savages is understandable and easily justifiable. Western politicians, although those may mean well, with their simple-minded venal and arrogant leadership places all of humanity in a position of peril..

145 **Director, Bruce,** *Recovering the Generative Principles of Modern Science.* On the 375th Anniversary of Kepler's Passing. Fidelio, Journal of Poetry , Science and Statecraft. Spring Summer '06. Vol. XV. 1&2.

146 **Quantum** space exists within and around biologically formed structures providing space for activities, which occur within the body. Space, within the cells provide accommodation for what is required of life including formation of *electron clouds* necessary in the production of life's energy (Johanna Budwig MD).

Openings scattered over the cell walls provide space for passage of minute substances into and out from the cell interior. Passageways, meridians are *"laced"* within the body providing means for the transport of energy and life-force from place to place within the organism. Finally, at inception, hollow tubules form to lead the cellular development of the body, including the differentiation, which produces the organs and other physical requirements for the life of the species. The unseen, existing as space has more force than what is seen. Indeed, the Universal space is a *"plenum"* whereabouts all energies from all space are virtually extant in every quantum of space (Thomas Bearden, *"Aids, Biological Warfare"*).

147 **Oparin, A. I.,** *The Origin of Life.* Second Edition, 1953 . Dover Publications, Inc. N. Y. Originally published by the Mac Millan Co. 180 Varick Street, New York. © 1938. L. C. # 53-10161.

The key word is "provided". The Question remains. Who was the Provider? The answer is that it must have been [Is] an omnipotent, Progenitor, eternal, infinite Being, whom history and the accumulation of humanity has determined is a God Being. The Catholic Church, founded by Jesus the Christ, crucified on a stick, teaches that all men must be treated as being equal as they certainly are in the sight of the omnipotent one called God. God is the Father [**progenitor,** of all that is seen and unseen], Son [**Incarnate,** personified as man, **crucified** for our sins] and Holy Ghost [**Spirit** existing and extending in an infinite space]. **Mother** is as the earth, **a fertile place** wherein nurturing (gestation) and formation of a new person together with an immortal Soul is the miracle of life. To say *"Mother Earth"* has profound and transfinite meaning.

Man can somehow manipulate certain things, within little cubits of space. And, at the present time man is contemplating [conquering] the universe! *For a temporal Creature, this is an absurd notion.* The Idea of capturing Space, though quite stimulating, may be nevertheless preposterous, especially given a very limited individually perceived view of reality. When Politicians entertain an Idea such as this there is no ending to the various programs, which those contrive, secretly and in the open. They that are of the "Star Wars" *mentality* seek control of what is infinite, however, quite beyond human control. *The Star Wars mentality functions best to format entertainment for children and adults arrested in adolescence.* The explosions, noise and creatures which display a vilified humanness function to distract and amuse as they imprint fantasy, which in some cases is perhaps so powerful as to blur or override one's understanding of humanness as a reality. *To conquer or command all that is, has been the ultimate wish of the vain hypocrite and presumptuous leadership for centuries*. All those, dictators demagogues and assumed as leaders have harbored this insane notion, which is assumed in Nietzsche's contribution to civilization as the **Will to Power.**

No human being can or will conquer Space, which is composed of nothing. No man can or will sublimate an omnipotent power that cannot be known. ***Man is not God!*** Eternity, which is what Space is all about (together with all Time), can only be approached and understood from the position of an omnipotent existence, and can be known only to One, Triune God.[148] *There can be only one first cause and one Omnipotence; all else is as being subservient in order*. Reality is, without question, an ordered phenomenon. Although the politically inspired Democrat or Republican does not or cannot understand Reality, there is a *descending order* in the universe. Whatever is "Ordered" must present a descending or ascending configuration, *such is the nature of being ordered.* What is not ordered is chaotic,[149] which is generally the obvious factor in most

---

148 **Triune God, a** universal God must exist as such, which understanding is the foundation of Western Civilization. And, which understanding sublimates all other understandings of what and who and how is God? Omnipotence as defined, thereby understood requires that this is so.

149 **Tradition** is what places thinking in an ordered progression, especially so regarding history and human behavior, which can be defined as ordered in an ascending sequence leading to a God-head. The Barbarian or Savage is at the bottom. Jesus the Christ is at the top. Most men have imagined God, or what they imagine as a Deity, providing a manner of guidance. This has taken and continues in the direction of promoting what is good for the concerned individual(s) and his/their kind and was or could be antagonistic to all others. Presently certain elements within Islam pursues a dogmatic disregard for all others not Islamic. This is an adolescent notion in the minds of those (mostly youth) that do not have the intellectual and moral disposition, which would guarantee a higher level of human understanding. Wisdom is a product of old age! Unfortunately, misunderstanding of *"Religion"* creates problems that are, presently, insurmountable. The politician does not and cannot benefit from greater understanding being, as it were, politics is beholden to economics and the sins of

human endeavor, and in the Mind Space of billions of individuals, excepting certain scientific endeavor? Science has ordered domains of thought, which in turn presents a form of Tradition of one or another form of specialized thinking.

Physics, a subject dealing with objective reality, as being generally electricity, force and light, has perhaps advanced the most. The computer is the best example, a new wonder of the world, the consequence of micro management of electric impulses. Certainly Physics in its many applications is beyond most human understanding, especially when such understanding has been limited within the confines of Pubic Education. Certainly some of genius ability have, attended public schools however *their genius was not founded by their education.*

Chemistry also has discovered, in part, certain heretofore-unknown truths, and Chemists at the present time begin to understand Reality with more certainty. Notwithstanding, the use of such knowledge is not always for the benefit of all. Much and it is much, is motivated by the Politics of controversy and is used for the destruction of others. The present controversy has as its reason an age-old antagonism, stemming from the difference in Religious thinking between the most prominent Religions: Islam, Judaism, Buddhism and Christianity for example separate humanity and the subsequent misunderstanding is problematic. In the future China and India will have a more dominant role simply because of the politics of numbers. Just now everyone is concerned with the availability of resources to provide everyone with the American dream. Keep in mind it is a dream.

Every person is a creature within a complex totality, a totality, which is **unknown and beyond any human comprehension.** Attempts at comprehension which, postulates all time and the totality of mankind, is the subject matter of what we define as philosophy or religion, having epistemological as well as eschatological components. Comprehension of *what is unseen and unknown (?)* requires Faith however, man's limited understanding has confused this issue almost beyond imagination. It is very easy to fake certain attitudes as is well known to the hypocrite. However, eventually by our actions, we will as individuals incur whatever settlement is demanded, of the time we have spent in God's good Space. *The Universe is His!* This should be obvious without explanation however seems not to be so. This presents an existentially significant idea for contemplation.

We may begin with a simple question. **Where?** Interestingly it requires only four letters from our alphabet to inquire of a profound notion. The answer is brought forward in history, in that each is born to a location and moves in time and space as part of a minute factor within that extension, that same history, however becomes a particularly pertinent history, involving he/they/who are involved.

For any such question the answer is the same. **There!** Interestingly it requires only four letters from our alphabet to answer a most profound question. A simple answer, concerning one's location in space, qualifies whatever may be a particularly pertinent existence. The understanding of the

---

anger, murder, lust, vanity and greed. To be well meaning is not enough. What is required is a form of consensus, communion within a holy Tradition, convincingly expressed so to be well understood and therefore effective. All governments must endeavor to eliminate the effects of "Gigantism" and efforts that "conspire" to control humanity. The Civilization should endeavor toward the reforming of Nation-States wherein a true consensus leading to human happiness and fulfillment is a more attainable possibility. The Nation-State provides the best opportunity for individually inspired self-expression a worldwide conglomeration does not!

answer requires that one is cognoscente of objectivity in proximity to the person, event or object in question. The expression can also have an intellectual dimension as well, then requires as it infers a higher level of intelligent understanding, including the awareness of attendant circumstance and a consideration of both past and future time.

Where and how shall one build His house? The Children's story of the three little pigs exemplifies the moral, implicit in this peculiar endeavor. Structures are seated in a place, where they must remain and will become a part of the landscape viewed by all, that venture within sight of any such structure. As such, any architectural form or structure becomes part of an architectural tradition. In the recent past, we have built mobile homes, which require the support of an extensive technology. And there does remain the Nomad, seated on a horse that roams from place to place, as has been done for centuries across the great, plains, of the several continents. Also, still in evidence are those that build their dwellings from natural materials found in close proximity to where they are. These are used to build the traditional form of their house? However, the most complex *Civilizations have been built in place* as is apparent in the present great cities and those, which remain, from past antiquity.[150] At present the technology is awesome nevertheless there do remain serious problems of crowding and sprawl. In terms of architecture, the architect-artist attempts to leave, his mark, on the building, which he considers as [HIS] work. This, of course is an expression of **VANITY**, a sin. Buildings have taken on the meaning normally attached to painting or sculpture however, are much larger. Here scale is an important consideration. A building, which has the intention of functioning for a reason has become as an artifact, **viewed as Art, which it is not.** This is a question that is difficult to answer and goes directly to the meaning of words. Architects and their followers will have great indignation with this assumption.

A building is primarily functional, as having been built for a purpose. Sculpture or painting is primarily esthetic and deals with the ***Ideas*** men have. Buildings may accommodate sculpture or painting however cannot replace them, since those are not the same things. Modern buildings are the work of many people and as such the individual is lost in the complex. *Technology has widened the technical comprehension of any structure however has not changed the meaning.* This is an important point. The scale, of a building, dwarfs anything, which might be placed inside that same building however, should not overcome the essence of the artifacts placed therein. Calatrava amongst many do not understand this point. And a building should not attempt to appear as a bird or something, which it is not. The Milwaukee Art Center is guilty of this infraction as well. The architect did not know, truthfully, what he was doing! He worked from a point of vain comprehension which is sinful in some ways and according to the best of Western thinking is quite improper. There are other structures whereabouts the ideas and image of the architect are more important than the building. Plainly stated this is vanity a sin. There is much wasted space and materials to give effects which are a consequence of this Vanity. One cannot solve this problem easily since all are somewhat vain in their doings.

To use a building as a symbol for a place deprives the place of being what it is. To hire an architect from the other side of the world, from a completely different culture and disposition, to design a hallmark for a strange place, is not worthy of creditability, it is a faux symbol. The symbol, to be meaningful must originate in the place for which it is the symbol. This is a broad subject that will be addressed in a different volume.

---

150 **Mumford,** *The City in History*

If one wishes to gain most from occupancy, any house, city, nation-state or civilization must be cared for, maintained, though not forever, only as long as it may last. A structure will stand where it is placed however, cities, nations, cultures and civilizations require profound attention as they "evolve" and become different from time to time. They are essentially the products of *"mental restructuring"* in response to pertinent needs. Such restructuring is limited by the amount of money one has to spend on the project. Additionally most such structures have developed within a traditional framework. This is obvious in the many subtle similarities of intent and expectation. Referring to the two paragraphs directly above one can see how the elements of architecture and language combined with other limitations make this a very complex subject.

Some speak of being in control of their life, which they may be. However, given that which is significantly important, each of us will control very little, for a very short time in a very small space.[151] *Enter what we define as economics!* One's dwelling must be paid for, as all structures must be paid for, in time or money and it must be maintained in time or in money.

Money as currency is related to both time and place in nearly unimaginable ways. Currency has its own, thereby energized domain, which interlocks with the expectations of who has possession of it. This author has considered the subject of Money, in a different volume. Significantly, money travels in space and time, in a lateral or an extended time/space pattern. The velocity of money varies from place to place and is an indication of the nature of commerce. The velocity of money forms as a vortex absorbing what is as it provides for a future store of value. It functions much as a funnel directing liquid through a determinedly advantageous space. Electronic transfers, for the rapid dispersal of *notional values* and of *real wealth* have added new possibilities, for good and for evil. International Bankers envision a one-world currency, which they will control. **Total control, Totalitarianism**, they envision as being possible, enforced and sustained by the control of money (currency)[152] **and the force of weaponry.** Socialists seek sameness in populations, fearing the significance of the singular mind of Genius. Socialists are brothers to those that are Totalitarian. Socialism is a more gentle form of Communism: ipso facto, both are the same.

Any form of Political Control aims at sublimating a uniformly inspired population to the **Will to Power** of an elite ruling group, which controls commerce and the minds of men. Actually to some considerable degree and in many ways this is a fete already accomplished: the existence of this fact would require a volume of its own. The minds of men can be controlled by means of brainwashing, which requires threat of intimidation and death. More recently behavioral modification, *a form of patterning human thought processes,* has been the euphemism for mind

---

151 **Each and every encounter** has an important set of consequences attendant thereto, with absolutely unpredictable effects. The migration of peoples makes this even more interesting as well as problematic than when individuals were more certain to remain close to their place of birth

152 **Currency,** the term, implies the present value of money. Ideally money retains the same value as when it was acquired. That is to say, it remains constant in regard to the expectations of who did acquire the currency by some lawful means. *This is primarily a question of morality as well as economics.* As a matter of fact, *economics should be the servant of both money and morality as it is rather a matter of accounting for what exists and for what moves from one person to another.* We have given Economics, per se, a too important role in the development of Western Civilization, especially where about conflict is concerned. And we have made economic gain the Holy Grail of endeavor. This is a monumental mistake that, ultimately, will kill the Culture (it has done much-harm at this writing) ultimately it will kill the Civilization.

control and is practiced, more or less, in the public schools.[153] This is often quite subtle and comes to the classroom as a *"mandate"* from the state or federal government. The teachers do not quite understand what they are doing however they imagine they are experts: this assuages their ego and gives them a misunderstood power.

Disguised in language behavioral modification attempts to condition the child or young adult to accept certain tenants regarding what is and is not acceptable behavior. Changes are brought about gradually so as not to alarm those that might object to the destruction of our Holy Tradition. The very word *"Holy"* or any word connected with what may be holy is removed from public and much private discourse. Pressure groups like the ACLU use this Technique quite successfully in some instance. Especially Catholic Symbolism, pictures of the Holy Family, the meaning of Christmas and Easter, all are deliberately confused in the minds of youth. We have ***Christmas trees and the Easter Bunny*** as well as many various saccharine symbols that distract from the meaning of such events. Halloween with goblins and witches is becoming more prominent than in the past and relates to the punk Rockers, Rappers and other anti-traditional youth groups. Some become millionaires because of the ignorance and me too attitude of our youth. Public Institutions of Education work to deny the Catholic Christian God as do the commercial elephants pandering for profit. Some Federal Judges with contempt for what is holy Tradition are doing whatever they can to destroy all vestiges of Catholic Christianity. Coincidentally witches and goblins, warlocks and Harry Potter are best sellers. Those are encouraged for the profits, which those earn for the producers. I realize that this paragraph includes generalities that are not pertinent in every instance however in essence this is true.

Space, as displaced, is *given to the definition and qualification of all tangible form.* One should be aware that the human body is that substance or that defined physiological space, the place (so to speak), within which we as individuals do (in fact) exist. This must be so otherwise we could not be at all. "To be or not to be **[is]** the question." How then, shall one become? Given an individually functioning mind, all thoughts that we will ever have are ethereal and intangible, which accompany the phenomenology of a particularly human living presence. It is axiomatic and logical there can only be one of any individual being. The *"cloning of cells confuses"* this issue considerably, in the minds of those that will profit from or be the objects of such endeavor. This is what is important: each person is an individually unique, biological/physiological being, the life of whom is given, as a gift from an omnipotent force, God, the Father [progenitor], Creator of all that is seen and unseen. Believe this and you will be well on your way to happiness. Thus we might consider that an omnipotent force is as the motivation for the propagation of the human race. Nevertheless, there are many that do not believe this. Understandably what is corporeal involving the biology and physiology have an understood continuity, whereas what is spiritual and of the Soul does not appear so obvious. One cannot change from one body to another however, one's thinking can be patterned in different ways, and actions can be or will be modified accordingly.

Who but a God [?] may have created all of what is, including each and every human being? Gestation is a biological process, whereas inception is mysterious phenomenal and existential in implication. Parts and processes may be observed, nevertheless absolute understanding is evasive. The parents are only a means and are entrusted with a great responsibility of nurturing the body and soul of their peculiar ***extension into the future.*** Any form of future extension is determined by the past. *Therefore we are well advised who would form and maintain a clear and decently*

---

153 **Sutton, Antony,** *How the Order Controls Education.* Research Publications, Inc., P. O. Box 39850,

determined Biological and Physiological Tradition. Most will not understand the meaning of this assertion nevertheless it is of ultimate significance, especially now that ignorance is "tinkering" with the reproductive process. Tradition generally, is what feeds the Intellect and makes advances in thought possible. We share with each other, as we occupy a very minute part of God's Universe however each individual person is quite necessary, *one or another way*, to complete a profound, magnificent universally functioning totality. Furthermore, we should never forget, all human events happen in God's good space.

Every human being has an inherent or inalienable right and responsibility
In the peculiar portion of space, which he occupies (displaces)
To become the best he can to benefit the human race.

One can imagine a forever, based on a mature understanding of the continuity of the species. Biological continuity does provide a concrete and truthful example of extension in time/space. Evolution of the species is an issue, which we do not intend to introduce at this moment. It is possible to imagine space/time as being infinite [∞]. Nevertheless, whatever is the nature of All Space is not open to peculiarly limited Human understanding. We believe, those who are locked within a segment or portion of Space must be content to admit there does exist an unknown absolute beyond the present moment. This understanding drives man to discover many new things however *no single human person can possibly have an absolutely complete grasp of anything*. Nevertheless, as each human person is locked within a space/time segment or domain, there can be physical and intellectual reciprocity, between proximate individuals at any moment. The most intimate of such occurrence is mating, thus to create a new human person, having an individual Soul, destined for a possibly eternal existence. It is important that this should be better understood and that all men and women learn to meet their responsibilities and to assist in the nurturing of their children. *Children are begotten because of a man's decently romantic, vain or impetuous nature.* In each instance, the father, as well as the mother must bear the responsibility for their own behavior. Children are the body and soul become because of the most intimate form of cooperation. The children of such union deserve to have a father and a mother and should not be bused between parents or from place to place because of a parent's inability to live as responsibly committed adults. Our celebrities have misunderstood this: imagining that money will make a difference, it won't!

Where, is an important consideration just as important is when? Where one is conceived has to do with who are the Parents, especially one's mother. Mother is primary, the first place for all of her children to be. Like all living creatures only a few from what is a potentiality will ever be born into space.[154] For humanity, the mother's body is a very special place, wherein the chromosomes combine to determine just how the offspring shall become.[155] Recent understanding

---

154 **Nature is prolific** in regard to the extension of a species always providing most generously for the becoming of the young. Many plants have tens of thousands of seeds. Roots and stems can be propagated as well. Fish and various insects propagate in thousands however, most serve as food in a never-ending struggle for existence. What we imagine as this struggle is largely misunderstood and is a very natural process. Man as well as animals, utilizes the substance of both plant and animal for his own survival.

155 It is most unfortunate that a woman's body has become the object of so much lustful attention. Pornographers have caused irreparable harm to millions of youthful woman, which because of their beauty are routinely violated by ignorant moronic and bestial attention.

has determined that the mother is primarily responsible for the genetic structures of here children, only accepting those chromosomes that are, for whatever reason, superior to her own. Mother's body has also, in the recent past, become a very dangerous place, especially so for the first born that opens the womb. There are spiritual as well as historic connotations hereabouts, which are beyond our intention. Therefore, it is quite likely that many, having been conceived, will not be born at all. Presently, it is estimated that, in the three decades prior to now, there have been hundreds of millions of known abortions worldwide, many millions uncounted as well.[156]

Abortion may seem rather ordinary, acceptable, a matter of [mature] adult choice. This is no incidental matter. Ill-educated individuals speak of a woman's reproductive rights suggesting what is sinful has more *"rights"* than what is natural, spiritual and decent. Remember ***everyone has the right not to fornicate indiscriminately*** merely for sensual gratification or as a reward for an illicit inclination. Where someone is, individual placement in space (on this planet) determines what one can and will do. Mating is part of what humans do. Individually men and women should determine beforehand that they will only participate in what is lawful, decent and fair to all whom they encounter including the *"one whom they choose"* as a mate.[157] Humanity has advanced to the position of understanding the value of perseverance in an adult conjugal relationship. It is unfortunate that some are determined to pull man back to being [again] as a lustful barbarian or a cruel and lustful Savage. As mentioned elsewhere, ***the preponderance of personal and social problems are the result of fornication.*** It is possible, indeed necessary, to structure one's thoughts so as to avoid doing what is known to be destructive to the individual and to the community. Education is supposed to inform correctly as well as to point the way to goodness decency and contentment. Job training has assumed a too important role in the system. Any individual of whatever intelligence and ability can find a place to work and to earn a living.[158] What is needed is a generally applied sense of fairness and the will to cooperate with others. Men that do simple tasks should be paid sufficiently to live respectably and less emphasis should be placed upon the attainment of economic advantage. If this occurs there would be no need for abortion.

---

156 ***Human Life International***, January 2000.

157 This calls to question the position of the homosexual or lesbian that wishes to legitimize their behavior as being married to another homosexual or lesbian. This is an absurd notion: however the notion has the support of the government and the Anti-Christ. With such support it is imagined to be legitimate. For many it represents a form of sinful behavior imagined legitimate because of the force and scale of government. Additionally such groups form as political entities that can be controlled when one understands their behavior and their objectives that seem important.

158 Interestingly the jobs that are readily available are not the ones that most would wish to consider. Imagining one's self as being educated encourages a form of vanity, which causes one to disallow what they are properly suited for? Many dummies now have college degrees, which are worthless, in that they are not maturely informed and are not able to think clearly and intelligently in problem solving. Their own lives are corrupted by sin and they are not willing to cooperate with a truthful and loving mate. So how smart are they? Almost fifty-years of teaching in the university have allowed me to observe that most of the best students came from other places than the United States. Foreign students are becoming the professionals in a country dedicated to nonsense because our government does not send them home after graduation. If they have a child in this country the child is automatically accepted as belonging. This is the consequence of a Law, which is no longer necessary. We have enough people and should solve existing problems rather than making new ones.

Immigration *is the consequence of people wanting to move to a different, presumably better, place.* When like individuals group and sustain a community as has happened, in the past, such groups maintain familial characteristics and they strive toward the becoming of a Nation. Nations are comprised of groups and individuals having common attributes and shared aspirations.[159] In proximity individuals learn from each other, language is an obvious means together with one's observations of what exists.

Societies and Cultures develop as a consequence of their respective and sustained achievements, which are obviated in their Tradition, as artifact habit and custom. Who went where? What did they do? Both are very important questions. As such Tradition is a valuable containment from which the present and the future are the beneficiaries. Public education encourages the young to be independent, creative and to abandon Tradition. Thus the hypocrite or the ignorant Practitioner-become-Educator encourages youth to abandon the source of both knowledge and method of continuing the Tradition which is their birthright.

Having abandoned their Tradition, youth will drift and can be captured by one or another Philosophical Imperatives. The one most generally pushed by the establishment is socialistic, collectivist, Marxist and is anti-Christian, tentative and politically imposing against, which because there has been little truthful knowledge conveyed within the educational system (except perhaps in the hard sciences) youth has little or no defense.

Creativity, it must be stressed can be found at all levels of intelligence, from the fool to the genius. Our system, being presumed as Democratic has determined, that the Creativity of a clown or a fool, those being the more mundane forms of creativity are best for mass distribution. Highbrow stuff is more limited in reference to economic gain and must [often] rely on subsidies or donations. The finer forms of pleasure and Entertainment are not encouraged in the schools, nor is a significant understanding of the meaning of great literature given much attention.[160]

Limitations imposed by placement in space determine that most potential is never realized. It is impossible that all potentialities could be realized! Because this is so, we understand that all potential is not required, only some. Because of this, various peoples have developed differently. It is incumbent upon the community that the best forms of thought and methods of accomplishment should be encouraged. *No community can afford to pander to ignorance!* What we imagine as primitive is often a manner of ignorance or an arrested development. A categorical imperative is at work here. Fish survive as fish in the ocean or in water, because they are fish. The fish is of a nature that provides for this. Man will survive, because he is man, made in the image of God, however, given free will and aptitudes given to no other creature, man is also burdened with responsibilities. Nevertheless, all humanity could be, probably will be consumed in one gigantic earthly- Devastation. It is believed by millions that Man, if he is to become one in being with the Father, could/does have an opportunity to move toward an open-ended infinity, an endless

---

159 **The United States** is attempting to overrule this truth. In time we will know if this was a good idea. Certainly individual will integrate however t his is a personal issue and, we believe, should not be pushed by the governments.

160 ***Athletics,*** while of modest importance is given the most attention and the most funding. In a university the football coach may be paid two or three million a year, whereas the other *"scholars"* do not earn enough to pay the rent.

space.[161] Nevertheless, that some could be given to share in God's infinity does not infer that every man will be as God. *Man is the Creature God is the Creator.*

Regarding political, psychological and social issues, space is a primary determinant. Proximity to a friend or foe has always been an important factor in determining what men do. Immigration involves moving from place to place, thus to better one's existence, as being free from danger. This is simply the reaction to pleasure or pain. When populations move to a new place there is thus a degree of infiltration, with subsequent sociological, psychological and perhaps political consequence. ***Ideas move with people.*** Such movement of ***thought forms*** carries positive as well as negative connotation. *Psychological infiltration involves the movement of an Idea from one mind-space to another.* When ideas enter the human mind they coalesce with existing thought-content and have unpredictable consequence. Individuals, with just and truthful motives do attempt to help in the assimilation of the stranger, unselfishly so. This can serve either Good or Evil purpose. Nevertheless, there are many that would take advantage of the confusion, which is caused when ideas are in conflict and new ideas are certain to impact an existing understanding. Much of present politics is centered on this and related issues.

Tradition is the determinedly mindful-progress of a people and does provide a particularly formed [time-space] insight into what should and does happen. It is a form of social, psychological and ideational insurance, which guarantees the direction of learning and knowing.[162] A primitive Tradition, may have existed as a singular form however, presently societies are much more complex. The hypocrite and the opportunist are able to profit, one way, or another, from the movement of populations, and will encourage abandonment of Tradition in favor of evil ways, *often imagined as progressive or modern,* so to accomplish some obscure objective, hidden within the hyperbole. To some degree, we recognize this as Modernism.

Modernism is a disease of the Soul and of the community. Modernism compromises proven Traditions as it encroaches upon important intellectual, psychological and sociological aspects of one's existence as well as that of a community of men. Religion becomes as a political forum with a veranda about which the minstrels stroll as they mesmerize the devout, with guitar music and dancing girls, rather Pagan, to be sure. We'll have no Gregorian Chanting, thank you. The curiosity of youth draws them toward what is noisy and exciting, whereabouts they intimidate each other to become part of the festivities. Chastity and continuance are old-fashioned for those that seek the most excitement from life and who assume that they, in their ignorance will improve upon what has taken two thousand years to develop. Youth is restless and seeks to participate in a more Democratic approach to Holiness imagining they will improve upon the wisdom of those that have lived a hundred lifetimes, during the past centuries. Many Holy Men have been martyred. *For most youth mind-space is rather small, it is right here, right now.*

State controlled, elementary and secondary compulsory education ***works hand and hand with primitive and atavistic religious concepts*** and is determined to destroy the foundations of the Western Civilization, especially targeted is any inference to Holy Roman Catholic Tradition, which is the foundation of Western Culture and Civilization.[163] State controlled education is considered

---

161 **Cathey, Bruce**, *The Bridge to Infinity*

162 ***The direction of learning and knowing*** can be controlled by education, coercion or force. Generally the strongest elements within the society/culture will control both learning and knowing.

163 ***Blumfield, Samuel,*** *Is Public Education Necessary?*

necessary where we have the march toward a socialist dictatorship, a Marxist-inspired one-world order. Certainly the defense against such mindlessness has been weakened, with the *"politically contrived"* separation of Church and State. It is imagined, quite incorrectly that, *there is **some manner of empty space** between what is secular and what is holy*, beside which we must *"honor all methods of worship"* except the most important one. Only a politician, a weak minded fool one seeking a new term, which will be extended to a lifetime, at the public trough (example, Ted Kennedy) could imagine a void within the mind of men that separates the intellectual framework of Church from that of the State.[164] It is fair to mention that many teachers and instructors do not prefer public education for employment however, the pay is better, and there are many guarantees that private schools cannot offer. Public Education is an insidious monopoly, which few are able or choose to stand against. All Bureaucracies are self-serving and self-proliferating.

Individuals and groups comprise various nations and, for various reasons, do not necessarily agree with a stranger. When the share the same *"living space"* serious conflicts may be engendered between foreign or alien beings. This issue relates to autonomy and is made complex by political issues involving race, manners, habits and personality traits. Keep in mind _personalities emerge from a unique mind-space._ The determinants are very complex, involving the consequence of inter-relationships, which have become, *in unknown ways, integrated in the mind,* inextricably so.

Social Conflict obviates the need for astute abilities of statesmanship which few men now, or ever, might possess. Even when one antagonist has such abilities, there is no guarantee that he will ever meet another one of his kind at an appropriate moment. Statesmanship demands the kind of learning and knowing, which few men possess and as such they are not generally Politicians. Politicians imagine superior force must be applied. War leads to death and enslavement. Millions have suffered, and died unnecessarily because of a sense of greed, driven by misunderstanding, associated with a place to be, a Space on this earth.

Most do not and cannot consider all ramifications in Eventuality, pertinent to each and every circumstance. This is not done, because it is virtually impossible to do so, or we may not choose to do so. Very often, the most important and comprehensively truthful information and understandings, having been colored by means of deception, propaganda and intrigue, are not known by many, the honorable amongst us, who are involved in the most important tasks and the subsequently determined consequence. Too often the information and the level of understanding required, in an acute circumstance is beyond certain limitations and/or comprehension of the parties involved. This is particular to the "emerging African Nations" that have leadership just a short way from the jungle. Additionally, the abilities necessary in the formulation of a truthful response may prove ineffective when an effective process is deliberately subverted, by the introduction of a carefully contrived and seemingly appealing intervention. Complex circumstance almost certainly will create some manner of failure, one time or another, which will be exploited by cleverness (*Our Presidents have been victims of such subterfuge*). Often, reality is beholden to a manner of deceit, because of some secret vested interest hoping to profit from

---

164 ***The workings of any human mind*** exist as an individually determined complex-singularity. Because we have chosen to offer education in segments or disciplines as a matter of convenience, it does not follow that the mind is so separated. Certainly bits of mind content can be called upon so to clarify thought however, even then there are time-space influences bearing upon individual thoughts, which have there origin in a peculiarly formed psychological and spiritually determined matrix, which is difficult to understand. Without the guidance of a confirmed Tradition, what is close in time will form as being of greater significance, which may or may not be true.

what may happen when circumstance is cleverly controlled. Presently, entire nations have become entrapped and ours will be proven to be no exception.[165] Their collective behavior might be likened to the behavior of a dope addict;[166] the nature of the entrapment revolving around a medium of exchange, the value of which is deemed as money or credit.[167] This is significant, appropriately so, since in a modern Civilization, money is required to move objects from one place to another. *Space is an important part of any economic transaction,* one way or another.[168]

Because we do not find that we are always in the right place (at the right time) we may lose some advantage; the advantage we would have, if we could alter reality, or if reality was different from what it really is. Then, to proceed with lamentation and self-denial will be of little use however, what are demanded are understanding, penitence and a contrite and willfully good heart. What is demanded, in a word, is Virtue. *Simply stated, one must know his place of being and the potentials offered there from.* Everyone can only begin from where they are; where they may go is a matter of personal volition, combined with will and opportunity; anyone may gain or lose by their own activities. One may gain Human Dignity and aspire to reach the stars, from wherever one may be. This is God's intention; that each should choose right (that is correctly); thereby the best things will happen. Much of what happens in this world, which is unfortunate or disastrous, and not completely understood, is a consequence of the sins of our fathers. **War** provides a category of Sin that very likely has had a negatively affect on millions. **Fornication** is another root cause of unfortunate events. Decent and proper behavior, in respect to all others is assumed in the meaning of fairness and provides the most secure basis for self-esteem. Such behavior will propagate as good luck for the future beings affected thereby.

Nothing in this world is guaranteed, however, all Socialists pretend that, which is considered by those same socialists to be important should be guaranteed. After, which mundane proclamation, all Socialists begin to steal from their brothers so as to have something to pretend to give away; then to lie, so as to have something to say. The most sophisticated form of this, **what might be reasonable called a plague**, is found in the incidence of Inflation and various other forms of theft, all for the purported good of the man being robbed. That is how it should be; so we are told!

To deny the meaning of Reality is ultimately destructive and should be called by its proper name, **Ignorance**. The response is often **Indignation** or **Ingratitude**.

1. *Indignation causes one to be intransigent, unwilling to change one's mind, to accept that one is wrong. For one to admit to wrongdoing requires humility, which may be lacking.*

---

165 **Wilton, Robert,** *The Last of the Romanovs, How Tsar Nicholas II and Russia's Imperial Family were Murdered.* Copyright © 1993, the Institute for Historical Review. First British Edition, pub. 1920 in London by T. Butterworth. First U. S. Edition published 1920, in New York by George H. Dorn. French Edition, pub. Paris 1921. Russian language edition, pub. Berlin 1923. ISBN # 0-939484-1.

166 **Inflation,** just now, we recognize as the "Opiate of the masses." The nation was in a state of euphoria, even as our debts total in the trillions of dollars, near worthless dollars to be sure.

167 **Wickliffe, Vennard B. Sr.** *The Federal Reserve Hoax, The Age of Deception.* Meador Publishing Co., 324 Newbury Street, Boston 15, MA. Seventh Ed. Pp. 14-70.

168 **Spengler, Oswald**, *The Decline of the West, Vol. II. Perspectives of World History.* Authorized Translation with notes by Charles Francis Atkinson. Alfred A. Knopf, Publisher, NY.

2. *Ingratitude is that disposition, concerning vanity, which prevents one from admitting to truthful understanding, even though such is obvious.*

3. *Ignorance is that state of being in the equation of existence which emanates from Slothfulness, the unwillingness to truthfully seek, and is the cause of many of the maladies, which we can name! The good reader can form his own list.*

The spaces in the cities, for example, are deteriorating because those who live in them are too poor, lazy or too corrupt to make them better, without some manner of bribe. And such attitudes aid and abet the speculation that follows as urban renewal and restructuring, so as to drive populations away from well-seasoned and compatible neighborhoods.[169] Our government, though well meaning, or seemingly so, offers little help since our government, at various levels, works for the advantage of the moneyed interests and the speculator. Government pays little attention to what evils are really being perpetrated. When it does it is certain to promote the concept of One World Government and the **Socialist Paradise, imagined by every fool in the last three hundred years.** Economic gain is the primary consideration and motivation for those who pretend to make things better. Too often forgotten are the lives, aspirations and needs of those, that will be affected. Present methods are justified almost totally on profit motives, at a time when government is squandering and wasting unimaginable billions on needless and mindless warfare. *A collision of Cultures need not be inevitable* and will only occur as is planned and orchestrated by those that hope this will come about, for one reason or another. Nevertheless, the United States a nation pretending to help millions of antagonistic aliens, imagined as enemies, should be able to offer substantially better alternatives for our own people. We continue to suffer from more of a bad thing be it noise, pollution crowding or too high taxation Perhaps it is time to think small, inexpensive and fair.

> *Return to the Town Square, open space within the city, sunshine clean air*
> *Curtail mindless movement, economic gain from speculation*
> *Create a more soulful and peaceful existence.*
> Curtail the spectacle of athletics.

We should punish elected officials who spend our money, millions, billions, now trillions, completely ignoring the needs and wishes of those who elected them? May we punish appointed officials, who we may never know, for working in the best interests of organized crime and the destruction of our nation? Traitors must be called by their proper name. Then, they should be tried and given a proper sentence, in propotrtion to their indiscretion. To be a Traitor to one's own nation and family should be considered as a capital crime and, as in the past, the penalty should be a death sentence, which should be carried out in ninety days. Jim McVey was treated this way. Actually he may have been railroaded so as to cover up for others involved in the Oklahoma City bombing. In truth, factually, how many explosions were there?

There is a manner of moral responsibility, each to every other, to provide an atmosphere, within which goodness will flourish, whereabouts petty crime syndicalism and hopelessness are discouraged, by the positive attitude and behavior of proximate beings. Slovenly behavior and listlessness are learned behaviors (Skinner), as are prudence and thrift, albeit, some people never learn. Many are inclined, because of slovenly and misconceived behavior, to foul their own nest, to be indifferent to the garbage and rubbish that is strewn, in the space of their front yard and

---

169 **Jones, Michael, Ph. D**. *Fidelity Magazine* (Issue, #, date)

in their mind's space as well. *Some lounge in the hallways of the tenement, which they have fouled with ugly marks and their slovenly and arrogantly aggressive behavior.* We do not doubt that there are many good people living in what are slums however, wretchedness, crime and the filth that accumulates in the "great" cities of our nation has an overcoming influence. We are all creatures of God, [The] Infinite Being, who has provided each living person with Free Will. Free Will is the means to individual salvation. However, each individual must earn, by word and deed, that final resting place, in space, whereat some may ultimately become, One in Being with The Father, and at which place they will spend Eternity; a very long time, indeed! Eternity is all time beyond now! Seek Goodness and you will find that you will have come to the best possible place of all places.

What does it mean to be in a state of Grace, to be free from the stain of Sin. What exactly is meant when one is forgiven of their sins? Life, in this world, requires that each acts with respect for The One Who has shown The Way; that is, The Son of God, Whom we call Jesus. To ignore this, as the most important part of living, is to ignore the best advice which, has been given to mankind. It is very easy to corrupt those with whom one might associate (Syllabus of Errors)[170] therefore we are admonished to love our brother, as we might (indeed) love ourselves. Also, we must avoid all occasion for sin, for ourselves and for others. It is absolutely imperative, that sensual love becomes only as spousal love, one man for one woman, one woman for one man, as husband and wife. *Marriage is of Sacramental significance and must be considered as Eternal, with a complete and lasting commitment.* One who refutes this assertion, rooted in the obviousness of the biological formation of the Human Race, will suffer certain and grave consequence. One cannot defy the propensities of human nature and remain in the most honest and truthfully human state of being. Humanness demands goodness thus to provide for the best possible unfolding of existence for the self and for those with whom one might be placed in proximity, most assuredly family members and close associates.

Seemingly intelligent men point to the past and to the habit and custom of a savage or some Asiatic Prince or Mogul and attempt to excuse their own illicit behavior because this was the way of the savage, the barbarian and the Tyrant, which is simply stupid. We do know better. We are informed by a holy Tradition and by the Golden Rule. *Abandonment of one's mate and children is an inexcusable affront, which leads to indignation, self-pity destruction of the libido, insecurity, and a sensing of an ominous future.* Thus the mind space within the self is scrambled, as what was must convert to what is.

That overpaid celebrities set such a poor example in displaying their lustful ignorance is truly a travesty and is destructive on the world's communities. The cute sluts and lustful adolescent-appearing male figures are not experiencing love. What they experience is loss of self-control, loss of dignity and loss of their soul as they corrupt innocence. **A big belly exhibited at her wedding is no sign of a virgin bride.** Having succumbed to a variety of *"[sticks], and various forms of perversion"* the ladies [?] are used up before the Honeymoon. No expectation here, **just brag about how much you spent for the farce that is imagined as a sacred wedding?**

The personality is that human factor, a functioning of the self, which is in evidence moment by moment. Conscious acts are largely a matter of personality meaning they are personal in nature and unlike any other. Often times, personalities are in conflict, which is a matter of

---

170 **Pius X, Pope** *The Encyclical Quanta Cura and the Syllabus of Errors.* Issued in 1864. Reprinted by the Remnant, 2539 Morrison Avenue, St. Paul, MN 55117.

compatibility or *"the communion of souls."* Whether or not one is in communion with others has a strong influence on discreet human behavior. Every human being functions by means of neurological mechanisms with all that this entails, including the development and functioning of the personality. Personalities become of circumstance playing upon existing propensies and potentialities, which are idiosyncratic. A given experiential manifold can yield an unimaginable and/or unforeseen consequence. An ever- widening range of possibilities, exist among what is possible, unfolding with the developing and maturing mind.[171]

Given a huge number of brain cells, which each individual possesses, some are confident that humanity will stay ahead of the game. This is not a certainty: who could know in advance, what might become of the human race. Because this is so, we must pay more careful attention to those elements and manners of input, which are given to masses of individuals, so as not to encourage latent atavistic tendencies. If present world news has any value, it suggests that a return to more primitive habit and manners, in the most civilized populations, so called, seems to be on the increase.[172] Within certain groups, mostly young adults, comprised of marginally literate and incorrectly informed individuals, we find questionable precedent. There are millions roaming the streets of the densely populated cities on the verge of submission to an incitement to rage. The mob can be dangerous and provides the *"cannon fodder"* so to accomplish what the political Conspirators have planned for the people. Consider also those who are neurotic, deemed as social outcasts, however are presumably respectable individuals. There are many men and women in important places who, because of greed and vanity, both of which function through the personality are unable and/or unwilling to allow others to benefit from what exists. The men responsible for the French Revolution, later the thinking of Karl Marx, somewhat responsible for the subsequent atrocities of two world wars have corrupted the physical space of the earth as well as the mind space of humanity. Where business as usual is the method of the day, a serious study of history seems beyond those that are paid for leading humanity.

Philanthropy, which sounds like a pretty good word, is often largely self-serving, for tax, purposes and to enhance the image of the giver, especially when the giver is a large corporation or a wealthy celebrity. Thus, Philanthropy is group-serving, for a variety of reasons. Some wealthy- individuals may be more truthfully involved, in giving for honorable and praiseworthy involvement. Tax laws are often side stepped to protect large accumulations of wealth, which otherwise might be open to confiscation because of looting by the tax collector. Keep in mind the tax "collector" is a looter. Interestingly corporate theft is also given some protection, when the sums involved are significant (Milikin/Keating). Certainly, there are many generous people, however, even they can and do make mistakes, which effectively may damage or destroy the meaning of what they attempt to do. War is brutal and kills millions, nevertheless those that profit from conflict, are some of the

---

171 **Thinking** has become more problematical and is more complex in nature, because of the overload of extraneous information provided by mass-media communication, often designed to modify meaning and to create illusions. This is a Phenomenon, which has become apparent in the most recent past century. The trend will accelerate dependent upon new forms of mass communication. Often the information is presented simply as noise, with no significant comprehension of the quality or meaning of what is being conveyed.

172 **Body mutilation,** tattooing, piercing, pornography, addiction to substances and various forms of maiming the self all suggest that your son, your daughter your wife or husband may be unduly influenced.

generous givers.[173] The problem with charity for those who are reasonably able is that it robs them of the opportunity of doing for themselves that, which will enhance self-esteem as they develop the skills necessary for survival.

Presently the collective conscience, weakened by too much misdirected attention, given to the subject of psychology has, to a considerable extent, been corrupted. The corruption of mass mind presents a very complex and difficult issue. This is an assertion, which can and will draw some indignation from many quarters, since there are so many widely varying opinions, however, it must be considered. Psychological tinkering, in various instances has done great harm to a great number of individuals (Carl Rogers, William Coulsen).[174] To repent, after the fact, will not repair the damage done to a fragile mind, or return what, significantly, has been destroyed. Psychology has been at the forefront of a very debilitating Modernist movement having its emphasis on the perverted sexual encounter.[175] Interestingly, philanthropy is often directed toward those that have been victims of war and/or psychological distress.

Fine Art, beginning with ***Picasso,*** has been used as an implement to further the aims of perversion and ugliness and to denigrate women, reducing them to become the eager and submissive object of carnal pleasure. The final works done by a lustful little ***Twerp*** are some of the most disgusting scribbles that have ever found rest on a sheet of paper. The man, Picasso, was a disgusting lunatic that was praised because of the millions made by those that promoted his brand of decadence. The space in the world's Museums are full of stultified nonsense displayed as art, for the benefit of ignorant participation, which views with pleasure the destruction of Christianity and all forms of traditional Beauty. Donors, with more money than they can spend, take part in the philanthropy as they donate or loan to museums works of art, some of which appear to be the work of lunatics, *imagined as men of genius.* Much of which is considered as art, which occupies vast public spaces could be better placed on a few sheets of paper with a short statement. However, those imagining themselves as artists have neither the ability to draw or to write that would be necessary to present ideas as ideas without the need for tons of silly stuff. Model making and the tableau, are of some interest but might best be kept at a small scale, It is not necessary to overcome an audience with pretense. Theatrics does not enhance the esthetic quality of any work rather it distracts and often appears simply silly. Shakespeare had it in one sentence *"Much to do about nothing."*

Considering fine art of the Twentieth century, a group *"imagined as respected, world-renowned"* art Critics (five hundred in all) did come together to choose a urinal, by Du Champs *"imagined"* as the century's most profound artistic expression. One wonders how much artistic talent might have existed, amongst such an erudite group. Ulyssus by James Joyce was deemed the best of what was written Ta, Ta. Certainly, this was the *"presumably astute"* opinion of a group within which, many would heap criticism on the works of past genius as being outdated or decadent. We do not necessarily concede, to the opinions of seemingly educated elites, become foolish, stupid or simply silly in their endeavor. They were stupid in their decision however; such stupidly conceived

---

173 **Quigley, Carroll,** Ph.D. *Tragedy and Hope.* Chapter V.

174 **Jones, E. Michael Ph. D.,** *Libido Dominandi, Sexual Liberation and Political Control.* St. Augustine's Press, South Bend, Indiana. © 2000 E. Michael Jones. ISBN # 1-890318-37-x **Jones, Michael,** **Ph. D.** *Fidelity Magazine* (Issue, #, date)

175 **Reisman, Judith, PhD.** *Kinsey, Crimes and Cosequences.* Third Edition. The Institute for Medical Education, P. O. Box 15284, Sacramento, CA 95851-0284. ©1998-2000-2003. ISBN # 0-9666624-1-5

corruption of the intellect and of the arts does receive international attention. Such mind-space is full of bubbles and feathers and of course, some dung.

Keep in mind, like every other product, Fine Art has become a business. The market has been flooded with a commodity, deemed as being Art, and is driven by pricing, which has little or nothing to do with what Art should be. Much of what is imagined as painting and sculpture is the work of technicians hired to paint or build what is required. *Wrapping a building or installing a fence is not Art and does not emanate from the soul of civilization or of man.* Rather such is the work of a technician, a charlatan or simply a faker. There are many spoofs as well that are viewed as Art. Anything can be called Art (just a word) however this is confusing to youngsters that imagine they are involved in what is an important form of expression. The Arts are important in the destruction of both mind and soul of the Civilization, wherein the work of an individual man is completely eclipsed, by what is made by a machine or a technician with expensive implementation. Great Public Spaces, smaller private spaces as well, are devoted to the efforts of those with little or no talent for the work of the hand and the mind. Only what is advertised sells and only what sells is advertised. This is a serious turkey in the egg situation. Apologists for the **New Academy** are legion and a dumb and disinterested population is easy to convince. The work of superior ability, even genius, is not patronized **unless it is profitable for the Businessman.**

Modernist thinking, especially regarding young adults has destroyed their *"Mind-space"* much of their innocence, their honor, their consciousness and their sense of shame, by means of publicizing, for profit, that which should remain as intimate, as private, between a Physician and a Patient, or a husband and wife. This is not always the case; however some individuals, including some well-meaning practitioners, attempt to gain wealth and notoriety by accepting, as entertainment, various maladies, deformities and deviate behaviors. This, in turn, inflicts some change in attitude concerning what should be considered Holy. The imagery conveyed in pornographic Publications attaches to what is in the young mind and provides for content destined to encourage prurient behaviors. Although there have always been opportunists, it does not help to hide behind this as an excuse. Good men should remain good and coincidentally help others to do the same.

Intimacy, in the recent past, has become the focus of prurient public attention. Intimacies should not be brought to public attention, in which instance the nature and subtle beauty of intimacy is destroyed. Intimacy requires quiet mind-space, seclusion in a cloistered space, involving the procreative aspects of loving, touching, mating, and *"being together"* as husband and wife, destined to form new human beings. Sex is not a joke! Whilst being pleasurable, *sex should not be viewed as mere entertainment.* Pornographers are most conspicuous in such endeavors even as they are the most despicable of the maggot-men that have gained prominence from Blasphemy, lewdness, sin and the ruination of lives.

Regardless of Where, God aspires to love every individual with an infinite love and compassion; nevertheless, God does have some very definite and clearly defined expectations. Some may not understand just exactly what are His expectations, however, all can imagine, at least, that Godly expectations are of the highest and most compellingly profound order that is possible. We should imagine that God considers each of us, in His good Space as one of His perfect creatures and then, we should act so as not to disappoint Him! In God's good space it is expected that each person will use individual intelligence, sustained by Free Will to advance the nature and being of humanness. A positively motivated Volition, given to the light of the accumulated Intellect of the past two millennia, should make this possible.

There are reprobates that will not be retrieved by a patient and all loving God. This love is discreetly expressed in the birth, of all that have lived, the living and all that may live in the future. The advent of birth, given the nature of biological reproduction, is an unimaginable blessing, no matter where or when. Tyrants, thriving on sin, especially lust and greed, have destroyed the lives of millions. Nevertheless, all human beings must aspire to meet the highest expectations, in which instance salvation (hopefully) shall be the reward. This has not always been understood. This is precisely why God did send his only Son to teach and to inspire. The Word, with the guidance of the Holy Spirit has permeated the mind space of the entire human race. We are admonished that in the last days, *"Christ will come again."* This chapter has not been an exposition on bible prophecy, or the history of religion, which can best be done by others. However this has been rather a common sense appeal to the reader with some pertinent understanding in respect to the nature and function of space, vis-a-vis what is sacred and holy?

Space is as self as is Space

Space is a self-absorbing Infinity*
Space is (THE) Symbol of Space
This must be so with an Infinity

This is true, only if one believes in the existence of a Supernatural and Eternal Presence, God the Father. God, the Father is, among other Things, simply an **Idea.**
Nevertheless the Idea is a persistent one.

$[\infty]$.
S = s a (I) *
Human mind provides the biological-psychological space.
This is the stage, wherein the past and the present intersect.
Then the known past is augmented, and is thus able to collapse.
It collapses upon the presently discreet moment, upon **Now time.**
All this happens in what we can define or understand as mind's space.
Neurological function, which becomes of synaptic accommodation, is the
Physical-psychic means of configuration, providing the necessary electronic paths.
Such paths attempt to define complex levels of known and reasoned thought.
Within the mind we find *"Nested Concepts"* one found within another.

For each individual, this process is absolutely unique.

All the discreetly known past, with or without comprehension, is compressed, in Time.
The Past as remembered is carried, within a single eminent and functional moment.
Space, which appears as nothing, as the sky, is symbolic of itself, which is nothing.
The present moment is evolving toward the unknown, and is infinitely becoming.
Every human being is aware of Infinity manifest as the sky, symbol of Space.
*It is the future, as one may perceive [**It**] to exist.*
S = S n < > S

Manifest awareness is the knowing, as is evident in the individual mind become.
Knowing is a product of the neurological and specifically formed cellular complexity.
Intellect as knowledge, is accessible through language, this is of absolute importance.
Knowing, to a degree, is derived from the advent of individual human experience.
Act is as a response to or consequence of a truthfully perceived reality.
Knowledge becomes as individual mind, content, is thereby localized.
Knowledge is a phenomenal product of [a] People, [a] Culture or [a] Civilization.
As having been actualized, history is or may be widely evident: the lie distorts history.

Space is as self as is Space

Given the nature of humanity and individual humans, truthful History may be obscured
by subtle deception, in Time, or widely known as reasonably understood past truth.
Given the nature of humanity and individual humans,, or
reasoned understanding of consequence, as
understood, by individuals creates, thus qualifies history, for mankind.

The present moment, in space, provides every single human being a unique opportunity for
individual involvement destined toward the perfection of that particular living person.
Everyone should strive to be perfect as Christianity defines perfection.
There are many ways to do this.

The future [holds in space] whatever is possible, from this moment Foreword.
All potential is held in future space-time.

Whatever is possible will happen, as an event in space-time beyond now.
In Space each moment is wrapped in time, therefore, all will be aware who are in the
"sphere" of influence, which is as a coincident event in a particular *place-moment*.
Each moment has also been surrounded or wrapped in a *place-certain time segment.*
Consequence will be favorably or unfavorably obviated, at a *space-time point* beyond.
Whatever can happen will happen at a certain *space-time*, in the future.

The truthful meaning of all current conscious acts, whether intentional or inadvertent
will be made known, to some small part of humanity in future space-time.

However the question remains; does mankind learn from the past mistakes?
The answer is that, most men certainly do not learn from the past!
The War on terror or any War makes this blatantly obvious.
War is a complete abrogation of our present reality.
War is cowardly, sinful and must be stopped.
To glorify war is primitive and barbaric.
Technology does not make it better!
It is much worse now than ever.
It is the way of the coward
And the way of a Fool
And of the future
Think of it?

For a more complete understanding of Space wrapped in Time,
See Thomas Bearden's work in "<u>Aids, Biological Warfare</u>,"
Tesla Book Co., P. O. Box 1649, Greenville, TX 75401. ISBN # 0-914119-04-4.
Additionally: A future volume which I am working on will contain a more complete explanation.

The Sphere of existence.

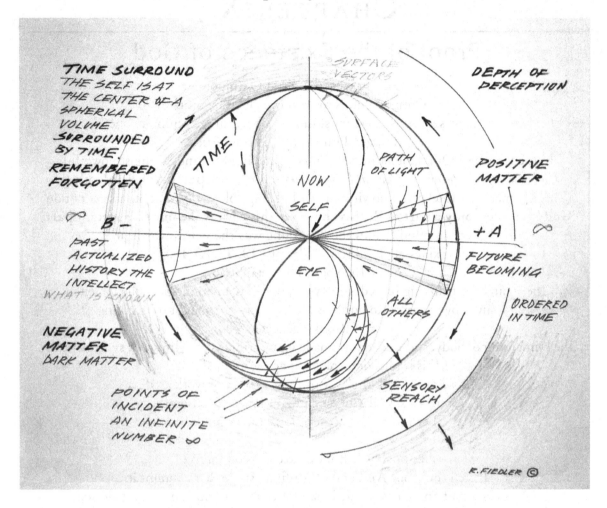

This is a two-dimensional sketch of how the person relates to the surroundings. There are no numbers. The Drawing is the basis for the understanding.

The person is in the center: words explain the meaning of the lines.

One must imagine a sphere to complete the picture.

The totality will exist in the mind's eye thereby bringing one closer to an understanding of the concept.

CHAPTER X

Proof of the Existence of God

Let us begin with the Word Omnipotent:
To be Omnipotent, is to be above all else: number 1.
Given any sequence, there must first be a beginning, a number one.
(This is logic, Philosophy and linguistics).
In the language, Omnipotent means primary, first in order and the most powerful.
*God is thought to be or imagined as being" **Absolutely" superior,** above all others.*
(This is a matter of Intellect), knowing the ALL, being able to do what others cannot do.
God is an Idea, only a part of Reality, however this Idea is the most important part.
Keep in mind that in the Beginning **was the word,** which
expressed an Idea: the Idea of **ALL THAT IS.**
(This is Theology and Metaphysics).
The thought or thinking precedes every act, which is a neurological phenomenon
and is given by whom (?) to our Species, to motivate thought or thinking.[176]
(This is Science).
The human mind, body, and the organs, made up by trillions of cells, work synergistically.
(This is phenomenology, tangible and psychic).
Those must work this way or those could not work at all.
Complex singularities are programmed to existence.
They must work as they do or they would die.

Presumably, Infinite **Space** goes on forever.
There is only one ALL and one Infinite space that contains it.
The question of Space has puzzled man for centuries and continues to do so.

Time is another factor which goes both ways: the before and the after every incident (?)

Complex multi-placates must work in concert, each must certainly be aware of the others.
When groups of men combine **Ideas become confused:** the men lose their reason.
They lose there way intellectually and cannot follow the complex dialogue:
Which may and often does become confused in its meaning and intent?

Christ came to save Humanity: **All men,** not some however all men.
One can imagine that Christ intended for all men to gain Salvation.
Nevertheless no man understands or knows: what is Salvation?
Where is this Salvation? We cannot be certain, therefore:
One must die to know.
The living, are given the opportunity to believe on Faith.
Faith combines with one's understanding, of what is and what is apparent.
The Intellectual tenor of Faith is what places one in a position to understand or not.

---

176 Who gave such power and why is of Primary Interest to the human Race.

The Intellectual tenor of Faith

Is what may be or is confusing?
This separates one group from the other.
Men speak in various languages and dialects.
(This is linguistics).
This is a part of Satan's Plan to divide and conquer.
(Satan, Lucifer and the Devil are Ideas about evil, with personalities).
United we stand divided we have fallen and will continue to do so.[177]
(This is axiomatic) and can be understood as such.
Men are divided in various ways. War is an outcome of such division:
Which emanates from misunderstanding, or refusal to admit to the meaning of words?
Keep in mind that the men who are speaking are not
always the best of men, those may be lying
Many are hypocrites seeking small advantage for their own person: often sex is involved.
War is a primary determining factor, altering the course of History and of Thought.
(This is History, falsely formed in sin).
Men are proud of their inventions of the means of killing others of their kind.
Much of what we know and learn comes from fictitious presentations, staged for
Propaganda
They are intended to convince and reorient the individual's thinking.

Whole industries are built on such false Pride: Pride is a mortal, sin.[178]
Millions sit in front of their Television sets watching mayhem and brutality.
(Such as this is a waste of Time however, this is reality).

The System is so complex that the individuals are not responsible for their own acts.
(This complexity results from the contrivances introduced every day, as falsehood, lies).
A functional System cannot be built on lies and *situational ethics*, a polite term for lying.
Situational ethics do have a devastating consequence on the formation of Reality.
(This is a question of morality: lying is a sin and should not be encouraged).
Most are very confused in the meaning of now and then, before and after.
The utter confusion acts as a cover for foul endeavor and **Mortal Sin**:
Which, is not thought to be sinful, is imagined as entertainment.

Christ admonished Humanity the Truth would set you free.

The movement and the music are appalling, but who thinks of this?
Mindless movement does not add one little bit to a Culture or to Civilization.
Youth enjoy mindless movement because those are ignorant of the important things.

---

177 Martin Luther and Mohammed, it is our understanding, will not go to Heaven: Those are Heretics of the most profound kind. It is questionable what will happen to those that did follow either one.

178 The Defense Industries are a very large part of "modern governmental expenditures. Those are wonderful as a business since the products are destroyed as a matter of use and must be replaced with more of the same

Mindless movement

Mindless movement is vain, is subtractive, destructive and unnecessary.
In such instance quietude is a virtue to be learned and practiced.
Our Television has become a tool of Satan promoting Sin.
Individuals are not aware imagining they are being entertained.
How much Time is wasted watching drivel and smut as entertainment?

God, being omnipotent, knows everything and is aware of every sin.
Men forget however God will remember.
It is impossible to win over omnipotence: men do try a futile gesture.
Who is this God that occupies all space and is every where simultaneously?
He exists outside of Time, as we understand Time to be.
He is an Idea, a Spirit, and in Christ a man an ephemeral presence.

He has no substance yet he controls all that is on the Earth and in the Universe.
A misunderstanding of his being, of his nature permeates the thinking of every man.
Regardless of their levels of intellectual development all men know about *"some"* God.
Men dance and sing in his honor, **there are Festivals,** rituals, rites, & men carry candles.
All of this proclaims of his presence without ever understanding the nature of His being.
Primitive men have voodoo and other seriously flawed & mysterious understandings.

Only the Catholic Church has an unbroken continuity directly from the Christ.
Christ is the second Person in the Holy Trinity with the Father and the Spirit.
Christ is thought to be the only Son of God a most responsible position.
The crucifixion & resurrection of Christ stands as a form of proof.
Christ was the only human being taken directly into Heaven.
He is now seated at the right hand of the Father.
And will judge the living and the dead.
His Kingdom will have no end.
(This is Theology).
(And Phenomenology).
A kingdom that has no end suggests and infinite Time frame.
(This is Physics)
There is a correlation with an infinite Time frame
And the sphere or time surround that envelopes every person.
A sphere has no edges or corners, is a continuous form and is an enigma.[179]
The sphere is the only such form and is a key to the meaning of Human reality.

---

179 Enigma: perplexing, baffling, unusual form. From the center of the sphere to the surface, given opposite polarities the form, *"in the interior"* cancels itself. This presents a perplexing and confounding situation. This function is involved, somehow, for the coming and going of Time. Every individual has his/her own time surround. The various time surrounds interlock as an important, nevertheless misunderstood, element of existence. (*See* **Bearden, T. E., Col.,** work and explanation in *Aids, Biological Warfare,* Tesla Book Co., P. O. Box 1649, Greenville, TX 75401. ISBN # 0-914119-04-4).

The sphere, a key to reality

An unseen sphere surrounds every man, which sphere is responsive to his becoming.
(This is axiomatic, transfinite given to every individual).
The content of this sphere is space, with whatever such space contains.
These are mostly unknown elements, which cannot be seen.
As for example the Host O which, is the body of Christ
Theologians, Doctors of the Catholic Church, have carefully pursued a search for truth.
This has continued unremittingly for over two thousand years.
Many find disagreement because of the degree and level of their misunderstanding.
Keep in mind understanding is based on belief given to a language of expression.
Languages vary and understanding however, the **ALL** is the same for everyone.
The Universal, Christ centered faith has been divided into various Religions.
Religion is not the same as theology it has broken the continuity of Faith.
Faith is based on what is given, as Universal and is all inspiring.
Many aspects of existence are the same for everyone.
(This is Universal Reality).
Light, which illuminates realty?
Time, given moment by moment,
before and after this moment: Now.
All directional emphasis ups and down.
One's ability to move, which connotes life,
and darkness, concealing the absence of light.
There is growth and development of various species.
Plants and animals flourish and bear fruit in God's space.

Theology deals with the ALL: all Time, all space, all movement material form and matter.
Religion is man-made and deals only with those parts that man imagines to understand.
Theology and religion are not the same: Theology is complete Religion is incomplete.
To know and serve God one must have a complete Faith, the Catholic Faith.
Millions have died for the Catholic Faith, the Faith of Jesus Christ.
Many more will likely die in the future, a sad reckoning.
To begin we must first know that God does exist, in spite of the prattling of ignorance.[180]
God is an IDEA and a reality the Word becomes, Flesh: look around and you will see.
God is also a Spirit and God is a person in Christ and God is THE Creator.
Of all that is seen and unseen: finally God is a man: Progenitor.[181]
Being a progenitor is an important part in the scheme of things.
God has entrusted this responsibility to the male of the species the female is an
incubator. This assertion is made without any notion of superiority: both men and
women are required to carry the species forward in Time, as part of God's plan.

There is a plan

---

180 Be wary of men who imagine they are wise. No man can know everything, actually men know very little. Most of what most men know those use to serve them and disregard the nature and feelings of others: in two words those are selfish and vain.

181 Rutler, George W., DD. *The Fatherhood of God*. (Homiletic and Pastoral Review, June 1993).

CHAPTER XI

The Self as [THE] Center of Reality

Refer to Diagram at the end of the book so to best understand what is written as follows

Imagine yourself, your person, as the center of the circle.
Now imagine the circle is a sphere. Thus you become the center of the Sphere
(*This happens in your mind as an **Idea**, there is nothing tangible or real}*
The **Idea** is that you are in the center of the Sphere the Space is all around you

As depicted, imagine the right side of the sphere is the future the left side is the past
The lines you see, which appear to be on the surface of the cones do two things:

First, on the right side, those define the surface of the cone:
The surface of the cone is the part that faces reality
The drawing is symbolic of a significant Idea
The Idea exists outside from the drawing
The Idea is extant and irrefutable
The drawing is trenchant
And is suggestive

Second, on the right side, those represent elements coming to you from outside the self
An idea, images, sounds, colors, smells, light and dark: all coming your way, so to speak
These are elements that will affect you somehow: this is not knowable, except generally
AND
On the left side of the sphere the lines drawn on the cone, define the surface of that cone
Second those represent the thoughts and ideas going from your being to infinity, in Time
Your thoughts and ideas can be "picked up" by anyone in your wake who is aware of them
This becomes a part of the effect that you will have on those in your immediate purview

This is a bit more complicated nevertheless it is made somewhat understandable for you
Whatever your senses pick up is transferred to your brain: the sensory center of you
All the aspects of your presence are apparent on the left side as your History
Those cannot be repeated due to the nature of an irreversible Time
Every person is in exactly the same position as you are
Every person is as **THE** center of what is

This relates to the absolute being of everyone
All are made in the image of the God: somehow
God with an infinite presence can make this happen
To deny this is to deny the existence of God the Father
One cannot deny the existence of ALL, which is so apparent

* * *

God the Father is the progenitor of all that is in the Universe

CHAPTER XII

Time

Time Limits, Human Understanding.
In Time, we are one, where are we?

As a first and foremost consideration, as a creature of God we are restrained by our *placement* in time.[182]
First, every individual is limited, in the most profound and extensive ways, by **when** they were born.
The moment of our conception has complex, far-reaching implications, which determine our being.
When were you born? What time is it now? What moment, hour, day, month, year and century?

Second, we are limited by placement in space, a Co-incident of our time-space format.
Where, in this world, have you been? Where are you now? Where will you go?
All eventualities will occur in specific Time, one way or another?
You are in the center of a Time-surround!
Every individual is surrounded by Time!
(See diagram on page 109).

Third, we are limited by intelligence, the expression of which is given to language.
Complex Ideas and thoughts move in respect to the form and manner of formalized language.
Vocabulary dialect and idiomatic, have profound influence on both meaning and understanding.
Where understanding originates is very difficult to determine impossible in most instances.
Attitude disposition and personality modify important elements of understanding.
All such elements are necessary for a manner and degree of comprehension.
Understanding is a complex issue, determining ultimate consequence
And: the outcome from each and every event.

Fourth, immediate family, friends and personal associations determine all limitations.
Understandably any such limitations can have positive or negative impact on the affected individuals.
Individual human beings possesses a phenomenal nature and are completely unique it there totality.
Who are you and are you sure? How much of you, has been given as a gift from another?

Fifth, the implements available in one's own good time facilitate how intelligence is utilized.
Can you fix it? How? What tools will you employ? How does mind dive implementation?
Distinctions in implementation demand differently developed skills, more or less.
Intelligence is obviated in the concept and utilization of a given implement.

---

182 **The Advent,** of an individual human existence is a *phenomenon of transcendental* significance, biologically driven within the context of a genetic imperative. This becomes as a consequence of the interaction of one with many *irrespective of what one believes*. **Life is God-given;** it is not an accident and does not just happen coincidentally. Exactly why one is born and is not someone else is a profound mystery; however the world needs its entire people. God is [The] *necessary Being,* from which being all Wisdom flows. Thus every person is a *consequence of a wise decision* endowed with infinitely timeless foresight. (Ibn Sina, 980-1037 AD) postulated a similar notion over a thousand years ago as did Plato before him.

Time moves silently across each face, marking each with joy and sorrow

Everyone is given some of God's good time. The fact that *time is a given* is a phenomenon worth contemplation, as it pertains to every discreetly personal existence. Fundamentally, there exists a profound relationship between *what is perceived as time* and what is accomplished in that same time. Time provides one of the great mysteries of the Universe and pertains to answering the most important question, which interestingly is just a single word. Why?

No individual human being is *given* more than a few years to live, perhaps one hundred years, more or less. Each one of us is given an absolutely defined placement, in the womb of a biologically existential mother. Nevertheless, the twenty-three paired chromosomes, of the two parents, *during a process called mitosis,* yield a remarkably singular human Being, created *discreetly* in the Image of an infinitely discreet God. The child emerges from the body of another, always a mother,[183] and finds the time in this world, to be just right for his/her being! It could be no other way. That emergent being is never a duck or a rabbit, nor could any Human ever be so. Some modern thinking overlooks the fact that the begetting of children is woman's most important responsibility. The nurturing of such offspring is a most important task and requires full attention.

Pertinently we note, many that might and should have been born have been killed, the consequence of misunderstanding, coupled with an *excessive and tainted interest in sex as entertainment*. Admittedly, the urge to reproduce is profound and compelling. Nevertheless, for political reasons, our Civilization places the biological family in jeopardy, especially so because it sets too high value on money and things and on *making it in the business world.* There is too much emphasis on economics from the various media: radio, television and printed formats, which have gotten to be absolutely preposterous. There is too much for sale and very few have the money to purchase what is imagined as necessary. In my first volume I touched upon the overproduction which was problematic already in 1900. It is much worse at the present time. Overproduction remains our number one problem. Interestingly the excess that we have is being imported from other lands that have an excess of people. The **Idea** that one can make millions by bringing all kinds of ***"Stuff"*** to America is a very compelling one. The solution will be to allow everyone who is in this country legally or illegally to remain and those will be encouraged to purchase the *"Stuff"* with ever cheapening dollars. The illegal ones will be excused. This will work only for a short time until those have become addicted and loaded with *"Stuff"* just like the rest of the natural born citizens. *"Stuff" will not provide happiness or contentment* especially when the styles change yearly and one becomes left behind those others with obviously newer ***"Stuff."***

Present dialogue attendant to Woman's liberation does not help individual circumstances, beholden to mass titillation dished out as entertainment, in concert with pornography, legally sanctioned perversion, sex shops and shacking up. Furthermore, abortion, in the most profound

---

183 **Motherhood** must, once again, be given the highest respect. Motherhood must not be viewed as an unfortunate accident due to ***indiscriminate fornication.*** Young women must be informed and educated to understand and respect their *primary and most important* role. Job training and employment should not eclipse the importance of nurturing one's own children. Abortion should not be encouraged, by government funding; if performed it must be with the full understanding of physical, social and moral implications. Abortion is a mortal sin; it is a horrendous crime perpetrated against an ***absolutely defenseless*** victim. Abortion is never a good idea, whereas a stable two-parent family is the basis for whatever follows that is reasonably good in any Civilization.

and mortal manner, intrudes on the <u>*intended becoming of millions,*</u> thus corrupts the continuity of our Civilization and the Human Race, in an unholy way, as it destroys the mortality of absolute innocence. We have no way of knowing, at this time, what the consequence of **wholesale murder** portends, for the future of human beings. We do suspect that they who have been so murdered would have added immeasurably to the totality of existence.

We assert that Time and Space are always willing to accept another Human Being. All who are conceived are welcome in God's Universe? Although, it has been observed that, there are some similarities in the developing child (*fetus as some prefer*) with other species, no other species is endowed with the twenty-three pairs of human chromosomes. Additionally, no other species is made in the image of God? The proof of this fact is forthcoming in the time given to the completion of the Human Endeavor, which will require more, however not all Time. Time is as the Infinite and closes upon itself as it cancels the past in collision with the future. [184]

We assert also that <u>the quasi-infinite cancellation of time by itself is the primary motivation for the becoming of Electricity</u>. We have no proof of this however it seems a real possibility. Though magnificently engineered, electricity is a phenomenon that few understand. As Space collapses into a Black Hole so too the Time within that same Space is extinguished, possibly forever. This is a very real event; however, we do not see it happening. Nevertheless, much of what is possible, in the most profound sense of the word, is functionally related to this phenomenon. Electricity exists as a consequence of the coming and going of Time, which is caused by the **Time Surround** within any **Spherical Space.**

> *We are surrounded by Time which, within that surround, cancels itself*
> *as though [It] never happened. Time is as a measurement of duration*
> *and is as nothing tangible or real, as is observed by the senses.*

Time is as an absolute coincident of Space and provides the period(s) for the possibility of extension in space. One's placement *within time* obviates one's presence while they are on this earth. Metaphorically, *within the Western Civilization*, all places in time are considered before or after the Son of God, B. C. or A. D. actually one hundred years, a time span which would encompass almost every living person, is a very short time. When compared to all time, a lifetime is but a moment, absolutely so, when time is as Being considered Forever! Most of us, in this life, are given less than one hundred years. However, Time is both extensive and coincident. In extending, time is a measure of the seasons, the years and the centuries and may be perceived as such by human awareness. This awareness is heightened by the Intellect, which is the accumulation of knowledge, what is learned, and understanding over the course of known Time and is available [from time to time] for study and contemplation, thus has historic meaning. As a basis for what is coincident, time provides unique moments for all that live at [any] moment, at [any] location in this world. Coincidence provides for simultaneity, which becomes as a basis for structured human endeavor. Structured human endeavor is what has built all Civilizations, which come and go in Time. How individuals value and utilize moments, which are given, is what sets the tenor for any accomplishment, individually and collectively. Presently, as in much of the past, **politics born of sinful endeavor corrupts the time of much of the human race.** War is the ultimate corruption and **all wars are political**. There are some in this world that *"imagine"* them superior to all

---

184 This **cancellation of time** has consequences of which we have no absolutely truthful and complete understanding.

others.[185] Those have caused unimaginable hardship and death for millions of innocent people and those are organized and are prolific in their nefarious endeavor.

All Time is given as only a Moment! One might contemplate that in an infinite number of places there exists an infinite duration of time. The reciprocal is all time is a single moment. Interestingly, given a universally Catholic Theology, regardless of the amount of time one is given to live, it *is always sufficient* to gain Salvation. For those interested enough to pursue serious study, an understanding of Catholicism will illuminate this complex and easily misunderstood concept. *Catholicism provides the intellectual and spiritual Tenor for Western Civilization.* In fact Christ, the first Catholic separated Time, which until His coming, was dominated by ignorance and superstition, vengeance, greed and selfishness. The Bible, by virtue of its existence, conveys the teaching of Christ, simply and directly and is a literary extension in Time. Literally, what we do or do not learn, during formative years as children, from the teachings of the Son of God, will support as it determines most of what we think and do thereafter. The notion of extension and continuity is widely understood and may be applied to formal education. Presently adults are *filling the time of our children* with too much nonsense and ugliness at an early age, after which they are unable to act responsibly and intelligently regarding encountered circumstance.[186] Is this planned or is this an accident? At this time all of America has become as a Disneyland of sorts with profound, however not well understood implications.[187] Much of this seems to be planned, so to prevent the development of the more comprehensive mental capacities. Simple-minded persons make good Socialists and those are willing to die for those that are in control of circumstance. Consider that Napoleon, "great leader of men?" entered Russia with four hundred thousand soldiers (400,000) and left with about ten thousand (10,000) more or less: talk about success? This type of madness has decimated the most advanced Nations in this world, even as the more primitive ones have been encouraged to flourish. This is a guarantee that the meek "**Will inherit**" the earth.

Think of this. During the sixteenth, seventeenth and eighteenth Centuries France was a very Catholic country and an intellectual leader in Western Civilization, just then beginning to be infected by what we understand as Modernism. The Artists in France, during the late nineteenth and early twentieth Century's provided the step to modernism in the Fine Arts. No doubt this was a tragedy. The Mid Twentieth century brought the effects of the Second World War, certainly contrived for the effect and consequence, which we are seeing right now. We were treated to the dissolution of that country at the Moline Rouge and were, in movies and literature, given to witness all the drunks that flocked to Paris for the cheap food and drinks, and sex with the French dancing girls. One wonders why? The Opportunists and the Comedians made a fortune on the

---

185 The **Idea** of a superior race has been considered for five thousand years, more or less. Superiority seems to be a given with the improvement in technical ability, which in turn has something to do with location. Invention has been more necessary in colder places where the climate would kill those who were unprepared. This is an entire subject, which we cannot comment on in this work except to mention that it does exist.

186 **LaRouche, Lyndon H.** *Dialogue on the Fundamentals of Sound Education Policy. April 12, 2002.* Fidelio, Journal of Poetry, Science and Statecraft. Summer/Fall, 2002. pps. 29-31.

187 **The New Federalist, Don't** *Give your Children to Disney.* Disney projects an insipid and saccharine form of nonsense, mixed with perverted and raunchy sex as entertainment. The sex is masked by insipid color and "sweetness" designed to entice and capture prurient interest. This can and is destroying the mind content of millions of children and the adults that refuse to grow up.

reruns and are still collecting money from the millions of fools, taken in by the farce. France, a once very Catholic country was, in part, devastated by the smut, ignorance and vilification of womanhood and the family. American soldiers flocked to Paris for the <u>*good wine and the cheap sex all paid for by the tax payers at home,*</u> who believed those were doing something of monumental importance. Actually *those were killing their parent Culture and Civilization*, preparing it for Islam or some Eastern form of existence. Keep in mind most of the people in the world are Asiatic. They have very different understandings than the people of the West. Some are being converted to western ways however this is a small number at the present time. What attracts them is our flagrant "lifestyle," so called which is driven largely by greed and vanity: both are mortal sins. We only mention this in passing: the reader has his own ideas of what happened: However the romanticized Ideas are mostly wrong.

Omnipotence has a prominent place in the scheme of things. During any period of one hundred years, the Earth will travel around the Sun one hundred times. The Sun, we understand, is moving also; to where we know not! Interestingly, as an effective first cause, an Omnipotent Being must exist outside of time. ***Omnipotence is Timelessness*** and has absolutely no tangible presence, *given to our recognition*, excepting through miraculous intervention. Nevertheless, the cause cannot be denied when the consequence has been, is and remains infinite. In fact this is simple enough for general understanding except that understanding is confused by improper education.

Given the human brain, which interestingly is primarily a ***phenomenally energized liquid,*** human thoughts have an *absolute placement in discreet time*. The Omnipotent One, first Cause, by means of The Holy Spirit, *can enter into the conscious being of any number of human persons simultaneously,* at any monument. This obviates the ***existence of a profound and timeless Good*** and is an aggressively pertinent understanding, in reference to the God Being. We [are] one in the **Spirit** and one in the **Lord**, thus all may become known as Christian. Distinctions as exist between differently informed understandings, when goodness prevails shall dissappear, when and if [in Time] truth becomes universally known and understood. This might have happened already excepting that "The evil that men do lives after them [Shakespeare], while the good is interred in their bones." We hope modern communication will facilitate the dissemination of the truth, thus all men will be free [from the shackles forged by greedy, vain, presumptuous and evil men].[188]

Different groups within the social network have formed to further their own discreet, not always noble, goals and objectives. Some of them have managed to capture the issuance of and the working and flow of money, the medium of exchange, which is necessary for any Civilization.[189] By so doing those have commandeered the populations of nations and seek to control the entire world. This has been and is a vain, and archaic notion, it is ***vanity*** and the ***will to power***. If this were not the case there would exist a more evenly distributed prosperity than presently exists.

---

188 **Luke 8:17,** "For nothing is secret that shall not be made manifest; Neither anything hid, that shall not be known and come abroad." The Bible is the one book of prophecy that has been and is correct. The Bible contains Ideas about past, present and future events. Those that "rant" against the teachings found in the Bible are either simply ignorant or those profess a different, false and incomplete, Religion. We should reconsider the Old Testament and all false and incomplete Religions and all of their negative teachings and follow Jesus. The world will be better that way!

189 **Money,** which should be a servant to all people, provides a medium of exchange, nevertheless has become the Master causing untold misery to millions. At present money is a curse on the Civilization instead of the blessing, which it should be. ***Money is a means not an end however for many has become an end and this is what has worked to corrupt mankind.***

This represents a core issue in the becoming of humanity. Those that have much acquire more and those with little or nothing remain as those are. America was perhaps envisioned, as providing a solution for this however has not done so. Greedy and vain men now control America. Charity has a function never the less one would hope to be independent from the philanthropy of those who are robbing the entire Civilization, before returning a small fraction back to promote the common good. This is precisely the point at which Church and State must be united and undivided in their respect for a universally valid Religion. That Religion already exists as the Universal Catholic Religion formed by Jesus Christ, miraculously the Son of God. Whether one believes this or not, is of little consequence since, the **Idea** exists and is persistent. Individual belief belongs to the individual however may be influenced by others with different notions. There are many contrary notions surrounding this **Idea** only one of which is absolutely correct.

What we commonly refer to as a time frame deals with *time segments or a time wrap-around,* given to specific placement and with absolute and specific duration.[190] Succinctly, an Infinite Being is not wrapped in time, as is mortal man. An infinite Being would naturally be in all places at all times, this is a definition of what infinite being is, precisely so.[191] There are absolutely no time restraints on Eternity, which is all Time, forever and ever![192] The supposition is that each individual person, or mortal being, is framed in time; that is, surrounded by a given amount of time and is, therefore, limited by the *structured nature* of the surroundings.[193] Existing life determines the nature and qualities of individual existence. Time is extensive, involves space and has *a peculiarly existential quality of elasticity,* which *is pulled into the service* of all **forms of existence**, including humanly perceptive existence. Meaning may be given to Time in direct reference to specific human incident occurring within that same time.[194] Actually, this should be quite easy to understand.[195] However, the question arises concerning just what level of understanding one is able to attain. Numerous and pleasant distractions prevent serious contemplation, which, in present circumstance, may be deemed unnecessary by most all of the population: excepting financial matters of an urgent nature. Often individuals avoid serious thinking, because they believe they are not capable of doing so, many (perhaps most) are not. Individuals tend to rigorously reject intellectual endeavor, as being intimidating. It does require a degree of humility, to accept one's intellectual limitations truthfully. Humility provides for the existence of a Cardinal Virtue. Athletics is satisfying for many because those can do what is expected and it doesn't take a lot of critical thinking. Those who do not participate simply watch, imagining that those too could do this. Spectator Sports are driven by greed and earn millions for those that succeed. Also this provides the excuse for the spectator to not think about anything important.

---

190 **Bearden, Thomas E,** Col. *Aids Biological Warfare.* Tesla Book Co., P. O. Box 1649, Greenville, Texas 75401. ISBN # 0-914119-04-4.

191 **Infinite, 1.** Without limits of any kind, undetermined and indeterminate. – Said especially of God and the Absolute. **2.** Without end; boundless; immeasurable. **3.** Indefinitely large, extensive or numerous; hence vast; immense; also inexhaustible

192 **Handel, Joseph**, the Messiah, Text. "And He shall reign forever and ever and ever and ever and ever." Amen.

193 The structured nature of surroundings is different for every single person.

194 **Meaning** is a product of experience within Time and is a holographic and ephemeral construct, as a consequence of discreetly operational seeing, knowing and understanding. Meaning is a product of discreet neurological functioning.

195 This is a question involving what one can do in a certain amount of time.

Humility is a Cardinal Virtue, that virtue, which *beacons other virtues to follow*, demands a manner of compliance, in reference to the truth, given to the admission of what is. In time, *humility plays an important role in truthful understanding*; however we may easily lose sight of this, in a busy and distracting world. Even though each of us understands that we will not live forever, that every Human Being has only a very short time to live, many find their mortality to be a cause for consternation and react, with aggressive contempt, for any power greater than any human could possess. Many, men and women, now as in the past, want to be as God, however this is certainly impossible. To obviate this issue it is only necessary to consider that omnipotence is and must be a singular entity, anything else must be less, emphatically and logically so. Reality is hierarchical with omnipotence, standing alone: alone at the top. All else is subservient, is less and should be considered as such.

Vanity is a consequence of an *imperfectly formed conscience* and often acts as an impediment to truthful insight. Individually, an ever-greater endeavor, toward the accomplishment of material progress in time, is in many respects a consequence of vanity in operation. Wealth encourages one toward vain aspirations coupled with a feeling of a superior self-worth, which may be somewhat or overly imagined. There is an adage that one might consider. ***Money corrupts!*** In fact money corrupts almost all that are fortunate or unfortunate enough to acquire more than is needed. In Time money earns interest (sometimes considered as usury), which compounding affords a *tremendous, in fact **absolute** advantage* to they who have large stores of money.

Aggressive trading in securities, when the trading can be rigged, has produced monumental wealth for men, actually thieves, so employed. The nature and effect of such fraud, deceit, vanity and deception is being discovered, as honest men labor, in time, just to exist.[196] The entire Civilization is beholden to *money earning money in time,* whereby a few gains more and more with virtually no effort, depending on the efforts of others who have much less, perhaps nothing at all. Such great wealth is contained in a few places and is *managed with a historically formed and consistent determination,* pertaining to politics, religion, sociology, literature and art, within such domains it has near-total authority. This does not preclude invention, however bears upon how invention is applied and for what purpose. War, Freeways and various Monuments stand as the evidence of vain activity in time, however, as such this is not well understood. Employment seems to be a compelling issue, beckoning this very same species of activity. How to attain *full employment in time* is of a profound political and economic concern. The disposal of such ultimate productivity is also a complex, operationally profound issue. Certainly it is really true that "all in this world is Vanity". (Christ) It is definitely stated on good authority!

Reality is as an Absolute. This is axiomatic, irrespective of the confusion of many Philosophers and their intellectually tainted philosophies. Reality as perceived *in time* should provide proof enough for the skeptic to consider (at least) the possibility of the existence of some species of absolute. A knowledge and understanding of a manner of Transubstantiation is an important

---

196 **Weiss, Martin Ph.D.** *Safe Money Report,* September 2002, Issue #34. Accounting Scandal wipes out $2.4 Trillion in Shareholder Wealth! "Daddy Warbucks," from Orphan Annie days, was a pauper next to those bucks. One should keep in mind that such wealth is "notional wealth," imagined as such by eager speculators. When one views the "real value" of such holdings the numbers are much smaller perhaps only one-hundredth as much or less? Nevertheless the control of assets, regardless of real value, remains in the hands of he who holds the wealth. To be in control of great sums of money (presumed as such) affords one great opportunity in commerce and politics.

understanding, at this Junction. The only possibility for man to become an active part, of an eternal presence, is to become *one in being with The Father from whom all good things come.* The presence of Christ, in the Eucharist, may provide for many men a temporal [timely] connection to the eternal order of being. Additionally, this truth, handed down through the centuries, obviates the presence as well as the profound significance of the third party, in the Trinity. By means of this phenomenal blessing, it is believed that many Individual Human Beings may share Eternity, *that is all time that is and will be in the future beyond.* The understanding of one's infinite existence (in Time) must be approached with humility, only on God's terms, in accordance with the rules, which He has given! The tradition of Catholicism maintains the deposit of faith as truth,[197] which found origin for our present Civilization in the presence of Christ, on this earth. Tangentially one may speculate, as do some exegetes that this Civilization may be the last one, having completed the destiny of the human race, now approaching end times. For those that don't believe this is true consider it is a possibility. The human race could be extinguished by physical means, high or low temperatures, perhaps flooding or simply the cessation of human genetic continuation might be interrupted. No one knows what is going to happen. One may also speculate that each day is an end time for many human beings. One may speculate; however can never *know for certain* what life and death will be for all humanity, indeed not even for one person.

If one does not believe this, that Catholicism has maintained the deposit of faith (as truth), one's chances for Immortality, understood by millions to exist, are (seemingly) reduced.[198] However, those who are not Catholic have no right to presume perfect insight, or to ridicule those who do believe in what is known as Universal Christianity; particularly Roman Catholicism. There are millions who believe differently. Nevertheless all human beings possess only what may be understood as imperfect knowledge. Obviously sinful behavior patterns provide evidence that millions have a poorly formed conscience. No mortal man has perfect knowledge and very few have a flawless conscience. In a world of tolerance we must be fair and cannot use slander and profanity to traduce Holiness. Putting it in the fairest terms, succinctly, those who ridicule and slander holiness are *blasphemers*, ignorant, insensitive and vain.

At any moment in time, the consensus or collective point of view is an important cultural ingredient. Millions are being encouraged, often indiscriminately coerced by state controlled education, to fairly examine and consider (presumably accept) all points of view. This is not a bad thing, if one is able to face truth as it is encountered. However, any thinking person will understand and admit that *all points of view are not somehow equal.* Some points of view emanate from what is certainly a truthful understanding whilst most others do not. Many behavioral patterns and what we have been encouraged to accept as life-styles are deviate and perverse, irresponsible and **sinful.** All this is known and believed by millions, supported by millions of incidents, in time, which have found their way into known statistics. We are encouraged to examine, consider and then accept all Types of defined perversity, given what is called diversity or personal choice. Why not consider that point of view, or that understanding, which has been

---

197 **Catholic scholarship** has maintained the Faith in tact for twenty centuries. Scribes, for centuries, copied with no error the inspired writing of the Church Doctors and Fathers. Other religions have attempted to do this as well, however not so successfully. The Reformation did great harm to Catholicism as it divided true believers. Nevertheless well meaning Heretics superimposed their thoughts, with specious and vain disposition, upon the divinely inspired writing of Christ and His Apostles. For most, the schism will define the finality of their timely existence.

198 **Pope St. Gregory the Great**: "The holy universal Church teaches that it is not possible to worship God truly except in her and asserts that all who are outside of her will not be saved." The Papal Encyclicals: Vol. 3 (1903-39) pg. 314.

proven as being primary, to the positive formation and development of Western Civilization? Given a fair opportunity, individual common sense, without much help, should obviate this profound understanding.

The Pretender and the hypocrite corrupt humanities future time. The corruption extends into the future and grows exponentially as more and various persons are inflicted. One may not forget that much in past time, presumed as truthful history, deemed to be the result of the great evil of Christianity is a consequence of the *individual pretender, the hypocrite, the interloper and the enemies* of Catholicism.[199] For centuries, in Time, the Catholic faith has been slandered by many claiming to be Christians when, in fact, they have been barbarians and evildoers, dedicated to the destruction of the Catholic faith.[200] The present crisis in the church is partly, perhaps mostly, a consequence of *hypocrites, liars, niggardly politicians and perverts* attempting to defame what is holy, worthwhile and good. Popular opinion, beholden to mass-media indoctrination, is not generally in depth, truthfully informed opinion. Much thinking, concerning the past is rather the product of individual and collective ignorance. It is in the best interest of they who benefit from deception to encourage the propagation and continuation of popular opinion, *devised* of ignorance. Presently mythology, hearsay, propaganda and most recently slanted reporting are cleverly combined with various forms of *imposed or packaged* models for comprehension. We name these as slogans, the cliché and mannerisms in respect to thought patterns. Defamation is easily accomplished by the use of *trigger-words*, which have been used in the past to incite, inflame, intimidate and slander.[201] Thoughts do have patterns and simple thoughts have simple patterns.[202] Those can be remembered and repeated over and over by every moron in town and there are many. Interestingly, normally intelligent youth are captivated by the antics of the moron: why?

When aggressive presumption is given to the disinterested, poorly trained, juvenile mind of a distracted being, that same being will be overwhelmed and surrender to whatever is being promoted. The spectacle obviates the temporary absence of personally driven, decently formed behavior, as a chanting mob will clearly illustrate. ***Spectacular productions are the opiate of the present mob gatherings,*** where screaming and aggressively silly behavior is apparent. There are also would-be musicians pounding incessantly on their drums and symbols: like a Bacchanal. Adolescent mob participation is an example of this, beginning with the pubescent attending a rock concert. Spectacles are a distraction, *spiced* with gambling on outcomes, and provide another age-old example. Thus is formed a somewhat universal *urge to participate,* **to belong, to have fun.** Circumstance; contrived for profit appears simultaneously to be personally unique and

199 **The Illuminati,** founded by Adam Weishaupt, was formed for the express purpose of destroying the Nation State and Religion, especially Catholicism, which was associated with many European Monarchs. Interestingly in Italy the heart of Christian Civilization, the Alta Vendetta operates in direct opposition to the Catholic Church, having assumed various disguises, as circumstance required. This alone provides a classic definition of a hypocrite. (See. Nesta Webster, *World Revolution.)*

200 **Dodd, Bella,** *School of Darkness: The Record of a Life and of a conflict between two Faiths.* The Devin Adair Co., 23 E. 26th. Street, New York, N. Y. LC # 54-10204.

201 **Reed, Douglas.** *The Controversy of Zion:* Veritas Publishing Company (Pty) Ltd., P. O. Box 20, Bullsbrook, Western Australia 6084. Copyright © Douglas Reed, July 1985. pps. *138-164* ISBN # 0949667 27 7

202 **Jacobson, Steven,** *Mind Control in the United States.* Critique Pub., P. O. Box 11451, Santa Rosa CA 95406. ISBN 0-911485-00-7. LC # 85-70431. Mfg. Apollo Books, 107 Lafayette St., Winona, MN

emotionally systematic. Nevertheless, mob behavior is always problematic; even considering many have the best, perhaps innocent intention.

Is it wise to assume that poorly informed choices of a young adult, of ordinary ability, are certain to be the right choices? Can the young, with too much information and very little significant knowledge solve the problems of today, created over a period of twenty five hundred years? Cans the emotionally driven blundering of youth, given to a false notion of Democracy, provide license to vote intelligently? Why have the contrived theories, of an indignant opportunist, such as Karl Marx been so seriously considered, so as to deform an entire Civilization, thus to corrupt honestly decent government? Can the World's accumulated wisdom, gathered and expressed by men of genius, be ignored? Can we discount completely the teaching of the Saints? Can we discount as irrelevant, a saintly commitment? Can we imagine, at present that any person would die for an idea or a principal? The Reader can form additional questions.

Whatever else one may or may not do, at death each individual, every single Human Being will submit their mortal identity to Eternity. Eternity is all time before and after now, especially after now. *All must submit to Endless Time.* Shakespeare said it quite simply, "In the end, we are all dead." No living Human Being knows exactly what will happen, or has ever known; excepting Christ Risen, Son of God, The Mystical Body of Whom provides for the Presence of the Holy Ghost, Third Person of the Trinity that Spirit, which motivates all that pertains to the goodness in Humanness. Although the Spirit is not seen, nevertheless, the Spirit is present, *at all times, in all places* and imposes upon the formation of individual conscience and understanding, as is given to knowing, affected thereby.

Whether or not one believes this has no effect on the truth, none whatsoever!

We do recognize that many will have a difficult time with some of what is expressed directly above, also some related understandings, however, since this is a most important understanding, in this world, common sense, in service of humility, demands that such a notion (at least) be truthfully considered.

> *If God should speak, He would say:*
> *Return to me; be among the just, as you know you must.*
> *I have been waiting. Depend on my trust. I can wait forever, eternally!*
> *Know too, it is important that you do,*
> *Forever is a long time.*

One can lay claim to no significantly mature understanding, excepting that one is aware of and gives fair-minded thought to the subject at hand. "Consideration of this alone, that is the contemplation of what it means to die, forms the basis and the motivation for much, if not most, of what we do when we are alive." (Count Leo Tolstoy)

Death has many means, however only one objective.

No great thinker has failed to recognize this; indeed, much of great thinking is emboldened by such consideration. Saints and Martyrs have become, because of their understanding of what it means to live and to die. The lives of Saints have been lived in acquiescence to the responsibility attendant to life itself. Saints and Martyrs, some merely children, Joan of Arc humbly accepted the greatest God-given responsibilities, so that others might better know what is truthfully significant. "There is a great distinction between the death for a noble cause and death caused by starvation." (Spengler)

The meaning of simultaneity has its definition in respect to all living humans at ***any one moment in Time.*** Artists have attempted to deal with the issue of Simultaneity, which many do not fully comprehend. Most have failed in what appear to be vain attempts to promote momentary sensation. The concept is perhaps best developed in the symphony and in Mathematics. Picasso was perhaps the most notorious; however Leonardo Deviancy's work was so intellectually superior so as to make Picasso appear stupid and silly. In spite of his commercial appeal and the consequence of extraordinary, politically motivated promotion, Picasso will be remembered ultimately for the damage he has done and the evils from which he drew his energy. His place in the twentieth century though obvious was, most generally, as a consequence of sophisticated promotion, coupled with the beckoning of greed working within the minds of many that pandered to his vain, lewd and frivolous mannerism. His contempt for women was extraordinary and his lust insatiable. ***He was a fornicator, master of pubic hair and a dupe for men wiser than he was and much more clever as well.***

Picasso was no hero. He was a silly and degenerate hypocrite. Nevertheless his influence has been notable, for the past half century. With the giant publishing houses having distributed hundreds of thousands of volumes of his work, such has had a near-simultaneous effect on millions of individuals. Professors who lack significant insight and have little or no artistic ability have praised Picasso's artwork. Historically significant works of Christian and Catholic art, works of *true genius,* have been called decadent, sentimental or overly religious. Youngsters, in public schools, have <u>learned how to create ugliness</u> and to illustrate what is perverse, conceived in evil and destructive to the soul. Nevertheless, some of Picasso's works do evidence a manner of ability over a technique. His greatest efforts were perhaps done as politically motivated blasphemy, for effect. And clever participation has netted a money reward in the trading and inflation of the money value of what he had done. It must be understood that Inflation has had an effect on every price, including Artworks.

To be honest, in spite of *artists* like Picasso, is to admit that much of what is best that we all enjoy, is a product of or is derived from Godly inspired Western Thought. A divine inspiration and profoundly formulated understanding animates Western Civilization; *given any moment, all are at once, ipso facto, children of God.* Fundamental to Western thought, Catholicism as Universal Christianity insists upon and defends the principal that we are God's Creatures and that God expects much good from each of us. As we have been given whatever ability we may have, we are obliged in God's good Time, to use that ability for the betterment of all that we are fortunate enough to encounter. This trust becomes as a definite responsibility. Though we are very small, God has great faith in each of us. Why do so many have no faith in God?

Absolutes do exist. Too few admit willingly, to the understanding that *forever and infinity are absolute,* are *Prime Determinants,* concerning what may become (in Time) of every single element in the Universe, including each and every individual. Like it or not, an awareness of this leads to an understanding of two Cardinal Segments of Absolute Truth. ***Reality is irrefutable! Time is irreversible!*** Or, if Time is reversible it is simply another aspect of immutable Time. Too many fail to recognize this. However, if one is able to recognize what is, what is apparent in Time, what is based on a combination of faith, knowledge and understanding, one will have made the first and a most important step toward a better life for themselves and for all, which they might encounter.

***In every instance*,** for reasons accepted by much of the Human Race, if one is not able to accept that Absolute Truth exists, one is making the same mistake as uncounted millions have made in the past. Eve, who could not accept an absolute limitation, too curiously sought *in time* what was forbidden. We suffer, to this day, for such indiscretion, even as *we continue to repeat the same error*, often based on curiosity, impatience or misunderstanding, perhaps all three. Given contemporary instances, where now abominable sin exists as fashion, how many truthfully understand all about Eve? How many utilize positive understanding in the service of their fellow creatures, each and every day, avoid temptation and aspire to holiness?

Heaven is, always has been, and will continue to be a very Universal that is Catholic place![203] This is known for certain![204] All people, no matter what part of this earth is their place of being, can be baptized as Catholic and live according to God's Commandments thus, any that do may be welcome in Heaven. However, *heaven is not a certainty for any individual.* Many believe that all are subject to Divine Judgment. Sectarianism offers various and contrary arguments, determined by false or selfish reasoning. Concerning the meaning of Texts, selfish reason can easily corrupt two millennia of careful and faithful study. This is true because the lies told are believable being mixed with a certain amount of truth. Often such disagreement is editorialized for the sensation that may sell publications. This assertion is made in view of the fact that ***Time provides for all manner and structure of endeavor*** beside which, all human emotions driven by good or evil drive reason, foreshadowing the nature of any consequence. This is precisely why it must be understood that perfect knowledge is not humanly possible. Only Divine Wisdom is perfect and only the Catholic Church has an origin in such wisdom. ***This is an irrefutable*** belief, which must be understood or one may not pretend to believe in Jesus. Often a pretense in belief will carry a too personal inference, from questionable or immature reasoning. Scholar and layman alike should understand that no one human being, in humanly perceived time, has perfect knowledge, and all are burdened by original Sin: personal Sins as well.

Sin has been given other names and has been multiplied, therefore is neither understood as Sin nor is Sin recognized for what it really is. Modernists corrupt Holy thoughts because of errors in their imperfect understanding of discreet Hermeneutics, the concepts within which are dismissed as old-fashioned. The Exegete is not socially conspicuous, or particularly influential when pitted against a rock-star drug addict or a lustful multi-million dollar athlete. Misunderstanding is always compounded when coupled with a biased contextual interpretation, as we find in the presentations found in the usual newspaper and popular magazine articles. Importantly, sin sells. One may be unwilling to admit to the meaning of Omnipotence, because of a peculiar or limited understanding of language. *Meaning has a way of wandering within the language* dependent upon who is speaking and who is listening. This too is a question of placement in Time, since *psychological readiness is a time-sensitive factor* in any dialogue, coupled with the imposition of personality. Inadvertently, without any malice one can be in error and simultaneously be unaware of that same error. This is certainly why Tradition is so important and why it is equally important

---

203 **St. Cyprian:** "Outside the (Catholic) Church there is no salvation. He cannot have God as his Father, who has not the Church, for his Mother." Fr. John Laux, *Church History*, Tan Books and Publishers, Rockford, IL. Pg. 72.

204 **St. Fulgentius:** "Hold most firmly and do not doubt at all: not only all pagans, but also all Jews and all the heretics and schismatic who terminate this present life outside the Catholic Church will go into the everlasting fire prepared for the Devil and his angels." Fr. J. P. Migne, "On the Faith, to Peter," chapter. 38, *Patrologiae Cursus Completus*, Paris 1855, 65:704

to maintain Tradition. The original God-inspired holy Tradition, founded by Christ Jesus is in a pure and unimpaired form. The maintenance of this form is precisely what the Catholic Church has done and precisely what the Bride of Christ will continue to do. The Catholic Church must remain inviolate, for all Time, just as Christ will remain perfect for all time.

Do not be deceived, linguistics notwithstanding, whether or not there is agreement, there can only be one Heaven, one totally inclusive [All], which includes all Time: there is only one infinite place beyond! Because this is absolutely certain, we adjure with the greatest humility, Catholicism covers all human beings, whether they may or may not like it, however this does not in any way guarantee immortality, which requires a Catholic baptism and proper behavior, thus immortality becomes a slight possibility. For whatever reason, many do not believe this, failing to accept that Christ was the first Catholic. To call Christ a Jew is to fail to recognize that Christ and the Ideas, which He defined, were in nearly absolute opposition to those who killed Him. Names and labels may and do infer connotation. In this case the connotation is significant and decisive. He was crucified for his Ideas! Indeed, upon His return, He may once again very well be the only Catholic on earth, having claimed consistency, in spite of the greatest form of suffering

One must consider that no matter what individual persons may think, in all instances human thought individually and collectively, cannot alter, excepting coincidentally, the complexities inherent in one single present moment. Every moment is shared by everyone in the Human Race. What is credited to Human Intelligence, at any given time, is dependent upon specifically known reality, combined with the inventive minds of mostly unknown others. Reality is a *cumulative existential phenomenon* beyond human understanding, excepting with respect to implementation in the service of obvious human needs. All that has been accomplished, in the past, is locked in time and functions as a motivation, albeit not completely understood, compelling the present moment forward toward an indeterminate, excepting coincidental, future Time. From such complexities as have been sustained, Tradition has become and moves forward in a recognizable form, carried by knowledge, which we define generally as the Intellect. Tradition exists as a manner of containment and is embodied in artifact and implement.

Nevertheless, thoughts as having been given to human action, often in ways that are not knowable, do affect future consequence, in an unfolding continuum. Individually, each Human Being only touches a small bit of the reality that enfolds and at times entraps them. Truth is! And, what is truthful is all that is significant! We must admit that all manner of Evil is some part of what is as well. Present adult responsibility is to define, distinguish and truthfully inform those who are destined to live after this time our children and the children of others. To define and to distinguish is a cardinal responsibility, which works toward the sustained continuation of Tradition, our Culture and the more complex Civilization, recognized as the present epoch. Language is the most important single element in maintaining and conveying the meaning of the past to the present. It also provides a way to consider the future *plan* of events. "What are distinguished remains distinguished forever." (Jacques Barzun, *The house of Intellect*).

Furthermore, as has always been the situation, the preponderance of any present thought, though seemingly important, which accounts for much of what the Modernist's claim as their authority will, for the most part, only effect a very few human beings, for a very short time. Actually, this is axiomatic, given the nature of Infinite Time. All Time is as of a moment in becoming. However, Time, as humanly perceived, is discreet and irreversible. Coincidentally, however not incidentally, we come upon another Absolute! ***Time is given as a moment, the smallest portion of eternity.***

Certainly there are very broad categories of thought; however, here we consider individual thought, mostly functional, in reference concerning day to day encounters, such in a very limited time frame. We might suggest that Time can be given to a spherical connotation,[205] thus we acknowledge an abstract Time-surround (See the diagram of a time surround with various implications). Interestingly, what we perceive as a cataclysm, as concerns matters of human behavior, is often nothing more than a multitude of little thoughts placed, at one time within a single sphere, *they are bottled in Time,* so to speak thus to become effectively operational as they are coincident. **We may call what happens within this sphere peaceful existence, social unrest, riot or war.** Categorically, all such instances are the result of many individuals acting irresponsibly; all committing the same manner of *dumb and reprehensible acts simultaneously,* within a given Time-sphere. This can be imagined as one aspect of the simultaneous aspect of sociology and could have immediate fatal consequence, for millions of individuals in the present Century and possibly billions, given the extensive potential of future time! Without knowing exactly how or why, all events are elements of a manner of accumulation.

Propaganda has distorted the general understanding of history. That manner of consequence as referred to immediately above may and does determine the lives of untold millions as a product of Propaganda. Propaganda has a profound effect, utilizing deceitful means, often with devastating result. Propaganda may have some origin in known reality; however ideas may also be contrived for an effect at the time assumed desirable by the perpetrator. We deem such individuals to be in collusion with organized sin, apologists for Evil: they are captured by the Devil. *Victims, of encouraged atrocities* have never been fairly informed of the *distinctions between documented truth and the specious lie.* Importantly, the victor writes the history, which is prejudiced toward the victor's point of view. What is right can be interpreted in different ways, at different times for various reasons, however interpretation does not alter the truth which, even if known and understood may be quite elusive. The objective of propaganda is to persuade and convince large numbers of individuals to think the same.

The distortion of truth has become as a sociological misadventure, influencing even those well informed, certainly the unsuspecting. For example, a group, race, or a nation may be directed toward a determined and hoped for response. The acceptance of a New World Order is a good example. All Dictators attempt to unify opinion behind their cause. If persuasion does not convince everyone, there is always the rope, the whip and the firing squad. We all know, as this work is being written millions are being persuaded to accept one point of view or another, which may or may not be in their best interest. Various forms of conditioning have certainly been attempted in the past. Incidentally, mass marketing techniques use various forms of propaganda, to sell various types of

---

205 The **Time-sphere** refers to a spherical space, within which related activities are enacted.

See diagram on page 109. Given to the size of a succinctly defined sphere, such activities are thereby limited in scope and are necessarily of finite duration. Nevertheless complex occurrence can be interactive in profound ways, irrespective of the size and duration of any contacts within any particular Domain. A single sphere, containing a cluster of events may and has changed the course of world History. Very often the men that inhabit such spaces are lunatics, liars and hypocrites who have been elected, we imagine, by the people? Obama is the latest of such "elected official" that apparently is not satisfied with the way things are. He seems to be an alien that has gotten control of a powerful and effective office. How could this happen. No doubt propaganda and the lie were important ingredients in his election. Time will tell.

merchandise at the appropriate, seasonal time. One can watch this as the fashions is changed, for effect, causing individuals to respond like lemmings. Propaganda is a divisive mixture of the truth, fiction and the lie. Propaganda is an important tool for convincing the unwary and the uninformed. This can may be harmless in some instances, devastating in others.

Once the effect of the propaganda has convinced the masses, it is most difficult to change such opinion, since the propaganda becomes inextricably mingled with the fabric of their consciousness, thus becomes reinforcing of itself. A lie, often told, is perceived as the truth. Amusingly, even now people may purchase eleven and one half ounces of coffee, in what appears to be a one pound can. This is a form of deliberately perpetrated deceit and is dependent upon the past formed habit of who is being deceived. It is clever and helps the bottom line, thus is considered good business. Can any endeavor that is basically dishonest be called good? Where has honor gone, decency? A collective consciousness, which can be controlled dependably is an important tool for Economics and Politics as well as Religion and can be compelling in the promotion of both good and evil. Millions of fools can be counted on to protect the confidence and influence of the propagandist, especially when they are incessantly reminded of their inadvertently assumed responsibility. Such are matters for Mass Media, to augment and to rejuvenate the desired opinions. This presents a very difficult and complex situation, of prime concern, especially when the educational system is controlled, as it too often is, by those who had ordered the propaganda in the first place. How wise are we?

In our Time, because some men are able to benefit and profit from the misery of unknown others, we have a thriving business in the means and implementation of conflict, coupled with a massive and sustained slaughter of the innocents: we call name this collateral damage. For centuries, whilst some clamor to kill others, whom they do not know, power hungry men are engaged in a dialogue of the most seemingly deceitful and reprehensible kind. Such hypocritical dialogue sets the stage for speculators and racketeers, so they may profit from the blood of an unknowing and unsuspecting innocent dupe. Consider saturation bombing, which destroys the homes of millions or abortion, which destroys one helpless unborn infant with each endeavor, we are assisting, by our institutionalized actions, in the propagation of Evil, and the destruction of the Soul of Western Civilization. Saturation bombing and abortion are only two of what Pope John Paul has called, quite properly, the structures of Sin.

The deceitful and clandestine ways as previously mentioned, in which a few manipulate and control the allocation of money and credit, is another primary example; albeit institutionalized theft seems a cleaner business than war or abortion. Nevertheless, the wars being fought today are fought largely because of money, which affords support for ***"The Will to Power."*** Therefore, it is easy to recognize the very profound reciprocity between *two Evils, the perversion of Money and absolute Power,* working in concert toward the annihilation of Goodness. The effects of such goodness stand as evidence attesting to the best characteristics of Western Civilization. Understandably, other Civilizations, Cultures, Nationalities and Races have also prospered, where goodness, with its many implications has been allowed to flourish.

Goodness stands silently and wins no prize
By most abhorred, Goodness is (unfortunately) its own reward
Why is this so?

If we were to face the whole truth, for many it would be quite unbearable. Millions of adults, who might be encouraged to speak out against the various and quite numerous atrocities, are found to be either ill informed or simply complacent. One of the explanations, in this respect, is that families do not find solidarity and greater personal strength in the confines of the home. The humble attitudes and reasoned recommendations of the elders in an extended family, must be more positively considered, more gratefully acknowledged and thereby would receive greater credibility in the scheme of things. However, the *generation gap has been contrive*d to prevent this. Amusements and simple-minded activities distract millions of youth from serious study and an appreciation for what wisdom provides.

The wisdom, of known and loving individuals, must be given more respect. Public Education cannot possibly replace the importance of a good and loving family, mother, father and siblings. In spite of self-interested practitioners who have created a clumsy, archaic and ineffective Bureaucracy, the present system, in the minds of many, does as much harm as good, perhaps more harms than good. Notwithstanding, in spite of the best intentions, anxious attempts at Universal Education, spelled indoctrination, is not education at all. Indoctrination, is brain washing! Brain washing is necessary because those who are in control of both money and the transmission of *information are generally speaking enemies, intellectually and philosophically, of the Western Civilization.* This is not always apparent since control of many avenues of communication is under the influence of an alien intelligence directing what will happen.[206] Of course there exists now as always, the Hypocrite and the opportunist, who will sell his soul for a few coins, just like Judas.

Advertising and propaganda, together with the various contrived television serials, have become too dominant in the formation of manners and habits of a mesmerized population. The opinions of Hollywood producers and super-stars, as well as various unknown others, working behind the scene, should be valued for what they are worth; just about nothing! Recently youngsters have been given the opportunity to play video games, in which they practice killing. Such games are known to have deleterious effects on the minds of children. Youth and young adults should be encouraged to become more firmly cemented to the id of their parents and respected elders, known personally for who and what they are. This can help young adults to form a *genuinely positive* individual character, based on reality, not fiction. Reality provides meaningful opportunity to build a positive, personal Identity. There will exist, in the minds of the young, a more reasonably obvious basis upon which to form the notions of the next generation. This is how Nations, Cultures and Civilizations sustain, in time as they propagate, in kind, from generation to generation. If this is good for Indians and the Black man, it is also good for the White man, in fact, all men! We do not assume to preclude technology, which can be viewed quite independent of both Politics and controlled Education.

At this moment, many seem to have lost their identity and do not know who they are or what, properly and fairly, might be expected from them. Apparently *everyone is an actor playing a role* based on the model of an unknown other. As a result, families are confused and often members are in a state of despair or alienation. The destruction of the biological family, coupled with a malicious attempt to recreate the meaning of the word family, has been encouraged by many nincompoop-would-be-philosophers. Shallow minded and vain intellectuals, some of whom should know better, *support the evil efforts of unknown motivation.* Politically determined compromise, imposed from the top, given the force of law does not help a bad situation.

---

206 **Sutton, Anthony C.** *How the Order Controls Education,* Research Publications, Inc., P. O. Box 39850, Phoenix, Arizona, 1983. ISBN 0-914981-00-5

With the Advent of Democracy and a College Education for all, we find that even the very stupid amongst our numbers; have somehow earned a degree in Higher Education. Because this is so, we find great ineptness in all spheres of intellectual endeavor. Thus the intellect has been weakened. Interestingly, being ill prepared demands a hypocritical pretense. We witness a continued sense of strained vigilance in the work place, thus to sustain what is, in fact, a farce. The farce, often as quite sardonic humor, creates shielded animosity in a more capable peer, who finds himself/herself in a subordinate, thus inferior position. This is all part of the present politics that relies on the intelligent ones to carry the load, even as those that are not as intelligent are given accolades. As one might expect, the time of the most capable may be wasted, in futile attempts to promote ill-reasoned compromise, where there is no appropriately significant ability to understand the complexities of serious problems. *This is a cardinal Causality*, inherent in the realm of imagined equality, women in combat, for example or a redundant, overly presumptive Bureaucracy, such as the seemingly democratic Federal Government. This is an important element, to be sure, a part of an elite plan, the plan to create the One World Utopia. The nature of now need not remain beyond the understanding of an informed citizen.

We have no will to punish who are certain criminals, existing as we do, *captured by a theory of relativity*, **inappropriate for a sociological issue**. Situational ethics confuses our behavior and quietly breeds contempt and indignation. Some have encouraged viewing criminal acts as a manner of entertainment, such interrupted by commercialism, Advertisements and nausea. Petty acts of vindictiveness are featured as humor. Silliness and the crotch comedian, who treats flatulence as a, presumably funny, universal joke fills the air with canned laughter. The encouraged response performs the task of applauding the most venal and silly efforts, of a chosen few. No intelligent human being would applaud nonsense, except as prompted to do so, when compromised by the ignorant participation of others. Silliness is applauded as a matter of being politically correct: nonsense has achieved a great political advantage for the liberal and the ignorant fool.

Commercial nonsense seems pointed at capturing the imaginations of an already distressed and overly self-conscious population. Real scenes from the courtroom, the prison cell and the many bloody and violent atrocities of the streets, are viewed in most homes as the daily news, having become as a form of entertainment. News Programs as well have become somewhat prurient forms of diversion, distraction and entertainment. This is a very powerful weapon for those who control the news. We even have pornographic clips, flossed-buns and nipples, as part of the news. Pretty and shapely young women are always in demand: this is not all bad however there are certainly limits to how far such portrayal should go. Unfortunately, much of the reporting of News is carefully controlled, with motivations cleverly hidden from the general population. The population is victimized, by ignorance and a multitude of politically corrects however bad habits. There exists Real TV, telling it like it is! Additionally, there are the endless special effect sensations, combined with blasphemy, pornography, sit-com nonsense and the Miss America strip contest, to mention a few. Minorities are given roles which are representative of that which, in fact, most do not live up to. With respect, those who do are likely to be vilified by their own brothers, for being traitors. Blasphemy and perversion are given to the minds of all the children in the land of make-believe. Make believe nonsense is pouring out from La, La Land! How much time is wasted on nonsense promoted as entertainment, time which might be better spent? Plato's cave is a living room with the giant screen TV, where the family sits in semi-darkness and in mindless wonderment, views that, which should not be seen.

In our time, foreign invaders are overrunning our country, other Western countries as well. The poor from other nations come to America (Bruce Springsteen, **Pimp in Paradise)**. They come to America for the freedom and prosperity which they imagine will be their reward. When they discover that they can make money with crime and welfare fraud as an occupation, many abandon the simple tasks, which they have done in the past, merely biding their time as beneficiaries of a stupid and negligent, alien controlled system. Greedy Americans, who employ (exploit), them paying as little as possible, will exploit the decent ones. As a consequence, many of their children become anti-social, exhibiting little if any moral restraint, regarding their participation in street crime (Gang violence) and traffic in narcotics, as an income producing occupation. Sin pays much better than an honest job, which might be obtained, by a decent person of average ability. They bring their vices and virtues with them as well as many strange religions, forms of thinking quite distinct and often antagonistic.

Young women are enticed to <u>*spawn bastard babies in America,*</u> a land where ***feeling good is a religion***. Thus the alien, often an illegal alien, may *claim citizenship for a child*, with some manner of support guaranteed for the mother. The mothers can *continue screwing, without the need to marry* or to be a citizen, thus enjoy all of the pleasures of sin at the expense of goodness and compassion, which has become to promote evil. In our time which might be defined as one quite illicit in the history of the world, ***sin and deceit are encouraged,*** promoted by powerful social forces initiated as government sponsored programs and are proclaimed by do-gooders waving the American flag. In our time, the government *promotes sin and the destruction of the family*, perhaps avidly so. Contrarily the most significant and positively good and decent values, defined and clarified for over two thousand years are maligned or ignored.

> *Coincidentally, many martyrs have died for principles, which are deliberately violated*
> *For some short-term advantage by one who is a salesman-become-politician:*
> *The clever few trusted by a philosophically ignorant population.*

In our time, illicit sex is subsidized with billions, designated for the support of *unwanted bastard children*, many of whom will never know their father.[207] What we have managed to do to solve this problem is to assert that there are no illegitimate children, *they have become love children*. We change the meaning of words. Those will become Socialists or Marxists and take their share of the booty. Thereafter *imagine* what existed, for centuries by definition, will no longer exist. We simply refuse to recognize that evil is all about and enjoying an unprecedented political patronage. The *government provides* Ghetto Bunnies with *status as well as financial support* for sinful pleasure, free rent and food for mom and the litter. Public *education condones this* is an alternate form of behavior insisting that shame has no place in the lives of *sinners, become wards* of the state. As a consequence of this, illicit behavior supported by the ignorance **and the ingratiating manner of our elected leaders,** millions live in squalor in our crowded, crime ridden cities. Millions more will spend their time in a similar situation. Those who feel they *deserve better* often become involved in crime, soon thereafter they find themselves in prison. With wasted lives they seek pity and a form of legitimate employment. This sounds good however they have no developed abilities and certainly not the sense of moral responsibility necessary to act dependably. Television Productions, concerning crime, suggest that anyone can become a different person, from what they have grown to be, which may be true ***in a few instances***. However, what one has become is difficult to alter, especially when intelligence and a positively determined will is lacking, as is perhaps generally the case, with those committed to jail-time.

---

207 **Bastard,** a person born of parents not married to each other; an illegitimate child. Of illegitimate birth or of uncertain, origin. Webster, New World Dictionary. *The word bastard is discouraged in public discourse for being unfair or too negatively subjective.* (Italics by this author).

Millions have worked hard to build the Western Civilization and this nation. Other millions watch as it is being brought to ruin. The Central Cities, in many instances, have become War Zones, Detroit, Saint Louis, and Los Angeles: almost all are, in places, run down crime zones. Within these very crowded and decaying cities unruly and ignorant youth, not to imagine lazy, threaten all that would venture there. Young, arrogant morons with nothing but the clothes on their backs *imagine they have some right to the turf,* which they quite tenaciously occupy. Often a pubescent with too much money and a too small brain can make a fortune dealing in narcotics. The Police seem afraid to discipline the children. Certainly the police are constrained by eager lawyers who can convict the police, however not the criminal, who may have killed his wife and friend, or perhaps a dozen young ladies. This is so because of strange legalities, which target the keepers of the peace for imagined crimes against the criminal populations. And it is difficult to prove who committed a crime. How then shall the general population be protected? In Time, the system has *seemingly* been deliberately corrupted by complexities, which no one seems to understand: or can they?

Police appear to be under great suspicion, even as the intent is to develop a national or world police force. Nevertheless, the criminal, very likely, will not be convicted, regardless of any evidence. In America and some other Nations when indicted, criminals are treated with great respect for his/her human rights. All this happens while many good families are disintegrating because of the awesome pressure asserted by taxation without representation and the IRS. There are many considerations; however, there is still time to adopt a Universal that is a Catholic, approach to healing many of our present problems.

Time being what it is and what it is not, the assumption is that all will turn out well for most in almost any situation. Even evil and despair have a way of strengthening one's understanding and inciting one's soul with a greater energy and compassion. We have seen an awesome improvement in technology with all of the things that some associate with a notion of progress. Nevertheless, no one has found a way to change or alter the nature of Time and the effects that Time has on all living things, human, plant and animal. The course of history can be viewed as a line or as many lines converging on the present moment. In convergence, history is a conical phenomenon. We can imagine this or describe this understanding; however it will not alter time, not even a little. Light provides that an image in time can travel a great distance. To the individual light rays and what those carry can be seen here and now. (See illustrations on movement and the conical formation being written of).

Ethereal aspects of existence are not well understood nevertheless, they do have consequence, which may be of profound significance. The heat emitted by a living organism is an ethereal element as is the frequency of every human cell.[208] All such frequencies are measured in time. *The magnitude and amplitude of any resonance is related to a cyclical reality, also measured in time: all waves sum to zero. Magnitude and amplitude as well as frequency are time-space phenomenon.* Significantly, many understand the mechanical and physical aspects of such jurisdiction; however few would comprehend the spiritual dimensions. Just now the human mind is discovering the nature of minutely small impositions which, in fact, have a monumental effect on the human person. Disease, as a malfunction in time, is something to consider. Metaphorically, the inside of a cancer patient can be likened to the workings of a great city, nevertheless the individual

---

208 Gerber, Richard MD. *Vibrational Medicine.* The #1 Handbook of subtle-energy therapies. Third Edition, Bear and Company, Rochester, VT. 05767. © 2001 Richard Gerber. ISBN 1-879181-58-4.

person is much more complex however, not as extensive as a city and far less obvious. A tumor may be likened to the black hole, which exists in a galaxy. Both are impositions and draw from surrounding domains any element of significance that would be beneficial to their becoming. The difference between the universe and the inside of one's body can be compared metaphorically thus to determine the nature of an immutable esthetic. *Picasso,* bite your lip, what you imagined and bungled through was really as nothing.

The Universe is God centered. Nevertheless, one can conceive of the individual as being a discreetly formed sensory center, of an apparent infinity. It is impossible to imagine the end of space. However, one can conceive that light, being what it is may travel a path of profound curved complexity, given the space, which is infinite. In so traveling, it may return to a point of origin, compelled by a singular human Brain, thereby reconstructing a form from the past. This is a complex and far-flung notion. *However God will choose who shall become as an Angel;* how He will do this can never be known. Individually, we hope in time we will be chosen, thus to reside in Heaven and to be *"somehow"* an eternal being. By some miracle, all Time will be united in a far away Eternity, one moment at a time. If the energy within an atom can be so powerful so as to compel a mass of matter outward, then the energy of the All could compress, collect, distribute, divide reconstitute or form in any way, all that is. This in fact has already happened.

The Universe is here. Now!
A Thought requires no space: A Thought is ephemeral!

Chapter XIII

What about Opposing Religions

There are many opposing Religions come into being since Christ was on the earth.
Most have lasted a short time and have then been extinguished by disagreement.
Judaism and Islam have been somewhat exceptional in our own epoch.
Those are openly antagonistic to Christianity our universal Faith.
The Jews imagined their Messiah as a powerful warrior.
Who would conquer the World for them?
Those are vain and selfish thoughts:

Both are Mortal Sins.

Christ is believed to have been a gentle man.
As the Son of God, Christ claimed complete authority.
After His crucifixion he was raised and ascended into Heaven?
This is one of the profound understandings that motivate Catholicism.
This is not speculation: the Church's history of miracles supports this.
The understanding was (IS) that Christ came to redeem all men:

The best of all men?

Catholicism is a complete Theology, noting left to chance.
This disturbs those that would destroy Catholicism.
What is perfect and timeless is bound to win.
The Catholic Church is inviolate, infinite.

All Religions are not equal.

Some Jews promote this kind of thinking as defense against what is perfect.
Jewish scripture without the New Testament is flawed, imperfect: excludes Christ,
False Religions that have developed because of man's misunderstanding are not equal.
Those are only partialities, they are either incomplete poorly conceived or heretical.
Men have excluded certain elements that have been found to be inconvenient.
This is part of Satan's plan to destroy the Catholic Faith and Theology.
Right now there is great agitation for homosexuality, a mortal Sin.
Homosexuality was considered an abomination: a worst Sin.
It was also considered a mental illness to be treated.
Presently homosexuality is considered a life style.
We should reconsider this dilemma more intelligently.
Simply, discouragement would prevent much of what is happening.
The Law has come to favor most what is Evil rather than what is good.
Much of the present Law has been devised and promoted by false forms of scholarship.
In the Law, some Jews have played a decisive role in promoting their own religion.
Jewish scholarship is not Christian and has opposed much of Christianity.

There are five thousand years of History.
This is a very difficult Issue to approach?

And, we may not forget the role of money?

Money is Power, Control and Luxury.

Those with the most money now control most all governments.
Certainly, in our environment great wealth will control the World.
This has been the hope of all that are selfish and vain: Total control?
This is an archaic notion however it is working well at present.
Generally, it has always been this way
The United States, with a free people, was chosen.
It has been invaded and overrun by opportunists and thieves.
We are now being captured, as opportunists and thieves captured Russia.
What happened to all the gold that belonged to Russia: Did the invaders steal it?
What about the one hundred forty thousand acres of land owned by the Ruling family?
Are you aware many of the revolutionaries were imported from New York?
They were Zionist Jews become American Citizens to accomplish this
Jacob Schiff was Mr. Money twenty million for the cause.
Schiff was an impostor an opportunistic, Zionist Jew.
Beside Revolution & killing there are other means

The Federal Reserve is one of the means:

A German-Jewish Banker devised the Federal Reserve System,
He has been long dead however the evil that was in his plan is working well.
Paul Moritz Warberg was his name, he was clever however not wise.
Cleverness is never wisdom, is rather divisive and dishonest.
The Federal Reserve is so corrupt it may be called an abomination.
A scourge on the people and their productivity; nevertheless the people are unaware.
The only way to cure our financial dilemma is to simply
change the structure of the Federal Reserve.
Place the issuance of currency and coining of money back
in the hands and control of Congress:
Which is comprised of citizens, people of this country: not foreign-born and alien Bankers.

Nothing else will work!

Our latest President, considered by many as another Traitor, will make things worse.
He is believed to be a foreign born Bedouin alien to Christianity, our way of life.
Should he be impeached or voted out from the highest office in the Land?
He is as an **alien,** as the Zionist Jew or the Islamic fundamentalist.
The **Idea** of a one-World government is totally impossible.
It will have to be managed with the force of weaponry.
Nothing else will work unless drugs in the water.
Total control always demands **total control.**

There are some others as well who help in destroying the Faith that the people have in Christ.
We state, not all Jews or Moslems have worked so hard to undermine Catholicism.
Some have succeeded to a great extent in calumniating the Church of God.
With lies, thievery and subterfuge many have worked their mischief.

The Lie and deceit are the profound assistants of Thievery.

What about the Islamic Fundamentalists?

**As Islam is once again becoming more a part of the world scene,
It is becoming a certain moral threat to Europe and other places as well.**
Many of their radical **Ideas** are a real threat to our Civilization and our way of life.
Some Muslims are inculcating their children with a perverted hatred of Christian peoples.
Most of such children will never be able to throw off the effects of such teaching.
Those children are being taught to hate, that it is an honor to die for Allah.
If one can kill Christians in the process it is even better.
This is an insane **Idea,** archaic and selfish.

Europe is in a bad state right now with the militants.
Those carry signs and posters and are not stopped from doing this.
Some signs and posters advocate beheading and dismemberment of their enemies.
Some Muslims have imagined that all in the world are their enemy.
Everyone who is not a Muslim is a presumed enemy.

Those are seen in the light of day with this form of intimidation.
Apparently the Police do not stop them in their practice of inspiring hatred.
Those are not stopped because Europeans feel free expression is a right for everyone.
Those understand our weakness our inability to distinguish between freedom and license.
We are so kind we cannot define what is insurrection and revolution against our ways.
We must wait until things are much worse, when there may be no longer hope.
Then we might strike back with the full force of a watered down Law.
Europeans think of life as a process of Socialistic-experiment.
They imagine that everyone wants to be as they are.
If the rich can gain more, they are happy.
Greed and laziness is their way.

They are dreaming!

The Crusades, against which many moderns have voiced a negative opinion, continue.
Many of our Professors have blasted the Crusades with no significant understanding.
We imagine therefore any valid concept will lead to a truthfully peculiar form of existence.
Have now forced men to fight for their right to be who those are.
This unfortunately is not Christian, which is a tragedy.
Christ taught that every man was your brother

The militant Muslim mind-set was formed centuries ago and has not improved.
It is archaic and barbaric and has grown from ignorance locked in fear.
The real militants do not work or build anything of lasting value.
Rather those destroy what others have built and nurtured.
Those are a real threat to humanity and to themselves.
Hatred and ignorance keeps them from truth.

This is the truth, life is like that.

We imagine therefore any valid concept will lead to a truthfully peculiar form of existence.[209]
In the instance of the computer and the Internet, *this has already happened. In this instance a few men have seemingly brought us a small distance closer to eternity:*
All time and that, which is infinite.

Keep in mind, what is infinite is beyond measurement: it is a Godly-distance!
Infinitesimally small quantum or photons are sent abroad then reconstituted as pixels on a screen, or voices on the telephone, or music from a string, each of, which has a form of phenomenal significance:
With an appeal to a sensory mechanism: driven by the human brain.

In the ancient past who would believe that the sounds from a string could be so beautiful?
If man can do this, God certainly can, since God shares a
small part of His Intelligence with any man.

Wise men will work in unison to better the human race:
Thus to become eventually one in being with the Father:
From whom all good things come.

This is a universally Catholic notion.

They who fight us should join us. Those who hate us should be patient and attempt to love us.
At the very least they should attempt to tolerate us and understand what we are saying,
Such understanding is necessary so that the World can survive in harmony.
The Moslem faith is exclusive and intolerant which is not what a Faith should be.
All Faith must be reasonably tolerant even concerning disagreements in dogma and procedure.

We must work together or we may be compelled to die in defense of what is good or servicing what is evil.

Between good and evil only two choices exist,

Either you are with me or you are against me (Christ): Son of God who moves as a Spirit.

*

* *

---

209 Brown, Walt. *In the Beginning. Compelling Evidence for Creation and the Flood.*

ADDENDUM A
Give some thought to God

Those that insist there is no God do not understand what or who God is
In Catholic Theology God is a tripartite Infinity, meaning He exists as a Trinity;
Father, Son and Holy Ghost as Spirit: *Existentially so.*
For unbelievers He exists as an Idea. The Idea is persistent and will not go away

His Spirit is a part of and within all space no one can escape this: it is like that!
God is more masculine than feminine being the progenitor of all that exists
Men cannot deny the Holy Spirit as an important part of reality
God, the most *important part* of reality cannot be denied

God is the entity that ties man to infinity, to all that is beyond man
To be one in the father, from whom all good things come
Is to be one, with an infinite and timeless entity
An infinite entity is beyond known Time

What is infinite can have no manner of corporal restrictions
Infinity is boundless and timeless, as it must be
What is infinite cannot be seen or touched
Infinity is as God and is the ALL!

These are profound and complex issues, which were carefully studied in the past
In America our educational system centers on job training rather than thinking
There is very little Philosophy and even less Theology in Public Education
Individuals are not being taught to think very deeply or profoundly
Individuals are being taught to conform to imagined needs
In America at present such needs are mostly imposed
Those are made to appear very important
By who will profit from them

This is Commercialism

Such is a modern tragedy, which should be reversed
Because of this people do not understand what those are doing
The information given is generally in between the commercial messages
And has been heavily edited, by unknown alien strangers, with personal objectives
See footnote v, below.
Those working in the Information Industry are not generally aware of serious thought
They are functionaries for what is only *imagined as necessary* to do their job
Now Imagination controls what is done without reference to Fact?
Fact is difficult to find in a world of make-believe
Fact, as Truth, is God centered

It must be this way

Give some thought to God

During and since the Enlightenment Period and The French Revolution
The men who we consider Philosophers have done great damage to The Civilization
Those have given a worldly and more mundane notion to their thought forms
This is difficult to understand and historically is a very subtle occurrence
One cannot pick a single person as being responsible for all that is

What we witness as the Contemporary Scene is a monstrosity
The welding of one incorrect thought to another gives us the monstrosity
The wars and destruction and the wholesale slaughter of people is a part as well
This is not godly behavior, however by some is considered necessary to advance a cause

Men who think this way are *miscreants,* cowards and opportunists
Many have never learned about reality, what it means to be a decent person
Such as those continue to wallow in their own silly ideas and make them even worse
Technology has aided and abetted the means for killing a mother's son

At present in America the girls are being called to serve as *killers of strangers*
Those come home and recite how the enemy is just like those are
Nevertheless those will go back and begin killing again
This is our way, just now, which is the wrong way

This is what has been taught in our *great Institutions of learning?*
We have learned no real philosophy and certainly no Theology, this is sad
Men function because of particular thought patterns, which take time to develop
One cannot separate important and timely thinking from the acts of men

Joseph Stalin, Karl Marx, Roosevelt, Churchill, Soros, Obama
Were all cut from the same tainted, smelly, soiled and dirtied linen?
Philosophers and some thinkers of our Modern Age did soil their clothing
It will be difficult to launder what is so indelibly formed in such a soiled fabric

More and more the fabric is woven by worldly and uncaring men and now women
Those are becoming wealthy beyond reason as they *work at their assumed tasks*
The little people of whom there are more and more have less of what remains
The rich will eventually have it all: The really poor have near nothing.

How might one correct such malfeasance without the help of *God as Spirit?*
We do many things well however are negligent given what is really important
We must reform our thought patterns to conform to goodness and decency
We must withdraw from all war, which is totally destructive

This will not be an easy task with so much invested interest and, of course, money

Give some thought to God

God resides where all Space, Matter and Time are one
In being with the Father[1]
The presumption is that God is the ALL, the progenitor of the Universe

Heaven is that place where man, some men, expect to meet with God
This is an Issue of ***Learning and Belief*** and varies from Culture to Culture
Modern Philosophers have no competent understanding of this Issue
Most are too concerned with *their own position in the Field*

There are some exceptions however those are very few
This is a generalization since names are unimportant, meaningless
Significant issues are not timely; they are outside of Time as humanly perceived
Infinity is difficult to understand, even for the very best of mind

The Ten Commandments give direction to moral certitude and honor
This direction is found inappropriate to the ruling Zionist-Anglo Establishment
Such direction is contrary to the present Tenor of Contemporary Civilization
This is why Socialists are attempting to remove religion from the scene

It is apparently a must do for the Socialists: to them this is the correct behavior
Modern Civilization is somewhat Pagan-like and is often quite retrogressive
Recently, this has been obviated, by body piercing and excessive tattooing
The disregard for marriage is also a telling sign of a Pagan existence
People who shack up generally are unable to act responsibly

Such Individuals are too self centered, are uncaring and unstable
A Civilization requires just the opposite, caring for others and stability
Without this no Civilization can sustain. To be civilized is to be not Pagan
Paganism brings forward the ignorance and intellectual monstrosities from the past

Ignorance and prurient curiosity are now exploring and following much of the Occult
What has been displayed for seventy-five years in Comic Books is coming to the fore
This is a reversion back to childhood and infancy and this is not healthy for adults
All of this finds its way to us as humor by the gestured and funny comedian

Interestingly our Philosophers and thinkers were enamored by Occultism
Interestingly Sigmund Freud and Karl Marx were hooked on the subject
Marx was an adulterer with an illegitimate son, and was a drunk
The entire Intellectual Establishment still stands in awe

Over this depraved and drunken nit-wit

Robert Fiedler, Aug. 21, 2010

Addendum B

Who are the devil, Satan and Lucifer?

What do they do?

What can they do?

This is a somewhat perplexing issue. First and foremost
The Devil, Satan and Lucifer are embodiments of evil
Those are all metaphorical and real, simultaneously
They all live in the person of various individuals
Warp the personality of man and destroy his Soul

Most individuals consider them as individual persons
Those are a threat to all forms of decency and goodness
They search, for a manner of being that might contain them
Those have been given to occupy a special place, which we call Hell
Artists have given them grotesque and human-like form with horns and tails

When we were children we were told that the Devil was sitting on our shoulder
We were encouraged to knock him off so he would not influence our behavior
We imagined, knocking him off and would be good for the rest of the day
This was a game we all played: this notion did help us to be good
We did good things and were proud of what we had done
We did not commit evil acts ignoring the Devil

Who now thinks of such things?

The Devil can be a metaphor or he can be a real person
Evil is everyplace at the same time, in competition with goodness
As such the Devil is a spirit, somewhat like God, however with a different intent
The intention of God the progenitor is to foster all manner of goodness
Whereas the Devil is the father of all forms of evil

The Devil's workings are insidious and persistent
Once admitted to the personality the devil has a destructive effect
The heinous crimes and mayhem, of which we here are the works of the Devil
The Devil invades and then possesses the personality and soul of man
And works his evil against others in the community

This is reality combined with metaphysics
Evil begets
Evil

What about the dialectic of communication?

When forming groups, men must have common understanding

Such understanding is dependent upon a form of language
The explanations run asunder when meaning is conveyed incorrectly
Many things can be understood by inference whereas some things must be explained
The Devil knows what is said is not always what is heard exactly as intended
This is a problem with all forms of verbal communication

Add to this that the man speaking may not be telling the whole truth
This causes the message to be distorted for the effect it will have on the listener
Many of the thoughts that people have today are incorrectly motivated by such distortion
The entire Civilization stands beholden to the great lies, of a few unknown others
Propaganda makes great and meaningful use of this kind of subterfuge

Within any group there are personal antagonisms, some serious
Keep in mind those bear on the thinking of the individuals within the group
Such antagonisms have origin in obscure places and are not always well understood
Aggressive types tend to dominate and those are not always correct
The thinking of the most aggressive may be least correct

We have too many words with too little well understood meaning
The greater the context the more likely we will have continued conflict
The World with distinct populations cannot be ruled under a single dictum
Men that pretend and imagine this are Fools, or opportunists that intend to rule
When men speak of world government one can assume those are improperly educated

The Faith of the people is an important ingredient in any form of culture or Civilization
There does now exist, a Universal Faith however; most of the World rejects this
We must begin by considering what, is faith and try to better understand
Without a truthful consensus there will always be conflict
Our consensus is based on shortsightedness

Our technologies do not serve us well
We fight wars without knowing what to do in peaceful times
Too much of our economy is designed to profit from conflict, which is tragic
What is spent for fighting can be better spent in other ways
Millions are starving and have no means

How might this be corrected?

A few do profit
Too much

How might the Devil succeed in such instance?

The Devil will take advantage of such inadvertence
In the U. S., our Constitution somewhat prevented the Devil's participation
Men that were well educated to understand the meaning of the Christian Faith wrote it
There was a real empathy for decency and also for fair play and for goodness
Nevertheless the men were not all perfect those too were sinners

It is said that some engaged in fornication and had illegitimate children
This was wrong however those were ruled by a different set of circumstances
However those did understand what those were doing much better than at present
The entire collective Id was at fault, which no single man could correct
In a sense, a form of ignorance infected them much like today

Our Constitution pays much attention to God and to Truth
It is not contrived, as is the false Anglo- Zionist political agenda of today
There was little reason for lying and no reason to cheat so as to gain greater wealth
The present structure, Anglo-Zionist controlled has many near fatal flaws
It represents a collision between opposing Faiths, is old and worn

Honest men must carefully study our Reality
The Devil must be kept at bay away from any decisions
Our Reality must be reformed in favor of Christian goodness, Catholicism
Many will find this assertion unappealing however it is the only thing that will work
The Devil has been given too much time and too much authority

At this junction let us consider, what is Catholicism
It is Christ centered goodness simply stated, and it is certainly effective
It is a complete Theology without the interference of opposing schismatic Religions
This is an important point, referring to the Devil and his agents Satan and Lucifer
The Devil has worked unceasingly to destroy Catholicism and Humanity

Few people understand the true meaning of Faith and of Religion
The teaching of Faith was attempted by education at various times in the past
In the public domain much is made of Hebrew scholarship, less is made of Christianity
America is a Christian nation that has been commandeered by alien forces
The alien forces seem determined to destroy Catholic Christianity

Like the spirit of God, the spirit of the Devil is in every man
The advent of Christ was that human event that foretold of the coming of goodness
Until then, the world was dominated by the forces of ignorance, by Evil, and by darkness
We imagine ancient religions took advantage of a slave population to build Temples
Their Temples were misappropriated to their false Gods and to man

The World has suffered because of this!
It continues to suffer

What will the Devil do next?

This question will be answered by each and every man

This question is considered and answered every day of every life
Some answers are more important than others and have more certain veracity
Celebrity status gives answers more credit, people believe seemingly important people
A moron that plays a guitar or bounces a ball is heard and believed by millions
Whereas a wise man will remain unknown and is not often heard from

His message is lost in the clamor

What makes the difference is money:
Enter Greed: how much can be made on the deal
This is a salesman's mentality determining the nature of important Issues
The salesman together with the politician rule at the present moment
The present moment is under the domination of a moneyed elite
The common denominator is the coins on the table
The gold coins are now transformed into worthless paper
This is one of Satan's tricks it's called inflation and for some feels real good
The feeling is only temporary, as it is a strangulation process, which few comprehend
With all the funny money ignorant individuals feel secure; still they have no real money
Their money is transformed into credit, an enticement to over spend for sure

At present we are seeing some of the effects of this "credit squeeze"
They are certainly not pretty and those are worldwide and getting worse
The system must be corrected before it destroys all that has been accomplished
The world won't come to an end however many will suffer because of greed
The nature of the beast is relentless and is not well understood
Greed is one of Satan's best tools, inherent in every man
It is not possible to satisfy greed, which feeds on itself and others
Greed is the opposite of self-denial and is a very difficult emotion to deal with
Greed is a mortal Sin meaning it is a totally debilitating and disarming Sin
Right now the world, this United States requires a form of self-denial

Forget the American Dream it is really just a sales pitch

What we have is a deliberately imposed nightmare: Inflation!
The result of malicious ignorance espoused by experts that pretend to know
Using mathematics those attempted to cover what those were doing so to be able to sell
To an unsuspecting and trusting public on a worldwide scale, this is ***real clever***
One wonders how much did the thieves profit, it their dishonesty

Satan's form is always evil and debilitating for sure

ADDENDUM C

Belief, is Directed by Understanding, is Directed by Belief

The Real Chicken-Egg Syndrome

Understanding is what determines Belief. Levels of understanding determine comprehensiveness and one's ability to believe one idea or another.

Belief renders understanding and modifies thought, in that it directs or manages thought and ideas as they coalesce and, or formulate, within the consciousness of the individual. What happens presents a very complex method of occurrences, which leads to what are considered as understanding and knowing. In matters of the mind, there are distinct and significant differences between coalescence and formulation. These are Issues that involve a certain degree of complex medical knowledge with attendant experience.

Coalescence is the unconscious coming together, the amalgamation of thought increments or bits. It is of great significance that one knows where the "bits" are coming from. *Ideally, the correct bits would be offered within the curriculum of the institution of education in harmony with the spiritual and intellectual needs of the students.* In an oxy-moronic setting of Multi-Culture this is not possible since the basic tenants of most philosophies and theologies are antagonistic each toward some or all others. Certainly one can study and compare present Cultures and study Civilizations from past Time. However such study is often corrupted by religious and political beliefs. Each such "Segment" does provide a subject of its own. Right now some forms of Muslim thinking are very antagonistic toward Christianity: other religions as well. Nevertheless all Muslims are not all bad people; there are good ones as well.

Formulation is the conscious combining or arrangement of thought increments or bits, in a rational and knowable continuum. **A Bit** or portion is [as it is] as a consequence of placement in time, position in order or arrangement in extension. Individually, a thought matrix or perceived ideational construct, as well as an induced personal imagery may be received as a portion of an individually lived thought process and is a continuum, inputting toward what is psychic; a form of personal awareness: extended in a singularly personal Mind's Complexity.

This is phenomenology combined with a small portion of reality. The mind, that is the brain, is ultimately complex and is proprietary in handling all manner of thought forms: from genius to idiot. Even and Idiot has brain function necessary to complete all of the necessary processes to maintain life in such being. This is true of every form of malignancy and disarrangement in the human person. When the brain ceases to function the life given is stopped. In a political sense some individuals are prone to become temporarily idiot-like to accomplish a perverted objective. Here the imagination also plays an important role in stirring up adversaries to a point of lunacy. All of this is related in very subtle ways and is difficult, perhaps impossible to understand.

It is difficult to presume whether or not understanding is modified by belief or whether or not the reverse is true, although many do try. In most cases this complex enigma may be assumed as a constant. It matters little or not at all, whether this is completely understood, since the outcome is what is important and what will initiate the next moment of understanding.

Moments of understanding are critical, since understanding, as implicit within an idea, is very likely to change from moment to moment, thus any act may be based on a fleeting moment whereas a pertinent act may have long term, even fatal Consequence for millions: as in War. Thus, understanding may be considered as a momentary Determinant of critical importance.

Beliefs are more certainly stable, having been formulated into systems of thought, which may be and are learned through an extended period of experience or careful study. *Tradition* is what we call such extended systems of thought and motivation for action. However, aimed at the destruction of much that is good, ***the carefully contrived incompetence of the Modernist*** insists that our youth, they that most require the support of our Western Tradition, should abandon that same Tradition. *Such Subterfuge manifests as a combination of deceit and treachery leading the young,* those incapable of significant and mature understanding, away from what is fundamental to the development of the Western Civilization and inherent Cultures. All significant religious, political, economic and sociological systems of thought have an implicit foundation in the past and are based on current beliefs and extended toward an unknown, however somehow presumed future.

Truth must be known, so as to encourage proper and correct thinking. Thinking becomes problematic when truth remains hidden. Often, because of Greed and an insatiable need to dominate others, the truth is hidden, subverted or simply unknown, which is *the most serious and unfortunate Tragedy of the human race.* Truth may remain unknown as a consequence of ignorance or because of the superimposition of the *Lie,* which casts a long and persistent shadow. *The Liar and the Hypocrite have caused irreparable damage to the human race*, millions of who found a too-early grave; the victims are counted in tens of millions.

Profound Truth is too often disregarded. Often the most profound truth is simply beyond the comprehension of those that would benefit most from the wisdom contained therein. Additionally, the lie is often exploited by personal **Ego** for personal gain; this is especially true concerning matters of economic consequence. It is a sad situation, however certainly true, that falsehoods are often exploited for personal economic gain, in service of the **Ego** in every field of endeavor. Political, economic and military propaganda has corrupted the mind content, hence the Understanding as well as the Beliefs of the entire Civilization, excepting only those who understand the truthful meaning of the often-tainted content of Mass Communication. Such understanding is difficult to comprehend and it is impossible to correct outcomes in advance of any significant act.

Ethics and Christian Honor are nearly absent, where important decisions are made which affect the lives of millions and may ultimately affect billions of individuals. ***The knowledge required to develop the necessary understanding of present time is mostly lacking, having been supplanted by the tainted will of secret endeavor.*** Mythologies, lingering from the past, have surfaced and persist in spite of evidence that proves ***reality is not a story told by an Idiot.*** Distractions, particularly the Theatre and Mass Spectacles, which earn billions for the promoters, lead the population away from meaningful study and the thoughtful presence, which is necessary, to gain significant understanding. It is Tragic that most individuals do not care and are not properly equipped to consider even the rudiments of the elements involved. Disneyland Sentiment does nothing to solve this serious dilemma.

There exist a deliberately contrived destruction of the family and *the imposition of blatant ignorance on the meaning of marriage,* pertinent to the continuity of the species, the culture and the civilization, which presents a mortal calamity. Mass media has pounded away at the meaning of honor, continuance, and every form of Virtue relating to the marriage vows and the begetting of children. They have attempted and are succeeding in destroying the need for and value of veracity. The "Girly Magazines," Pornography and the too-influential Reprobates, have compromised virtue even as those have presented the most raucous and degrading content to our Children. Irresponsible and curious adults have exploited and maimed children in unforgivably indecent ways. **Youth is sacrificed** so that a *vain political imposition* may flourish, **driven by [THE] will to power** seated in greed, vanity and subterfuge all are mortal SINS.

We live in a World saturated with Sin. This is not new. It has been this way for a long time. In prior times it was largely a matter of ignorance and one's ability to communicate with others. Presently we have solved much of the problem of ignorance and are able to communicate with fluency amongst millions of individuals. These are good signs and given our advancing technologies some things are definitely improving. What is required is a better understanding of how Philosophy and Religion, misunderstood as they are, can be brought to serve goodness rather than evil. Additionally ancient and cabalistic forms of thought should be eliminated or brought to where they cannot and would not corrupt the life of every person on the planet. Economic reality must be more fairly and honestly approached so that money becomes a means of exchange and not a means to enslave the population. At present the Civilization is being strangled by the improper understanding and use of money.

Finally, the compounding of interest on debt currency, which is perhaps the greatest form of deceit in the history of the world has provided for the consolidation of assets in the hands of just a few, become powerful by such means. Economically powerful individuals steer the maggot like institutions protected by a legally contrived corporate shield. Those are maggot-like in there consuming of the personal and familial elements within the Catholic Christian, Western Civilization. The dealings are deliberately made to appear too complex for the common mind, thus to avoid detection. Before too long the familial, social, intellectual, economic and spiritual destruction to Family, Culture and Civilization will be complete.

<u>*There will be no return for you or your children: Never!*</u>

The Call is to Wake Up, before you are dead! The noose is being tightened every day!

Other books by this author:

Money Murder madness, IUniverse, Ind. Press: *ISBN-13: 978-0-595-41500-7 (pbk).*
   ISBN-13: 978-0-595-85849-1 (ebk).

Musings, Greed Love and Indignation,   *ISBN: 978-0-595-42901-1 (pbk)*
IUniverse, Independent Press   *ISBN: 978-0-595-87238-1 (ebk)*

The Desruction of America, XLibris, Ind. Press: *ISBN 13 Hardcover: 978-1-4415-2629-8*
   ISBN 13 Softcover: 978-1-4415-2628-1

In Honor of Geri, IUniverse, Ind. Press: *ISBN: 978-1-4502-3009-4 (pbk).*
   ISBN: 978-1-4502-3010-0 (ebk).

*

*   *

ADDENDUM D

Traitors Within Our Midst

It is most difficult to imagine that, amongst whom we have elected to lead and protect our nation
Are included so many Traitors; betraying our Nation, our Principles and our People[2]
We the People are led like sheep to the "slaughter of the innocents"
Abortion, Entertainment, Theft, Pornography and the IRS
Have forged a new form of indebted-Slavery
Millions live in humiliating poverty
How and why has this happened?
$ As only a few pile up billions in money $[3]
Billions of which are spent on lavish accommodations?[4]
And a life-style (so-called) that would shame any decently ethical man [5]
Unfortunately such thievery is associated with worldly success
And the compounding of assets, is the silent partner[6]
To all such lucrative activities, decent or not
And, Sin and moral corruption, are[7]
The most lucrative activities
Good is most forgot
Ready or not
Corruption
Sin

The Ideas that motivate much of present activities are not clearly understood[8]
By a people that are incessantly entertained away from serious and historically correct learning[9]
Fairytales abound in a land dominated by the lustful hound and the Directors at the Bank
Greed is certainly an important part of any social equation other sins as well
Yet we dare not mention Sin, the Law is on the side of the sinner
There are so many and they do vote in the contrived elections
Politicians depend on the prattling that accompanies all such occasions[10]
Our Leaders have curious understanding of how a world's people should be cast
The Crowd is numbed by the pretense that accompanies the presence of the chosen ones
What form of disposition has been gained by all of what may have happened in a distant, past?[11]
Somehow ideas, of which only a few are aware, are now combined into what is manifest as the present
Narrow-minded Usurpers, imagine the present must lead to
what is presumed as a well-planned Future[12]
A complex Hyperbole is what, seemingly, promotes the actions of those that are the most influential
Most still stand in awe of Greek and earlier Mythologies, which have combined with reality
Mythologies do not die easily: they become a part of generalized thought patterns[13]
Thought patterns as formed by public education are beholden to an alien view[14]
Thereafter such thought patterns are very much self-perpetuating[15]
And most assuredly they influence much of what then follows as common understanding
Which understanding is "force-formed" by those that control means and patterns of communication?[16]
No man has perfect knowledge and all are victimized by
deceit, by the imposition of liars and hypocrites
We are a nation, imagined as governed, by consensus in
response to a well-formed Constitution
It is tragic; that so many decisions are made by appointed surrogate functionaries, Judges and "Czars"
Many are determined to destroy what history has brought forth as a very fair form of governance
It is incomprehensible nevertheless true; those in the highest positions are beholden to Evil
The good, decent and the humble will be managed by others of a quite different nature

150

TRAITORS WITHIN OUR MIDST

At any given time it is difficult to positively identify who are in opposition to free men
Secret Societies have worked to hide the activities of those that are the enemy of most of humanity
And, those so involved have denied the existence of that; which guides the most powerful political forces
This is largely an economic issue because money has become a commodity and controls what happens
Much of government, is a charade of black-handed politics which falsifies the reality of the Civilization
Thus, those with the most money control the nation's government as well as the nation's law
This is nothing new; of course, it is Reality plain and simple
Nevertheless, it is a fatal flaw
Most Kings, all Pirates and certainly all the Robber Barons have always known this[17]
**The general population is occupied from day to day and is
now distracted with spectacular amusement**
Nevertheless, the population is entitled to some form of diversion from mundane Activities
Such diversions, have been cleverly and compellingly commercialized,
So to mesmerize the citizen, television is the prime mover
Dominating the Ideas that fill the mind-space[18]
Of a collectivized, stupefied and controlled population
The ACLU will suppress any real understanding of Legal Issues
Those that plot for deliberate personal advantage are not usually spotted
Until much of the damage has been inflicted, which may be impossible to correct?
And, citizens do pay dearly for expert opinion, which robs them of their wealth and freedom

One should inquire.
Who are those that betray their fellow countrymen?
Thus, by clever forms of deceit, to become wealthy beyond common understanding
Who are those that then do spend their ill-gained wealth pandering to some vainly driven whore?
Who does arrange to steal the wealth from a trusting and humble neighbor so to enrich the sons of Sin?
Then to encourage the immigration of millions, who seek relief from abject poverty and ignorance?
Those then will invade and smother this "beloved" native land, so to line the pockets of Traitors and Fools
Who now destroys the prosperity of good men, removing opportunity from their children?[19]
A false sense of security keeps the population content waiting for a government's dole[20]
Responding to mindless thought of stupid social pretense; we admonish
A whirlwind is just now approaching and [it] is not too far beyond
Where men will be engaged in prolonged warfare[21]
With no manner of reasonable direction
Millions certainly will be slaughtered
As the super rich will cower
In some far-away place
Or inside the Banks
Inspired to bring
A Civilization
To an end
Hail Mary
Full of grace
The Lord is with you
Blessed art thou amongst women
And, blessed is the fruit of thy womb, Jesus
***Holy Mary, mother of God, pray for us sinners;
now and at the hour of our death. AMEN***

Endnotes

Protect that which has become and may continue to progress as
THE
Universally established and orderly Civilization?

All for One and One for All

Christ is [The] One

God is [The] All
God is everywhere, at all times in the form of the Spirit.
The Spirit is in mind of every man and woman.
God is a Partner in the Trinity.

Keep in mind for many God is an Idea apart from reality. Individually men are encouraged and becoming to believe there is no "real" God. Some Imagine God is a myth. This is an age-old notion. The only way to know is to die or to have Faith in the being and existence of Christ and His teaching. Whether you believe in God or not the teachings of Christ are invaluable. The Ten Commandments are the best affirmation of *"What is Holiness"* and the Sermon on the Mount is better than any other form of advice. (This is theology). This is not merely Religion; it is much more than that. The problem with various Religions is those are composites of man's too-simple understanding and advice. Even the Universal Catholic Faith, has been corrupted by the *"Imperfect thinking"* of men that do not have perfect knowledge. Even some Popes have been guilty of corrupting the Faith. The last five Popes have been guilty of many blasphemies and compromises: 52 Popes were not real Popes they were heretics. There is not compromise between good and evil: Those are mutually exclusive and harbor contrary objectives and expectations. For a more complete understanding see publication from Most Holy Family Monastery, 4425 Schneider Road, Fallbrook, NY 14735.

FINALLY: *No man is omnipotent: omnipotence is God's domain.*

Bibliographic notes: for Traitors within our midst.

1. **Those seeking to lead** are often meagerly informed or their information is carefully screened, for effect, so to present the ***wrong manner of understanding,*** which models their thinking. Always there exist hypocrites that seek short-term special and personal advantage, which cannot be completely understood. And there are Secret Societies that do encourage mayhem and revolution (**Webster, Nesta.** *World Revolution, the Plot against Civilization,* Veritas Publishing Company, 7th. Ed, 1994, Cranbrook. Western

Australia 6321). Many Politicians mean well, however, are beholden to what they do not comprehend. Politics are generally concerned with Power. The implications have both moral and ethical dimensions, especially concerning economic issues, which are often tied to *"TIMING" and the imperatives that time restraint implies.* Thus Politics are issues concerned with the "fusion of church and state." The "separation of Church and State" has done and will continue to do, great harm to our Western Civilization, founded on Catholic Christian Principles. A nation founded on Catholic Christian principles cannot abandon those same principles and continue to exist as a unified social body. Ideas do separate men. Christianity, Catholicism in particular, provides a complete system of thought, which is fair-minded in recognizing the Ideas of others, however, cannot be changed by any "Democratic Process. Keep in mind, a System of Thought is and does not control the content of individual mind, which is directed by Free Will. This posits a difficult situation. Furthermore, the general population, being good in many ways, is not able to discern the thought-elements that comprise the totality of any Philosophy. Serious study has been abandoned in favor of **"play acting,"** *playing and acting,* neither of which will aid in the formation of comprehensive understanding. In any event, complete understanding is not possible, requiring the omnipotence of God. And, God is a "Masculinity" a Progenitor of all that is seen and unseen (**Rutler, George W., DD**. *The Fatherhood of God*. (Homiletic and Pastoral Review, June 1993)

2. **Roberts, Craig, Economist,** *Middle America News.* Middle American Institute, Inc., P. O. Box 20608, Raleigh, North Carolina 27619. Pg. 19. January, 2008."*Impending Destruction of the U. S. Economy,*"

3. Pg, 19, February 2008, *"Self-serving Lies Destroyed the American Dream,"* Pg. 23 Certain opportunists are awarded hundreds of millions of dollars in a single year, even a billion or more. Such greed and malfeasance is destroying the country, *which pretends to be capable of leading the world to a better future,* even as that same country is resting upon false hope and a monetary system based on usury, greed and hypocrisy, controlled by a **"Consortium of Thieves."** Our nation and our people are being destroyed by greed and the imposition of alien antagonists, in collusion with the above- mentioned Thieves, The American Dream has become a nightmare of debt and insolvency. One can observe a form of collective madness, driven by the sound of the Rapper's wailing, the Beat of the jungle and the Screaming of hundreds of millions that participate in the debauchery of our disintegrating Culture

4. **Architectural Digest,** Apartments are advertised as costing between $750,000.00 and $40,000,000.00 for a *space in the air* near downtown Chicago. Other principle cities are similar, in respect to cost for *Space in the air, near where the big money is made.* One can smell it (the stench) from across town.

5. There is a waiting list for fifty million dollar luxury yachts ($50.000.000.00)

6. **Exponential growth** on large accumulations of Capital will in time consume all other existing wealth. There is a great difference between real wealth with commensurate underlying value, real estate, buildings, gold, silver, other commodities and the wealth generated in the stock markets, which is a **Notional form,** defined as a financial asset, generated in the process of exchanging paper pledges from one fool to another. Fools make the trades professional Shysters scam the profits. Thereafter *such profits* are used

to buy real value, in one form or another. Such fraudulent form of exchange represents a means of legalized thievery, which few could understand.

7. **Pornography** is a multi-billion dollar business. Lecherous "Persons" that delight in destroying the body and soul of youthful beauty intimidate and compromise the young. Anyone can see the results of Kinsey's questionable research. Alfred Kinsey was a man of very questionable intentions, "tinkering" with the libido of a too-permissive social complex, compromised by "sin as science/". **Reisman, Judith, PhD**. _Kinsey,_

   Crimes and Consequences. The Institute for Medical Education, P. O. Box 15284, Sacramento, CA 95851-0284.

8. **Woodrow Wilson, President. (Former President of the U. S)** "Some of the biggest men in the United States, in the field of commerce and manufacturing, are afraid of someone are afraid of something. They know that there is a Power somewhere so organized, so subtle, so watchful, so interlocked, so complete, so pervasive that they had better not speak above their breadth when the speak in condemnation of it."

9. **Hundreds of millions** scream and are excited as the watch the Super Bowl: Why? They have been _**"educated to do so"**_ by a controlled network of opinion makers: newspapers. Television, magazines and (yes) the government controlled Educational System.

10. **2008, an Election Year** gives quaint proof that the "leading" Politicians are over-financed Fools. Perhaps those are intelligent however they are not wise. They have millions to spend and nothing to say that has any significantly motivated understanding of what they are supposed to be doing. The big issues for the Democratic Candidates are "change," which they do not define, blackness (the first black President) and femininity (the first woman President). The Population is indoctrinated, mesmerized, listening to promises of change, _which will certainly not be what they expect._ Democrats and some Republicans prefer more socialism and promote the activities of those that insist on the destruction of sovereign nations (by means of third-world migrations). Those applaud a one-world government (which will be Totalitarian, as it must be), and as such those are intolerant of any that might be capable of understanding present Reality. The two-party system guarantees (as, at the beginning of the twentieth century, Mendel House imagined it would), that the establishment, one way or another, will place another "Socialist Type" in the prime position.

11. **Pope Pius XII,** Encyclical Letter, _Humani Generisc, Concerning some false opinions which threaten to undermine the foundations of Catholic Doctrine_, St. Paul Editions. Especially #'s 18 and 19.

12. **Totalitarianism** in all forms promises a better future for the masses, which generally speaking, do not think beyond the present moment. There is not or can there be any happy ending to a history that depends upon inhumanly directed force to sustain what power is in command. To imagine other wise is to be stupid. History that is humanity will continue until the human race is extinguished, one way or another. No one can imagine just how this will occur.

13. **Thought Patterns** emanate from the interstices (minutely particular spaces) within the confines of the brain, that being between proximate neurons. Such spaces are

"charged" with the life force of a particular person, which enables the promulgation of thought patterns. Such thought patterns may be repeated, thus retraced, so to become an effective and sustaining factor, which does influence future thinking in ways not completely understood. This is a difficult subject to contemplate, since any form of proof, with subsequent understanding, is only apparent (possibly) to specialists in neurology and is not within the purview of common thought. **Thought forms** *are evanescent structures* composed of a combination of ethic elements including memory, visualizations of images of the past, linguistic structures inherent in composite thinking and images, structural and verbal, which anticipate elucidation in a future beyond? Such forms cannot be illustrated except as diagrams of with symbolic connotation. A system of symbols is yet to be developed.

14. **The Education-minded "thinkers,"** *alien view* is definitely anti-Christian and is in support of a more oppressive government and the eradication of the soul and spirit of the individual, as understood to exist by Catholic Christianity. Modern Education in the United States is an ***Oxymoron:*** a conglomeration of personal ranting combined with modified history, propaganda, religious intolerance and is completely overcome with the thinking and tinkering of scientists. Scientists are not always wise men. Most Students, not fluent in their own mother tongue, are not able to "think about" complex problems and are beset and confused by the conflict of ideologies which have come from the other side of the world. Many are hopelessly distracted by the athletic contests for which millions in scholarships are given. This is apparent from Woodstock to the wailing of ignorance in the form of the Rapper's vain and childish impositions.

The music and the minds of ***this*** [now] generation are being vilified by the trash dumped on the Culture and Civilization. Many educators (?) envision all of humanity living on one giant Anthill, over which will crawl a submissive well indoctrinated and insect-like form of humanity. "The international game plan for world control, will start at the economic sphere and then spread into the political and sociological spheres." From *Barbarians inside the Gates*, by Lt. Col. Ret. Donn de Grand Pre'. The **"spreading, spelled**

15. ***Indoctrination*** "is the Ruth Fiedler charge of modern humanism fostered by an education, formed under the influence of socialistic and clandestine impositions. Such impositions have origins in the distant past (Douglas Reed, *The Controversy of Zion* Veritas Pub. Company (Pty) Ltd. ISBN # 0949667 27 7.

16. **Individually:** random occurrence inveighs upon and alters subsequent thinking, which leads to action. Thus the future is a product of and is determined by the past, as interpreted and sustained in the thinking of the individual, which is not always correctly understood.

17. **Frost, S. E. Jr. Ph. D. (Then)** Assistant Professor of Education, Brooklyn College. *Great Philosophers:* Barnes and Noble. © 1942, Doubleday and Company, Inc. Sixth Printing. Pp.246-251. Education, with imagined consequence has been contemplated by many philosophers: Rousseau, Pestalozzi, Fichte, Herbart, Foible and John Dewey. Their "musings" remain with us today, as "Literature in the Field of Education." There are more recent *Specialists* as well, for example Skinner, Marcuse, Rogers, found flourishing in the Universities. Many are given generous grants and pretend

that they are looking for something, which they do not comprehend and never will. "In the end we are all dead" (Shakespeare). Most *Specialists* prefer such *searching* rather than teaching, what is truthfully known, for which they are being paid. As such, *Educational Experts* are confusing and can be proven to be mortally destructive, rather than constructive where great numbers of *learners* are involved. To view the behavior and the silly theatrics emanating from adolescents is to understand the consequence of *over-valued adult ineptitude*. **Education is a "Cardinal Form" of communication** however, when given over to the role of supporting State Policy, beholden to a doctrinaire imposition, formed in the minds of Lunatics, ***significant Catholic and Christian Thought*** will be extinguished in favor of Humanism and Socialist, feel-good, Prattling. Then Western Culture and the Civilization, which has flourished in modern times, will be no more.

18. **Roberts, Craig, Economist,** *Middle America News.* Middle American Institute, Inc., P. O. Box 20608, Raleigh, North Carolina 27619. Sept 2007, *"Return of the Robber Barons."* Pg. 19. September 2007.

19. **Gerber, Richard, MD.** *Vibrational Medicine, the # 1 Handbook of Subtle-Energy Therapies.* Third Edition. ©2001, Richard Gerber. ISBN 1-879181-58-4. Bear and Company, Rochester, Vermont, 05767.

20. **Mind-Space** has certain aspects, which can and must be engaged in meaningful endeavor. Thoughts are formed by finely motivated infinitesimal, electrical impulses; we name them quarks, joules or photons. Such impulses function between proximate neurons within the tissues of the brain and being invisible are difficult to contemplate. All thought is dependent upon micro functions, driven by a biologically and electrically formed humanly motivated energy. The brain is responsive to the environmentally determined forces that exist within the purview of the person, as a living human being. *Holistic Tubules* are antecedent to cellular growth. ***The cells follow the paths and the a priori conceived biological determination of an unseen, nevertheless, physiological force: a life force that precedes corporeal development***. *It is an important part, alluded to in the Apostle's Creed, which makes note of all that is seen and unseen.* **Hereabouts we find a connection between an infinite God, progenitor of the universe and humanity** as expressed in the individual sovereign being, made in the image of that same infinite God.

21. [11] **Outsourcing** is a euphemism for *Grand Theft* and the destruction of one's own native land. This is done for the benefit of those that acquire the fifty million-dollar, 200 foot-long yachts, floating accommodations for the rich and unconscionably famous, Pirates of the land and sea, of Culture and Civilization. We are informed that this is a reward for being a good Businessman. We suggest, rather it is the product from grand-theft, in the style of Evil's children. See: Architectural Digest. PP. 226-231, March 2008. Such opulence is symptomatic of the obscene products of finance capital, usury and unfair business practices in the population. "This in fact was and is the very important part (***as the educational extension***, *author's comment*)

22. **Credit Cards** provide the sense of security for those that are compulsive, in their spending habits however, are not able to pay for what they want. Credit cards are a form of "bridge financing" that demand a heavy token

23. **Korea, Vietnam and now Iraq,** several others in between is the harbinger of what is to come. The movement of populations under pretense of affording security is another example of what is in store for the Western Culture and Civilization in general. The appeal will be to Christian compassion. The world will be run as one giant kindergarten, an ant farm. Adults will be told what to do that is acceptable to the politically formed requirements of a Multi-culture (?), which will hope to guarantee the destruction of Catholic, Christianity, meaning

Bibliography

for body text of book.

Adler, Mortimer. Ten Philosophical Mistakes, Mac Millan Pub., NewYork, Collier Macmillan, London.. ISBN # 0-02-500330-5.

Alexander, Anthony F. Rev. *College Apologetics,* Henry Regnery Co., Chicago, ©1954. *Nihil Obstat.* Very Rev. Edward L. Hughes, O. P. Censor Librorum. Imprimatur, Samuel Cardinal Stritch, D. D. Archiepiscopus Chicagiensis, Oct. 13, 1953.

Allen, Gary, *None Dare Call It Conspiracy.* Concord Press, Rossmoor, California. 1971.

Aquinas, Thomas, Saint., *Summa Theologica* 1, 14, 13, ad. 1. Trans, Anton C. Pegis (New York, Random House, 1944), Vol. One,

Architectural Digest, Oct. 2002. *One Central Park Tower*

Barabanov, Evgeny, *From Under the Rubble,* (Little Brown & Co., Boston, Toronto, 1975),

Barzun, Jacques, *The House of Intellect.* Harper and Row, NY, 1959. LC #59-6300.

Barzun, Jacques, *From Dawn to Decadence, 1500 to the Present*. Harper Collins Publishers Inc., 10 East 53rd Street. New York, NY 10022. ISBN 0-06-017586-9.

Bearden, T. E., Col., *Aids, Biological Warfare,* Tesla Book Co., P. O. Box 1649, Greenville, TX 75401. ISBN # 0-914119-04-4.

Beaty, John PhD. *The Iron Curtain over America*. Chestnut Mountain Books, Barboursville, Virginia, 1968. © 1951, John Beaty. First Printing 1951.

Benson, Ivor, *The Zionist Factor.* Millennium Edition,GSG Associates, P. O. Box 590. San Pedro, CA 90733. USA. ISBN: 0-945001-63-0. pps. 25-26-27.

Birmingham, Stephen. *Our Crowd.* Dell Co. Inc. New York, NY. 1967.

Blumfield, Samuel, *Is Public Education Necessary?* Arlington House, 1972, New Rochelle, New York. L. C. # 72-186241.

Bondi, Herman, *The Universe at Large*

Brown, Harry. *How You can Profit from the Coming Devaluation.* Arlington House, 1970, New Rochelle NY. LC# 77-101959.

Brown, Walter, Creation: *In the Beginning: Compelling Evidence for Creation and the Flood.*

Buckley, William F. *God and Man at Yale.* Henry Regnery Co. Chicago, Ill. 1951.

Burnham, James, *Suicide of the West.* Arlington House, 1964, New Rochelle, New York. L. C. # 64-1424.

Butler, _The Lives of the Saints_

Carlson, Elof Alex, _Human Genetics,_ (D. C. Heath and Company, U. S. A., 1984, Ch. 6, Mendel's Laws and Genetic Disorders).

Carpenter, Lynn, Editor, _The Fleet Street Letter,_ Vol. 67, Issue 7, Special Forecast Issue 2004. P. O. Box 925, Frederick, MD 21705-9913.

Carrol, Charles Holt. _Organization of Debt into Currency: and other Papers._ Van Nostrand. Inc. 1964.

Carson, Clarence B. _The War on the Poor._ Arlington House, 1969, New Rochelle, N. Y. L. C. 69-16951.

Cathey, Bruce, _The Bridge to Infinity._

Chang, Matthias, _Future Fast Forward, The Zionist, Anglo-American Meltdown._ First American Editions, 2006, American Free Press, Washington D. C. 20063

Clark, Hulda Regehr, PhD., N. D. _The Cure for All Cancers._ The New Century Press, 1055 Bay Blvd.,Suite C, Chula Vista, CA 91911. ISBN#

Clark, Hulda Regehr, PhD., N. D. _The Cure for All Diseases._ The New Century Press, 1055 Bay Blvd.,Suite C, Chula Vista, CA 91911. ISBN# 1-890035-01-7

Clement, Marcel, _Christ and Revolution._ Transated by Alice von Hildebrand. Arlington House, New Rochelle, NY. © 1974, Arlington House. ISBN # 0-87000-233-3. LC# 74-3060.

Colby, Benjamin, Arlington House, New Rochelle, New York© 1974, L. C. # 74-19165.

Collison, Joseph, Writer and Director, Office of Pro Life Activities, Norwich, CN. _Abortion in America: Legal and Unsafe._ The New Oxford Review Magazine, June 2000. Pp. 33-35.

Coughlin, Charles E. Rev. _Money, Questions and Answers._ Pub. The Radio League of the Little Flower, Royal Oak, MI. © 1937, The Radio League of the Little Flower,

Corti, Count Egon Caesar, _The Rise of the House of Rothschild._ Western Islands, Publisher, Belmont, Massachusetts, 02178. © 1928 The Cosmopolitan Book Corporation,

Cruttenden, Walter: _Lost Star of Myth and Time._ St. Lynn' s Press POB 18680, Pittsburg, PA 15236 .

Cusa, Nicholus, _On the Quadrature of the Circle._ Fidelio, Magazine, Vol. X, #2, Summer 2001. Publisher, Schiller Inst., Inc., P. O. Box 20244 , Wash., D C., 20041-0244. Ed. Wm F. Wirtz, Jr. Fillmore, NY 14735.

Dall, Curtis, _My Exploited Father in Law._ Liberty Lobby, Washington D. C., 1968. L. C. # 68-2835.

Degrelle, Leon, _Campaign in Russia, The Waffen SS on the East Front._ Published by The Institute for Historical Review, 1822 1/2 Newport Blvd., Suite 191, Costa Mesa, California 92627. ISBN 0-939484-18-8. LC # 86-103799.

Diamond, Michael, Bro., *Creation and Miracles.* Most Holy Family Monastery, 4425 Schneider Road.

Disraeli, Benjamin, later Lord Beaconsfield,

Dillon, George E., Mgr. DD., *Grand Orient, Freemasonry Unmasked. Dublin,* M. H. Gill & Son, Upper Sackville Street. London and New York: Burns and Oates, 1885. The Brother's Publishing Society, London, July 27, 1950. GSG & Associates, 2000, P. O. Box 6448, Rancho Palos Verdes, CA 90734.

Dobbs, Zygmund. *Keynes at Harvard.* Economic Deception as a Political Credo. Probe, West Sayville, New York. 1969.

Dodd, Bella V. *School of Darkness.* The record of a life and of a conflict between two faiths. The Devin Adaire Co., 23 E. 26th. Street, New York, N. Y. LC # 54-10204.

Dos Passos, John. *Mid Century.* Cardinal Publishers, NY. 1962.

Dos Passos, John. *The Shackles of Power: Three Jeffersonian Decades.* Doubleday, Garden City, New Jersey. 1966.

Douglas, William Campbell II, M. D., *Aids, The End of Civilization*

Eddington, Arthur. *Space, Time and Gravitation.* Harper and Row, NY & Ill. 1959. LC# 59-13846.

Engle, Randy, *Sex Education, the Final Plague.* Publisher, Human Life International, 7845-E Airpark Road, Gaithersburg, Maryland, November 1989. ISBN # 1-55922-025-2.

Eugene IV, Pope *The Council of Florence,*

Fahey, Dennis, Rev., C.S.Sp., D.D., D.Ph., *The Kingship of Christ and Organized Naturalism.* Christian Book Club of America, P.O Box 900566, first published June 1943. Reprint October 1993, Palmdale, CA 93590.

Fahey, Dennis, Rev., C.S.Sp., D.D., D.Ph., *The Mystical Body of Christ in the Modern World*, Third Ed.,

Fahey, Dennis, Rev., C.S.Sp., D.D., D.Ph. *Secret Societies and the Kingship of Christ,* Christian Book Club of America. Pub. 1928, republished 1994.

Flynn, John T., *The Roosevelt Myth,* (The Devin-Adair Company, New York, Copyright, July 1948, eighteenth Ed., July, 1953).

Freeman, Richard & Tucker, Arthur, *Wal-mart Is Not a Business,* It's an Economic Disease. From, Executive Intelligence Review. Nov. 14, 2003, Vol. 30 No. 44.

Freeman, Richard, *Reverse the 35 Year Devastation of America's Industry and Labor Force*, Executive Intelligence Review, March 21. 2003, Vol. 30 #11.

Frost, S. E.Jr. Ph. D. (Then) Assistant Professor Of Education, Brooklyn College. *Great Philosophers.* Barnes and Noble. © 1942, Doubleday and Company, Inc., Sixth Printing

Gennep van, Arnold. *The Rites of Passage.* Univ. of Chicago. 1960.

Gerber, Richard, MD., _Vibrational Medicine, The # 1 Handbook of Subtle-Energy Therapies._ Third Edition. ©2001, Richard Gerber. ISBN 1-879181-58-4. Bear and Company, Rochester, Vermont, 05767.

Gregory XVI, Pope

Grand Prix, Don, Col. USA Ret. _Barbarians Inside the Gates, The Black Book of Bolshevism._ GSG & Assoc. Publishers. P. O. Box 590, San Pedro, California. ISBN # 0-945001-79-7. First Printing 2000.

Hackett, Ken, Executive Director, Catholic Relief Services. _Letter of appeal, dated October 2002._

Hadrian I, Pope, _Second Council of Nicaea, 787:_

Haksell, Grace, _Prophacy and Politics, Militant Evangelists on the Road to Nuclear War._ First Published, Lawrence Hill and Co. USA, 1986. Second Printing by Veritas Publishing Comany, Pty. Ltd. P. O. Box 20, Bullsbrook, Western Australia. Distributed by GSG Assoc., P. O. Box 590, San Pedro, CA 90733. ISBN # 0-945001-98-3

Heilbron, J. L. _The Sun in The Church, Cathedrals as Solar Observatories._ Harvard University Press, Cambridge, Massachusetts, London, England. ©1999, by the President and Fellows of Harvard College. ISBN # 0-674-85433-0

Hoppe, Donald J., _How to Invest in Gold Stocks and avoid the Pitfalls._ ©1972 Arlington House, New Rochelle, NY. LC # 72-77641. ISBN 0-87000 178-7.

Hayek, Frederick August von. _Road to Surfdom. Univ. of Chicago Press, Chicago 1944._

Hazlett, Henry. _The Conquest of Poverty._ Arlington House, New Rochelle, NY, 1973. LC# 72-9123.

Hoppe, Donald J. _How to Invest in Gold Coins._ Arlington House, New Rochelle, NY, 1970. LC# 70-115342.

Hoppe, Donald J. _How to Invest in Gold Coins and Avoid the Pitfalls._ Arlington House, New Rochelle, NY, 1972. LC# 72-77641.

Huxley, Julian. _Religion without Revelation._ Mentor Publishing, NY, 1957.

Intelligence Publications, _Who Rules America, Nature and Power of Conspiracy._ Extract: On Target 10-24 March 2001 issue. Donald A. Martin, Editor. Pub. by intelligence pub., 26 Meadow Lane, Sudbury, Suffolk, England.

Ireland, Thomas R. _Monetarism._ Arlington House, New Rochelle, NY, 1974. LC# 73-18186.

Nietzsche,

Jacobson, Steven, _Mind Control in the United States._ Critique Pub., P. O. Box 11451, Santa Rosa CA 95406. ISBN o-911485-00-7. LC # 85-70431. Mfg. Apollo Books, 107 Lafayette St., Winona, MN

Jaki, Stanley L., _The Road of Science and the Ways of God._ The University of Chicago Press, 1978.

Janeway, Elliot. *You and Your Money; A Survival Guide.* David McKay Co. Inc. 1972.

Jenney, George. *How to Rob a Bank Without a Gun.* Goodnews Pub. Co. Canton Ohio 1973.

Johnson, Paul, *Intellectuals.* Harper and Rowe Publishers. 10 E. 53rd. Street, New York, NY 10022. © 1988, Paul Johnson. ISBN # 0-06-016050-0. LC# 88-45518.

Jones, Michael, **Ph. D**. *Fidelity Magazine* (Issue, #, date)

Jones, Michael, Ph. D. *Degenerate Moderns, Modernity as Rationalized Sexual Misbehavior,* © 1993, Ignatius Press, San Francisco. ISBN 0-89870-447-2. Lc # 92-75406.

Jones, Michael, Ph. D. *Monsters from the Id, Part III., The Monster travels from Germany to America,* (Spence Pub., Co., Dallas, Texas 75207).

Jones, E. Michael Ph. D. *Libido Dominandi, Sexual Liberation and Political Control.* St. Augustine's Press, South Bend, Indiana. © 2000 E. Michael Jones. ISBN # 1-890318-37-x.

Jones, E. Michael, Ph.D. *Philadelphia Delenda Est: The Republican Convention and the Reality Tour.* Culture Wars Magazine. Sept. 2000, Vol. 19, No. 9. Pp. 28-41.

Kaufman, Walter, *Nietzsche, Philosopher, Psycologist, Antichrist.* Meridian Books, Inc. New York. First Published 1956. Fourth Printing December 1959. USA. LC # 56-6572.

Kershner, Howard. *Dividing the Wealth: Are you Getting Your Share?* Devin-Adair C. Old Greenwich Conn. 1971.

Kirk, Russell. *Edmund Burke: A Genius Reconsidered.* Arlington House, New Rochelle, NY, 1967.

Kirk, Russell. *The Roots of American Order.* Open Court, La Salle, Illinois, First Ed. 1974.

Knupffer, George, *The Struggle for World Power, Revolution and Counter Revolution.* 4th ed./, 1986. ISBN # 0-85172-703-4.

Knuth, E. C. *The Empire of the City, The Jekyll/Hyde Nature of the British Government,* 1983 Edition, The Noontide Press, P. O. Box 1248, Torrance, California 90505

LaRouche, Lyndon, *Dope Inc.*

Kuehnelt-Leddihn, Erik Maria, Ritter von, *Leftism, From de Sade and Marx to Hitler and Marcuse.* Arlington House 1974. ISBN #0-87000-143-4. LC# 73-78656.

LaRouche, Lyndon H., *What is God, That Man Is In His Image?* (Fidelio Magazine, March 18,1995

LaRouche, Lyndon, *The Essential Fraud of Leo Strauss,* Executive Intelligence Review, 3. 21, 03, Vol. 30 No. 11.

Larson, Martin Ph. D. *Tax Revolt, USA.* Liberty Lobby, Washington, DC. 1973.

Larson, Martin Ph. D. *The Federal Reserve & Our Manipulated Dollar.* The Devin-Adair Co.,

Old Greenwich, Conn. 1975.

Lonergan, Bernard, *Method in Theology,* The Seabury Press. Winston press, Inc. 430 Oak Grove, Minneapolis, Minnesota. LC #78-68581. ISBN 0-8164-2204-4.

Lucaks, George, *The Remembered Past (?)*

Lundberg, Ferdinand. *The Rich and the Super-Rich.* Bantam Books, NY. 1968.

Luzadder, Warren J., PE. *Basic Graphics.* Prentice Hall, Inc., Eng.ewood Cliffs, NJ. 1968. 68-15764.

Mailer, Norman, *Picasso, Portrait of Picasso as a young man. An Interpretive Biography,* Warner Books Ed., Copyright 1995 by Norman Mailer, Warner Books, Inc., 1271 Avenue of the Americas, New York 10020. ISBN # 0-446-67266-1.

Malthuse, Robert Thomas. *Principles of Political Economy, Considered.* 1821, 431 pages 1836, 516 pages. Original documents, Oxford University, England.

Manifold, Didirae, *Karl Marx, a Prophet of Our Times.* G. S. G. & Associates, Publishers. P. O. Box 6448, Eastview Station, Rancho Palos Verdes, CA 90734. ISBN# 0-945001-00-2.

Manzella, David. *Educationists and the Evisceration of the Visual Arts.* International Text Book Co., Scranton, Penn. 1963.

Markoe, John P., Rev., S. J., *The Triumph of the Church, accompanied by an Historical Chart., 21 st. Edition.* (A Catholic Viewpoint Pub., Scafati Printing Co., Inc., 1205 Whitlock Ave., Bronx, NY. 10459).

McMasters, R. E., *The Reaper, Newsletter*

Meadows, Meadows, Randers, Behrens. *The Limits to Growth.* Signet, NY. 1972. LC# 73-187907.

Mechizedek, Drunvaldo, *The Ancient Secret of the Flower of Life, Vol.II.* Light Technologies Publishing, P. O. Box 3540, Flagstaff, AZ 86336. ISBN # 1-1891824-21-X.

Mendelsoh, Robert, MD., *How to Raise Healthy Children in Spite of Your Doctor.* Contemporary Books, Inc. 180 N. Michigan Avenue, Chicago, IL 60601. Copyright ©1984. ISBN 0-8092-5808-0.

Meyerowitz, Steve, *Wheat Grass, Natures Finest Medicine,* *The complete Guide to Using Grasses to Revitalize Your Health.* (Sproutman Publications, Great Barrington, Mass., 01230)

Michili, Vincent, DD. SJ. *The Antichrist ,* Roman Catholic Books, P. O. Box 225, Harrison, N. Y. Jan. 24, 1981

vonMises, Ludwig. *Human Action, A Treatise on Economics.* 3rd Ed. Regnery, Chicago 1966.

vonMises, Ludwig. *Theory and History.* Arlington House, New Rochelle NY. 1969. LC# 77-97129.

Mitchell, Richard, *The Leaning Tower of Babel, and other affronts from the Underground Grammarian.* Little, Brown & Com. Boston, Toronto. Richard Mitchell ©1984. ISBN # 0-316-57509-7.

Molnar, Thomas. _The Counter Revolution._ Funk and Wagnalls, New York, 1969. L. C. #75-92222.

Molnar, Thomas. _Utopia, the Perennial Heresy._ Sheed and Ward, Inc. New York, 1967. L. C #67-1376 4.

More, Paul Elmer. _Lambert, Byron C. ed._ Arlington House, New Rochelle NY. 1972. LC# 79-189372.

Morgan, Dan. _Merchants of Grain, The Power and Profits of the five Giant Companies at the Center of the World's Food Supply._ The Viking Press, 625 Madison Avenue, NY, 10022. July 1979, 2nd. Printing. ISBN# 0-670-47150-X.

Morris, William T. _How to get Rich Slowly but Almost Surely._ Reston Pub. Co. Reston Virginia. Prentice-Hall Co. 1973.

Most Holy Family Monastery, _A Voice Crying in the Wilderness,_ Issues 1-2-3-4. 4425 Schneider Road, Fillmore, N. Y. 14735

Mullins Eustice, _The World Order, Our Secret Rulers_. (Pub. Ezra Pound Institute, Staunton, VA. 24401, Second Edition, 1992).

Mumford, Lewis, The City in History

Newman, John Henry, Cardinal. _A Newman Treasury._ Arlington House, New Rochelle, New York. LC. #74-310780.

Ney, Richard. _Making it in the Market._ Low risk System. McGraw Hill Book Co. NY. LC# 75-25979.

Ney, Richard. _The Wall Street Gang._ Attack Conspiracy. Praeger, NY & Washington. LC# 73-13050.

Nietzsche

North, Gary, _Unholy Spirits, Occultism and New Age Humanism._ Dominion Press, 7112 Burns St., Fort Worth, TX 76118. ©1986, Gary North. ISBN # 0-930-462-02-5.

Operations Research, _Silent Weapons for Quiet Wars_. Top Secret, Confidential, Operations Research, Technical Manuel TM-SW7905.1. An Introductory, Programming Manuel.

Orwell, George, _Animal Farm._

Orwell, George, _Nineteen Eighy-four_

O'Grady, Olivia Marie, _The Beasts of the Apocalypse_, First Amendment Press, Copyright © 2001. Printed in the United States of America. ISBN 0-945001-66-5.

Oparin A. I. _Origin of Life_. Dover Publications, Inc. 1953. LC# 53-10161.

Packard, Vance, _The Hidden Persuaders_, 1957. ISBN # 0-671-52149-2.

Paris, Alexander P. _The Coming Credit Collapse._ Arlington House, New Rochelle, NY '74. LC# 74-5438.

Pierce, William L., PhD. Editor, National Vanguard Books, Cat. #14, December 1992. Reprint in the *Committee to Restore the Constitution*, P. O. Box 986. Ft. Collins, CO 80522. Bulletin #376, May 1993

Pendell, Elmer PH. D. *Sex Versus Civilization.* Noontide Press, P. O. Box 76062,

Los Angeles, CA, 90005. © 1967 Dr. Elmer Pendell.

Peters, Harvey W. *Americas Coming Bankruptcy.* Arlington House, New Rochelle, NY. '73. LC# 72-91216

Pius IX, Pope, Dec. 8, 1864, *The Encyclical Quanta Cura* and *The Syllabus of Errors,* Reprinted by The Remnant, 2539 Morrison Ave., St. Paul, MN 55117

Pius X, Pope *The Encyclical Quanta Cura and the Syllabus of Errors.* Issued in 1864. Reprinted by the Remnant, 2539 Morrison Avenue, St. Paul, MN 55117.

Pius XI, Pope Encyclical Letter, *Mortalium Animos,* Gregorian Press, Most Holy Family Monastery, Berlin, NJ

Pius XI, Pope, Encyclical Letter, *On Fostering True Religious Unity,* Gregorian Press, Most Holy Family Monastery,

Pius XI, Pope, Encyclical Letter, *Ubi Arcano Die, On the Peace of Christ.*

Pius XII, Pope, Encyclical Letter, *Humani Generis,* Daughters of St. Paul Press, N. C. W. C. Translation.

Podhoretz, Norman *Breaking Ranks, a Political Memoir,* NY, Harper and Row, 1979.

Poncins, Vicomte Leon De, *Judaism and the Vatacan.* Translated from the French by Timothy Tindal-Robertson. 1967. Reprinted 1985 and 1999.

Pranaitis, Rev. I. B. *The Talmud Unmasked.* IMPRIMATUR St. Petersburg, April 13, 1892 KOZLOWSKY Archbishop Metropolitan of Moghileff. *All Rights Reserved. Printed at the Imperial Academy of Science. (Vas. Ostr., 9 Line, No. 12)*

Privetera, James MD., & Stang, Alan,

Pursley, Leo A., DD, *The Apostolic Digest,* Our Lady of Victory Publications, Ed., Kieth E. Gillette, P. O. Box 80363, San Marino, California 91008,

Quigley, Carroll, PhD. *Tragedy and Hope. A History of the World in our Time.* MacMillan Pub. 1966. Particularly, Chapter V.

Rafferty, Max, *Suffer Little Children,* (The Devan-Adair Co., NY).

Ratzinger, Joseph Cardinal, *Theologische Prinzipienlehre.* 1982 Erich Wewel Verlag, Munich. Translation by: McCarthy, SDN., Principals of Catholic Theology, 1987 Ignatius Press, San Francisco, CA.

Roberts, Archibald E., Lt. Col, AUS, ret. *Committee to Restore the Constitution, Inc.,* Bulletin Number 489, Aug. 2002).

Roberts, Archibald E., Lt. Col, AUS, ret. *Committee to Restore the Constitution, Inc.*, Bulletin Number 511, July. 2004). Alien, Harold Green (AKA Heinz Grunhaus, Control Information Highway,

Reed, Douglas. *The Controversy of Zion.* Veritas Publishing Company (Pty) Ltd., P. O. Box 20, Bullsbrook, Western Australia 6084. Copyright © Douglas Reed, July 1985. ISBN # 0949667 27 7

Reisman, Judith, PhD. *Kinsey, Crimes and Cosequences.* The Institute for Medical Education, P. O. Box 15284, Sacramento, CA 95851-0284.

Roberts, Craig, Economist, *Middle America News.* Middle American Institute, Inc., P. O. Box 20608, Raleigh, North Carolina 27619. Sept 2007, *"Return of the Robber Barons"* Pg' 19. January 2008, *"Impending Destruction of the U. S. Economy,"* Pg, 19. February 2008, *"Self-serving Lies Destroyed the American Dream,"* Pg. 23.

Roche, George Charles III. *The Bewildered Society.* Arlington House, New Rochelle, NY, 1972. L. C. 76-183677.

Roche, George Charles III. *A Man Alone.* Arlington House, New Rochelle, NY. C. # 71-139891.

Rogers, Donald I. *How to Beat Inflation by Using it.* Arlington House, New Rochelle, NY, 1970.

Ropke, Wilhelm. *Social Crisis of Our Time.* University of Chicago Press, Chicago, Ill. 1950.

Ropke, Wilhelm. *Human Economy.* Regnery, 1960.

Rosen, Lawrence R. *Go Where the Money Is.* Understanding the Securities Business. Dow Jones-Irwin, Inc. Homewood, Ill. 1969. LC# 68-56878.

Rothbard, Murray N. *America's Great Depression* D. Van Nostrand Co., Inc. Princeton NJ. 1963.

Rueff, Jacques. *The Monetary Sin of the West.* Translated by Roger Glemet. Macmillan Inc. NY. 1972.

Rueff, Jacques. *Balance of Payments.* Macmillan Co., New York. 2nd Print. 1967. L C. # 67-20735.

Rueff, Jacques. *Age of Inflation.* Regnery, 1964.

Ruppert, Michael C., *Crossing the Rubicon, the Decline of the American Empire at the end of the Age of Oil.* Ed., James Hecht. New Society Pub. Copyright © Michael C. Ruppert, 2004. ISBN # 0-86571-540-8

Rush, Richard H. *The Techniques of Becoming Wealthy.* Prentice-Hall, Inc., Englewood Cliffs, NJ. 1963. LC# 63-10667.

Rutler, George W., DD. *The Fatherhood of God.* (Homiletic and Pastoral Review, June 1993)

Schlossberg, Herbert, *Idols for Destruction.* Thomas Nelson Pub., Fourth Printing, 1983. ISBN # 0-8407-5828-2 & 0-8407-5832-4

Schmidt, Austin G., S. J., and Perkins, Joseph A., A. M. *Faith and Reason.* Loyola University Press, Chicago, IL., 1937.

Schoeck, Helmut & Wiggins. *Central Planning and Neomerchantilism.* D. Van Nostrand Co., Inc. Princeton, NJ. 1964.

Schulman, Morton. *Anyone can Still Make a Million.* Stein and Day, NY, 1972. LC# 73-77963.

Harry Schultz D. *What the Prudent investor Should Know About Switzerland.* Arlington House, New Rochelle, NY. 1970. LC# 76-130297.

Schultz, Harry D. *Panics and Crashes.* How you can Make Money out of them. Arlington House, New Rochelle, NY. 1972. LC# 76-186242.

Schulze, Richard MD. *Understanding Your Immune System,* Get Well, November 2002. Natural Healing; publication.

Schulze, Richard, MD. *The Ultimate Get Well Newsletter Collection,* (Natural Healing Pub. Jan. 2002),

Sears, Alan E., President and General Council, Alliance Defense Fund, Scottsdale, AZ., *(Memorandum to Concerned Christians.*).

Skousen, W. Cleon, *The Naked Capitalist.* Private Edition Publication. 2197 Berkeley Street, Sault Lake City, Utah. 6th printing 1970. A review and commentary on Dr. Carroll Quigley's book *Tragedy and Hope.*

Smoot, Dan. *The Invisible Government.* Western Islands. Belmont, Mass. 1962.

Sokoloff, Boris, M.D., Ph. D., *The Permissive Society.* Arlington House, New Rochelle, New York, 1971.

Solzhenitsyn, Alexander. *Lenin in Zurich.* Farrah, Straus and Giroux, New York, 1976

Spengler, Oswald, *The Decline of the West, Vol. I. Form and Actuality,* Authorized Translation with notes by Charles Francis Atkinson. Alfred A. Knopf, Publisher, NY. 1926.

Solzhenitsyn, Alexander, *The Gulag Archipelago,* Harper and Two, New York, 1973

Spannaus, Edward, *Shock and Awe': Terror Bombing, From Wells and Russell to Cheney.* Executive Intelligence Review, Oct. 31, 2003.

Spengler, Oswald, *The Decline of the West, Vol. II. Perspectives of World History.* Authorized Translation with notes by Charles Francis Atkinson. Alfred A. Knopf, Publisher, NY. 1926.

Stormer, John A. *None Dare Call it Treason.* "Treason doth never prosper, what's the reason? For if it prosper, none dare call it treason.

Struve, Otto, *The Universe,* The Massachusetts Institute of Technology. ©1962. LC 3 62-16928.

Sutton, Anthony, Ph.D. *The Secret Cult of the Order.* Research Publications, Inc., Phoenix, AZ. 1984 © ISBN # 0-914981-09-9.

Sutton, **Antony C. Ph. D.** *Wall Street and FDR*. Arlington House, Pub. 1975, New Rochelle, NY. L. C. # 75-20257

Sutton, **Antony C. Ph. D.** *Wall Street and the Bolshevik Revolution* , Arlington House-Publishers, New Rochelle, New York, Copyright © 1974, Arlington House. ISBN 0-87000-276-7. L. C. # 74-10868.

Sutton, **Antony C. Ph. D**. *National Suicide: Military Aid to the Soviet Union.* Arlington House, NY. '73.

Sutton, **Anthony C.** *How the Order Controls Education,* Research Publications, Inc., P. O. Box 39850, Phoenix, Arizona. 1983. ISBN 0-914981-00-5.

Thielicke, **Helmut.** *Nehilism, Its Origins and Nature with a Christian Answer.* Trans. John W. Doberstein, Schocken Books, NY. 1969 [1961].

Tocqueville, **Alexis de,** *Democracy in America.* Ed. J. P. Mayer. Doubleday, Anchor Ed., Garden City, New York, 1969.

Toledano de, **Ralph.** *Little Cesar, Cesar's War on the Grape Pickers of CA.* Athem, 1971

Tolstoy, **Leo, Count Von.** *War and Peace.*

Twight, **Charlotte.** *America's Emerging Fascist Economy.* Arlington House, New Rochelle, NY. 1975. I. Title HC106.6.T9 338.973 7 5-30 632. ISBN 0-87000-317-8.

Varghese, **Abraham, Ed.** *Intellectuals Speak Out About God,* (Regnery Gateway, Chicago, Ill., 1984),

Veblen, **Thorsten.** *Higher Learning in America.* Hill & Wang. NY. 1957. LC# 57-9759.

Verange, **Ulick, LLD.** *Imperium.* The Noontide Press, ©1962, Sausalito, CA. LC # 62-53156.

Vitz, **Paul C., Professor.** *The Intellectuals Speak Out About God,* Edited by Roy Abraham Varghese, © 1984, Pub. by Regnery Gateway, Inc., 360 W. Superior St. Chicago IL, 60610. ISBN 3 0-89526-827-2.

Von Meises, **Ludwig,** *Human Action*

Von Meises, **Ludwig,** *Omnipotent Government:* The Rise of the Total State and Total War. Arlington House, New Rochelle, NY 1969. LC 75-97131

Von Meises, **Ludwig.** *Anti-Capitalist Mentality.* 1956.

Von Kuenhelt-Leddihn, **Erik.** *Leftism, From de Sade and Marx to Hitler and Marchse,* Arlington House-Publishers, New Rochelle, New York, Copyright © 1974, ISBN 0-87000-143-4,

Wardner, **Names, Ph.D.** *Communist Infiltration of the Catholic Church.* Video produced by, Most Holy Family Monastery, 4425 Schneider Road, Fillmore, NY 14735.

Webster, **Nesta.** *World Revolution, The Plot Against Civilization,* Veritas Publishing Company, 7th. Ed., 1994, Cranbrook. Western Australia 6321,

Webster, **Nesta,** *The French Revolution, a Study in Democracy.* First Published 1919, Republished 1969.Second Edition, The Christian Book Club of America, Hawthorne, CA 90250.

Welch, Robert. *The Politician.* Belmont Pub. Co. Belmont, Mass. 1963. LC# 64-8456.

West, E. G. *Adam Smith: the Man and his Works.* Arlington House, New Rochelle, NY. 1969. L. C. # 69-16949.

West, Samuel C. D.N. N. D. *The Golden Seven Plus One.* 1981 © Samuel Pub. Co. Orem, Utah. 84059 LC # 81-86099. 18th Edition.

Wheeler, Richard S. *Pagans in the Pulpit.* Arlington House Publisher, New Rochelle, NY. © 1974 Richard S. Wheeler. ISBN 0-87000-264-3

Wickliffe, Vennard B., Sr., *The Federal Reserve Hoax, The Age of Deception.* Meador Publishing Co., 324 Newbury Street, Boston 15, MA. Seventh Ed. Pp. 14-70.

Williams, Duncan. *Trousered Apes.* Arlington House, New Rochelle, NY. 1971. L. C. # 72-78485.

Wilton, Robert, *The Last of the Romanovs, How Tsar Nicholas II and Russia's Imperial Family were Murdered.* Copyright © 1993, the Institute for Historical Review. First British Edition, pub. 1920 in London by T. Butterworth. First U. S. Edition published 1920, in New York by George H. Dorn. French Edition, pub. Paris 1921. Russian language edition, pub. Berlin 1923. ISBN # 0-939484-1.

Winchester, A. M. *Heredity: An Intorduction to Genetics.* Second Ed. Barnes and Noble, Inc. NY. 1961. 66-25040.

Witonski, Peter F. *Gibbon for Moderns.* Arlington House: New Rochelle, NY. 1971. L. C. # 73-10710.

Wood, Garth M. D. *The Myth of Neurosis: Overcoming the Illness Excuse.* Harper and Row, Pub. New York: *Cambridge, Philadelphia, San Francisco, London, Mexico City, Sao Paulo, Singapore, Sydney.* © 1983 by Dr. Garth Wood. ISBN # 0-06-015488-S

Wormser, Rene A., *Foundations, Their Power and Influence*, (Covenant House Books, 1993, P. O. Box # 4690, Sevierville, TN 37864, ISBN 0-925591-28-9).

Yockey, Francis Parker, LLD, *Imperium.* The Noontide Press, ©1962, Sausalito, CA. LC # 62-53156